POOR PEOPLE

POOR
PEOPLE

WILLIAM T. VOLLMANN

An Imprint of HarperCollins*Publishers*

HarperCollins books may be purchased for educational, business, or sales promotional use. For information, please write: Special Markets Department, HarperCollins Publishers, 10 East 53rd Street, New York, NY 10022.

A slightly abridged form of "Crime Without Criminals" was originally published in *Gear* magazine in 2001. I made money off poor people's backs. On the other hand, *Gear* never paid me.

"The Rider" was first published by *Time Asia* in 2002.

A portion of my discussion of Nan Ning originally appeared, in a considerably different form, in *Time Asia* in 2002.

A few of the photographs were previously published in the unabridged McSweeney's version of my *Rising Up and Rising Down* (2003).

Designed by Joseph Rutt

Library of Congress Cataloging-in-Publication Data

Vollmann, William T.
  Poor people / William T. Vollmann.
    p. cm.
  ISBN: 978-0-06-087882-5
  ISBN-10: 0-06-087882-7
  1. Poor. 2. Poverty. I. Title.
  HV4028.V65   2007
  362.5—dc22   2006048547

07 08 09 10 11 WBC/RRD 10 9 8 7 6 5 4 3 2 1

This book is dedicated to my interpreters, without whom I would have remained more deaf and ignorant than is already the case. Because I sought to give my interviewees center stage, and even so could not avoid distracting you with various interpretations and misunderstandings of them, the interpreters' presences got suppressed wherever possible. Only where their own reactions illuminated the poor people themselves did I leave them in the picture. I am grateful to each and every one of them. Their patience, in many cases their bravery, and above all their local knowledge made this book possible.

CONTENTS

PHENOMENA

CHOICES

HOPES

PLACEHOLDERS

INTRODUCTION

Recently I finished writing a longish book about violence. I wanted it to be theoretically "complete"—that is, capable of judging the multifarious but nonetheless finite categories of excuses for violence.

This essay about poor people was written in a different spirit—neither to explicate poverty according to some system, nor to erect a companion monument to *Das Kapital* in the cemetery of hollowed-out thoughts. I certainly felt inadequate to sustain a meditation on any specific incarnation of poverty, as was so passionately attempted in *Let Us Now Praise Famous Men*. I say "attempted," for even that masterpiece repeatedly expresses its own insufficiency, and above all and therefore, its *guilt*.

I can fairly state that I have studied, witnessed and occasionally been a victim of violence. I cannot claim to have been poor. My emotion concerning this is not guilt at all, but simple gratitude. Jack London and George Orwell both lived the poor life, but they managed to give us *The People of the Abyss* and *Down and Out in Paris and London* precisely because they escaped that state. Good books do arise out of poverty and its memory—for instance, the unjustly forgotten *Manchild in the Promised Land*. Masterpieces have been written by those who renounced worldly things (Christian monks, Buddhist hermit-sages), or by individuals fallen into comparative impoverishment, such as Ovid in his exile. But how many of these latter address lifelong involuntary poverty? *The Grapes of Wrath*, which is one of the best books about poor people I have ever read, and which surely owes something to Steinbeck's poorish origins, succeeds thanks to a combination of the author's great-hearted empathy, his visits with its Okie subjects, his education and, not least, the leisure for writing and thinking that he was able to buy.

2

This point is so obvious as to demand restatement:

Let Us Now Praise Famous Men is an elitist expression of egalitarian longings. The tragic tension between its goal and its means contributes substantially to its greatness. Its Communist sympathies, expressed, I am sad to say, in the midst of the Stalinist show trials, expose its naiveté, without which that greatness would not exist; for despite its fierce intellectualism it is essentially an outcry of childlike love, the love which impels a child to embrace a stranger's legs. What can the stranger do, but smilingly stroke the child's head? Few of its subjects could have read, let alone written it. James Agee sought to know them, to experience, however modestly, what they did; his heart went out to them, and he fought with all his crafty, hopelessly unrequitable passion to make our hearts do the same. This explains the necessity for Walker Evans's accompanying photographs, which record the poverty of those sharecropper families calmly, undeniably, heartbreakingly, inescapably. Their project falls repeatedly on its sword. It is a success because it fails. It fails because it consists of two rich* men observing the lives of the poor. The stranger's legs

---

* For a definition of this word, see the dictionary, page xxi.

may be approachable, but the stranger himself in his immensity stands too tall and far off in poverty to be ascertained in the easy way that our observers can see each other. Had this easiness existed in the portrayal of the book's subject, it would have been patronizing. Accordingly, Agee carries his sincerity to the point of self-loathing, and Evans escapes into the tell-all taciturnity of photography. A picture is worth a thousand words, no doubt, but which thousand? Is your caption the same as mine? A poor man stares out at you from a page. You will never meet him. Is he grim, threatening, sad, repulsive, determined, worn down, unbowed, proud, all of the above? What can you truly come to know about him from his face? As for the photographer, he need not commit himself.

Agee does commit himself. He wants us to feel and smell everything that his subjects have to, and comes as close to accomplishing this as it is possible to do using the sole means of an alphabet; so he fails, despising himself and us that it must be so, apologizing to the families in an abstruse gorgeousness of abasement that only the rich will have time to understand—and of these, how many possess the desire? For to read *Let Us Now Praise Famous Men* is to be slapped in the face.

The Grapes of Wrath is a more populist work. Okies have read it indeed, and achieved the painful pleasure of seeing themselves. But the novel's beauties of effect required their own hours of toil to create.* Although the migrants in the California camps might have lived through hours of nothing to do, their idleness never equaled leisure: Worry, malnutrition, crowdedness, illiteracy and kindred damage, all inflicted by poverty, made it "no accident" (as a Marxist would say, but never in this context) that this most powerful work ever written about Okies was not written by an Okie.

---

* In this connection I recommend *The Harvest Gypsies*, which is not art but which honestly and compassionately describes the situations of Okies. Steinbeck did his homework. That is why *The Grapes of Wrath* is not only "universal," as any vague emotional overflow can be, but accurately particular.

I do not wish to experience poverty, for that would require fear and hopelessness. Therefore, I can glimpse it only from the outside. This essay is not written *for* poor people, or for anyone in particular. All that I dare to do is to note several similarities and differences which I believe pertain to the experience of being poor. I began by asking a few of my fellow human beings: *Why are you poor?* The answers follow. Although these vary by region, their particularities may well mean nothing. People can be poor in anything and everything, including meaning itself. This must be why one great writer who truly did know poverty wrote: *Poor people never, or hardly ever, ask for an explanation of all they have to put up with. They hate one another, and content themselves with that.*

3

Thoreau once said that most of us lead lives of quiet desperation; but if this is so, the people who live those lives manage to deny it. With some exceptions, the protagonists of this book are not desperate. They are happy or sad; they have their good days, and their extremity, such as it is, half-mercifully attenuates itself by being quotidian.* The Russian beggar Oksana, for instance, soldiered on quite cheerfully, although whenever she discussed her family's situation with me she had to acknowledge its implications, and so she wept. I tried to seek out poor people whose circumstances bore a degree of ordinariness, or at least of *pattern*, so that there might be something to generalize from. The drug addicts, street prostitutes, and criminals who appear in so many of my other books get smaller representation here.

---

* We all survive somehow. Some make their money by getting you to feel sorry for them, while others make money by pretending that you need not feel sorry for them, for instance by bestirring themselves to perform unnecessary obsequious little services, as do the men who wash the windshields of captive cars in line to exit the Mexican border; while still others make money from their stories.

People who are poor but not in imminent danger of perishing have more of a chance of catching their breath and actually conceptualizing their poverty.

Needless to say, my own interpretation of how this book's heroes and heroines see themselves is damaged by the brevity of our acquaintance, which in most cases endured a week or less. I know how little I know. All the same, these snapshots of the ways in which certain poor people experienced their poverty at random moments bear meaning of inexpressible value to me; I've been able to pore over them long after my interviewees forgot me and spent the money I gave them. The impossibility of my gaining any dynamic understanding of these lives *over time*, my very lack of relevance to them, may enhance the truth of this presentation—for what do I have to prove? How could I be fatuous enough to hope to "make a difference"? I'm left with nothing to honorably attempt, but to *show* and *compare* to the best of my ability.

Any primary source is precious, being near to reality itself. Although this book swells with speculations and interpretations, those are my honest attempts to make sense of phenomena. Céline again: *They hate one another, and content themselves with that.* Such may be their privilege. It is not mine.

INCOME TABLE

Daily Incomes of People
Interviewed for This Book[1]

These are rough estimates of fluctuating quantities, especially in the cases of the beggars. The seeming precision of digits to the right of the decimal point is nearly spurious. An asterisk (*) indicates that the amount was explicitly expressed to me as the minimum required to survive for a day. I have assumed this to equal daily income, since none of the people I interviewed saved any money to speak of.

All available 1994 U.N. Human Development Index (HDI) rankings have been included (Canada = 1, Sierra Leone = 175),[2] as well as income aggregate (IA) rankings from the same source and for the same year[3] ("high" indicates a per capita Gross Domestic Product of $8,995 or more; "middle," $726–$8,995; and "low," $725 or less).

COUNTRY	LOCAL CURRENCY	US $ EQUIVALENT[4]	OCCUPATION	CHAPTERS MENTIONED
Afghanistan 2000 HDI rank: Not listed. IA rank: Low.	50,000 afghanis per	$1		2, 6
Cambodia 1996 HDI rank: 153 IA rank: Low	220 riels per	$1		19
China 2003 HDI rank: 108 IA rank: Low	8.2 yuan per	$1		
Lady in conical hat	10 yuan[5]	$1.21	garbage hauler	4
Retired road mender	13.33 yuan[6]	$1.62	pensioner	4
Retired railroad worker	13.33 yuan[7]	$1.62	pensioner	4
Colombia 1999–2000 HDI rank: 51 IA rank: Middle	1,770 pesos per	$1		2, 10, 13, 21
Japan 1998–2005 HDI rank: 7 IA rank: High	117.5 yen[8] per	$1		2, 5, 23
Erica		??	hostess/ prostitute	14
Big Mountain } Little Mountain	3,000 yen[9]	$12.76 ea.	{ bottle collectors homeless	5 5
Kazakhstan 2000 HDI rank: 93 IA rank: Middle	100 tenge per	$1		15, 19, 21
Avg. daily wage		$3.33[10]		
Mexico 1998–2005 HDI rank: 50 IA rank: Middle	10.5 pesos[11] per	$1		2, 12, 13, 21
*Jose Gonzalez	100 pesos[12]	$9.52	beggar-accordionist	12
Hugo Ramirez	??		beggar	21

COUNTRY	LOCAL CURRENCY	US $ EQUIVALENT	OCCUPATION	CHAPTERS MENTIONED
Pakistan 2000 HDI rank: 139 IA rank: Low	50 rupees per	$1		2, 19
Kachagari Camp	10 rupees[13]	$0.20	teacher (male/female)	
Philippines 1995 HDI rank: 98 IA rank: Middle	25 pesos per	$1		18
Gary	250 pesos[14]	$10	numbers runner	18
Juvy	3,500 pesos[15]	$140	bar prostitute	14

Russia 2005
HDI rank: 67
  (of Russian
  Federation)
IA rank: Middle
	28 rubles per	$1		2, 10, 13

Natalya			beggar	3
Oksana	110 rubles[16]	$3.93	beggar	3
Thailand 2001 HDI rank: 59 IA rank: Middle	45 baht per	$1		6, 8
Avg. BKK household	480 baht	$10.68		1
Beautiful Golden	167 [per 9 hours][17]	$3.70	cleaner	1
Unnamed woman	167 [per 9? hours][18]	$3.70	cleaner	1
Sunee	160 [per 8 hrs]	$3.56	cleaner	1
Wan	??		beggar	1
USA 1846	$0.007 (old value)[19] per	$1 (current value)		2
Avg. daily wage, 1860	$1.30[20]			
*Henry David Thoreau[21]	$0.10	$14.36	farmer- philosopher	2

COUNTRY	LOCAL CURRENCY	US $ EQUIVALENT	OCCUPATION	CHAPTERS MENTIONED
USA 2005				2, 21
HDI rank: 4				
IA rank: High				
Avg. daily wage, 2003		$103.47[22]		
Median daily wage, 2003		$124[23]		
Avg. Sacramento janitor, 2004		$88.64[24]		
Avg. Sacramento house cleaner, 2004		$74.88[25]		
Lotus, 2005		$114.29[26]	call girl	14
*Carmen Morales, 2005		$66.66[27]	cleaner	21
*Reverend Steele, 2005		$5[28]	homeless[29]	3, 19
Tiffany, 1993		??	street prostitute	14
*William T. Vollmann, 2005		$100[30]	author	21
Vietnam 2002	15,000 dong per	$1		2
HDI rank: 121				
IA rank: Low				
*Hong	19,500 dong[31]	$1.30	sidewalk vendor	6
Yemen 2002	180[32] ryals per	$1		2
HDI rank: 148				
IA rank: Low				
*Annah in Lahij	450 ryals [33]	$2.50	beggar	2
Beggar near Ta'izz	500 ryals	$2.78	beggar	2
Tuna fisherman in Shabwa	2,500 ryals[34]	$13.89	fisherman	2

DICTIONARY

COMMUNITY   A dream. Sometimes we do not know that we had it until we wake up from it.

FALSE CONSCIOUSNESS   A charge leveled against the perceptions and experiences of others whenever we wish to assert that we know their good better than they do.

THE MARKET   What Marxists used to refer to as *the cash nexus*. More generally, an ideology of ranking and valuing everything according to its perceived monetary value.

NORMALITY   The local context from which relative poverty, individual well being and other such abstractions ought to be considered. I often italicize this word to remind myself of its arbitrariness. Normality may partake of insufficiency, desperation, superfluity, or many other states.

POOR   Lacking and desirous of what I have; unhappy in his or her own normality.

RESPECT   An expression of protective tenderness or self-effacing homage. Alternatively, a thoughtless or even hypocritical strategy for consigning someone to invisibility.

RICH   Satisfied with one's normality, and reasonably able to apprehend it.

SELF-DEFINITIONS

I THINK I AM RICH

(Thailand, 2001)

I

The first time I met Sunee, I was in Klong Toey seeking a poor person whom I could ask why poverty existed, and she rushed right up to me, drunkenly plucking at my sleeve, pleading with me to come home with her. In the opinion of my interpreter, she was surely a former prostitute since she could speak a few words of Japanese and since when she poured out water for us she cried laughingly in English, exactly as the bargirls did in Patpong: *Dlink, dlink!*

Against the interpreter's advice, I decided to accept Sunee's proposition [photographs 19–21]. We had been in Klong Toey less than five minutes. Turning into the nearest slum, which began fifty steps away, we found ourselves in the accustomed maze of dank, sloping sidewalks, with house-crates close enough to touch on either side. The inhabitants inspected me slyly from their window-holes: Would I buy heroin or little girls? Sunee staggered triumphantly ahead, clutching at her heart. In two minutes more we'd arrived home, which is to say Sunee's mother's shack, whose ceiling and walls were planks nailed together, with warped gaps here and there for the greater convenience of Thailand's mosquitoes. The four of us sat down cross-legged on a blue vinyl sheet which mostly covered the concrete floor.

What I noticed was firstly the scrawny, reddish cat licking and gnawing at itself, I assume because it had fleas, secondly the round mirror which unfailingly expressed the corrugated wall (jars on a shelf), and thirdly the smell of bad water all around. What my still resentful interpreter for her part noted were Sunee's mother's household goods, particularly the pair of fans, one of which, the good one on the ceiling, our hostess had plugged in for a welcome; I should also enumerate the water filter, television and midget refrigerator. The interpreter sullenly informed me that Sunee couldn't be the least bit poor, for Sunee, or at least Sunee's mother, owned more appliances than she did! —My interpreter was shrewd, experienced, and, except when bitterness of one kind or another misled her, never wrong. In this case, her appreciation proved as accurate as it had been rapid, for I soon learned that the old lady owned this house; she'd bought it with her own money. Fine; so they were rich. Meanwhile Sunee kept looking at me, half caressing her breasts through the shirt, with whose tails and collar she continuously wiped her face.

She'd taken her first husband at seventeen, in those lost days before her father died. The result: four children. He was a construction laborer. In Sunee's words, *he didn't love me true*, since he left her for another woman. A decade later, she married again and got rewarded with the next baby. If I understood properly, this man also abandoned her, although Sunee, swaying and drunkenly weeping, passed over his memory in a confusing manner which might actually have been the reticence in which one clothes a private grief; nor was the bored, disgusted interpreter as helpful as on prior occasions. At any rate, the two husbands seemed less important as protagonists of the tale than as impersonal impregnation agents who'd passed through her like illnesses. Sunee woke up and found herself the mother of five; that was that. She'd worked hard to take care of them all, she sobbed, blowing her nose in her shirt, leaning against her mother's shoulder. Three were at university now; they never came to visit. The fourth worked in a bank. The youngest still lived with her.

The mother's fine, well-kept silver bangs trembled in the breeze from the ceiling fan as she traced S-shaped patterns in that blue vinyl floor covering whose edges had been repaired with brown packing tape. She herself had given birth to eight children, three of whom were already dead. She was sixty-seven, and Sunee was in her forties.

Now, my life is only with my mother, Sunee insisted to the world. My only power is my mom. She's always told me, Sunee, you try to be strong because I am here and I'll never throw you away.

And her mother, with a broad, gentle, broken-toothed grimace, gazed steadily at the drunken woman.

Every few moments, Sunee made a *wai*, the clasp-handed Thai bow of greeting, gratitude or respect, and then she said *kap kum kah*, thank you, sometimes to me, sometimes to her mother.

She worked for an illegal Chinese cleaning company which never allowed her any holiday; her boss had *a very bad heart*, and the memory of his existence shrilled her voice quite out of fervent mother-worship; for a long, long time she clawed at the air as she denounced him, until, exhausted by her own anger, she blew her nose in her shirt again.

The mother gently controlled her extremest gestures. Sometimes she told her not to speak impolitely.

Since you're unhappy, do you want to be a nun? the interpreter inquired.

No, I don't want to. Give me your telephone number, she said to me. The mother mournfully touched her knee; but Sunee, ignoring this warning, all the sudden began to plead and demand, leaning forward, gesturing, smoothing back her hair. My interpreter, who liked and helped almost everybody, including terrorists, could not squeeze out any respect whatsoever for Sunee, who kept saying: *My daughter is good; my mother is good. I'm a drunk.*

What do you like to drink? Mekong?

Local whiskey.

If you could have any one thing, what would you hope for?

She clutched her fists to her breasts and said in a tearful voice: Money! About ten thousand baht for the youngest's education. My daughter is good. My own life doesn't matter now.

A mosquito was biting my arm.

Sunee supposed that I must be a Christian missionary. Why else would I, Caucasian and a man, have agreed to enter this house? After all, *she* was too old to be sexy, right? If not, why wouldn't I give her my telephone number? Staring at me roguishly or perhaps defiantly, she cried out: *Jesus said, I can die for humans. Me, too, I can die—for my daughter.*

At this assertion, which might indeed have annoyed a Christian missionary, the mother sadly slapped her on the knee. Ignoring the reproof as she had all the others, Sunee pressed on in a louder tone: I don't make anything for others, only for my child. Why did Jesus make things for people all over the world? Why not for my daughter?

Her mother slapped her knee again.

Do you consider yourself poor? I asked.

Yes . . .

Whenever I think of Sunee now, I remember that habit she had, that gesture of touching her breast and flinging her arms wide, as if gasping for air. I remember somebody who was suffocating.

I don't want to be rich like the Prime Minister, she whined. If I had money, I'd just give it to my children . . .

Forty-five baht made one American dollar that year, so the sum of Sunee's visions worked out to about two hundred and twenty-five dollars, which I could easily spare. Would it do any good?

My mom calls me uneducated, but I'm actually very clever . . . — and she leaned forward, milking her breasts at me. My daughter works in the bank; she has a car, but she never gives us anything.

Well, I don't want to cause her trouble! Actually, she sometimes gives me five hundred baht and like that . . .

In short, Sunee the provider might be Sunee the leech. The mother stared down, embarrassedly caressing the floor.

When I'm not drunk, I'm a quiet person. I've been drunk for twenty years. If I'm not drunk I can't sleep. Whiskey respects me more than men do! My mom never takes a whiskey . . .

Why do you think some people are poor and others are rich?

She grasped at air and said: We believe in the Buddhist way. Some people are rich because they were giving in a previous life. What they gave gets returned in this life.

And what about the Communist idea that people are poor because the rich take everything from them?

Yes, because when I was in Japan before—

Don't believe her, the mother said. She's never been in Japan!

But the interpreter was sure that she had. Most likely she had indeed, and never told her mother. Many a year I've seen the Patpong girls all in a row under **YOUR'S HOUSE,** a dozen of them in long lowcut gowns red or blue or pink, standing on the very edge under the lights and arches, the door behind them almost never opening; at the passport office in Bangkok I once met a literal busload of girls who resembled them right down to the pastel gowns; a nice Japanese was paying for their visas to his country, doubtless because he possessed a pure heart. Ladies of Sunee's nationality have filled my glass in Kabukicho, which is the red light zone of Tokyo; once I asked three hostesses in lowcut gowns whether their mothers knew which country they were in right now; they clapped their hands over their mouths when they laughed.

Anyhow, our King is very good! Sunee patriotically shouted. He's always giving.

I asked her mother whether she too thought that rich people, corporations or nations might be at least partially responsible for her

poverty (oh, excuse me; she wasn't poor), to which she assented in
that ready Thai way which means nothing. Buddhist like her daughter, she knew that her past existences determined this present one.

So, if you are poor in this life, does that mean you did bad things
in your previous life?

Of course, Sunee answered for her. A moment later she was pulling up her shorts to show me her wrinkled thighs.

Sit down! she shrieked in gleeful English to a tattooed old neighbor man who was peering in through the window, and when he entered, she slapped her thigh.

But she couldn't forget the illegal cleaning company that owned
her, the company that never gave her any holidays, which was why she
took her own holidays, right now for instance, anytime she needed to
get drunk. Here she sat, unpaid, in the abode of her choice, the half-
bottle of whiskey already sweetening her blood, and she still couldn't
leave work! Without self-expression there is no self. That must be
why the victim of an atrocity, no matter how many times well-wishers
advise him to "just get over it," returns again and again to the horror.
Sunee's working day ran from eight in the morning until five-fifteen
at night. Presumably she got an hour for lunch and a fifteen-minute
rest somewhere, because the company paid her for eight labor-hours.
I became quite familiar with *eight in the morning until five-fifteen at
night*, because every time I met Sunee, she recited it three or four
times; it was a benchmark of her life. Most of us wouldn't consider an
eight-hour working day excessive, so we may as well agree right now
that Sunee had nothing to complain about, that her need to protest,
and therefore to poison the happy oblivion which she ostensibly
sought, deserves contempt. After all, the Victorian prescription, *quiet
renunciation*, remains the most widely sold elixir in our pharmaco-
poeia of expectations for the poor. But for some reason Sunee just
wouldn't keep quiet. Whenever she returned to the topic of her job,
which she did as often as a lunging mastiff gets yanked backwards by

the recoil of its own chain, she'd begin to slap at the air, her voice shrieking and coarsening. She hated her boss so much; she hated the company so much. —Like extortion! she kept exclaiming.

You talk so much! yelled the lady three houses away.

Sunee picked up the cat and reasonlessly slapped it, not hard. It fled. She said to me: Maybe I can work in a restaurant again. I can be a waitress! See, I'll show you: What kind of coffee do you want, strong or not strong? My boss likes my mix. I make it for him with one and a half teaspoons of sugar.

Winking at me, the neighbor man said: You mean one and half kilograms of sugar, and then lots of whiskey!

People say I'm clever, Sunee ran on. I could have been a Bolshevik! Better I stayed in Russia . . .

No, better you stayed in America, in that World Trade Center they bombed yesterday! Then they would have knocked you off!

Everybody laughed at this, even the staid old mother; Sunee chuckled chokingly, punching the air . . .

2

Destiny was what they always said. In other countries, to be sure, people treasured different explanations. I remember the young Algerian babysitter who, widowed and stranded just before she was to be married, quietly told me that nobody was poor because we'd each been given something by Allah, so that it was important to thank Him; that was how to pass His test. The Mexican cleaning lady, who was almost Sunee's age but didn't drink, had only two children, and happened to be working illegally in the U.S.A., credited a circumstantial explanation for her own poverty: namely, lack of documents. She remained here only for her husband's sake, she said. Back in Mexico she'd been a schoolteacher, hence enfranchised into the middle class. Since she hadn't sprung from poverty, she felt no compulsion to believe that it must be her destiny. When I requested her opinion on the broader question of why so many people in this world were poor, she replied that too few people owned too much money, so I then asked whether a revolution which killed the rich would better the majority, and this woman, who was brown, strong, freckled and in an impersonal way which never affected her capacity for friendliness very bitter, hesitated, trying to decide whether to trust me, which I took for a token that like so many of her countrymen she did in fact advocate violent revolution (the Algerian woman, as beautifully unworldly in her way as any Buddhist, cried out in horror: *But it's not right to kill people just for money!*) — but just then the mistress of the house entered the kitchen and commenced screaming that this half-day of the Mexican woman's life belonged to *her* because she had bought it; should I utilize one additional instant of it, I would literally have to pay; and the Mexican woman, who anyhow had never stopped scrubbing the sink during the five minutes that she had been speaking with me, turned quickly and expressionlessly away. No, *destiny* was hardly every explanation everywhere; but in Sunee's neighborhood, where beggars *wai*'d whether they received money or not and temperance meant swimming through the heat with as little effort as possible, not because Thais are "lazy" but because exertion in that climate was as unhealthy, even dangerous, as attempting to sprint throughout a twenty-mile race, people murmured *destiny*. Just as men carry boxes upstairs, while fat, craterfaced women sell sugarcane juice in plastic bags, just as foreigners swarm sweatyhaired or heat-defiant in the most expensive districts, just as schoolgirls in white blouses and blue miniskirts wait together for the buses, so poor people know that they were poor before they were even born. And these cleaning women, so many of them came from the northeast—the zone with a third of Thailand's area, a third of the population, too, and a tenth of the income. They came without vendible abilities except patience and the experience of rice-farming and in some few cases the wherewithal to attract the lust of men. Whether they fell into the slums of Klong Toey or found a shack near Phetchaburi Road with its American hamburger chains, chicken franchises and ice cream parlors between which taxis, trucks and the last surviving *tuktuks* crawled, destiny had tattooed them in their grandmothers' wombs **[photographs 22–23]**.

In your idea, are you poor or not? I asked another of them, a person who described her job as *clean—mop—sweep*. She was in her late thirties and looked at least fifty.

Poor, she replied nervously twisting a piece of paper in her hand. Although she'd clocked out for the night, she remained afraid that somebody might report her for talking with me, which is why after this half-hour interview, even though I'd paid her more than she made in a day, her friends advised her not to meet me anymore.

What kind of house do you have?

A wooden house, in the Ratchutori area. It's twenty minutes away by walking. I pay twenty-five hundred a month.

There went half of her salary.*

Why are poor people poor?

Just destiny, she said, politely half smiling, twisting the paper to shreds in her swollen-veined hands.

Can you change your destiny?

Impossible. Always poor.

If someone gave you one million baht, what would you do?

She smiled at the joke. Finally she said: Stay home, make a new house. No work in Bangkok anymore . . .

Can you read and write?

I attended secondary school, she replied uncomfortably, and I knew the answer.

Are men and women equally poor?

---

* It was also half of the average household monthly expenditure for housing in Greater Bangkok.

Women are more poor than men, since we cannot work hard like men . . .

So her gender became one more reason for fatalism, which she expressed with a smile of crooked teeth.

Her work was very very tiring, she murmured. She wanted to look for another job, but found no time to do it . . .

3

Never mind the Marxists; their notion of false consciousness has been adopted by busybodies down the ages, from the Jesuit missionaries who set out to save the Iroquois from damnation, no matter that the Iroquois didn't want to be saved, to the American legislator who sends his fellow citizens to jail in order to protect them from harming themselves by smoking marijuana cigarettes. What a world! But if Sunee, who's condemned to a moderately atrocious existence, chooses not to call herself exploited, should we take her word for it? If my interpreter can prove that in a relative way Sunee's mother isn't badly off, may we fondly dismiss them both?* If Sunee ever said, *I am rich*, which she won't, would that make her so? Where lies our responsibility for her life?

4

Her daughter Vimonrat, slender, shy and dark, was always waiting in her grandmother's care by the time Sunee and her bottle arrived. The girl spent weekends in that shack with the corrugated wall and the smell of bad water, since she had nothing else to do, school being out

---

* Pontius Pilate was lucky. After he had literally washed his hands of the blood-guilt which he would otherwise incur for condemning a certain troublemaker, the multitude conveniently shouted: "His blood be on us and our children!" I've never yet found a crowd who were willing to do this for me.

and her mother at work if not drunk. On the night that I first made her acquaintance, she and her grandmother were in the neighbors' shanty watching television news, which continued to be mainly about dead Americans, a topic of considerably less interest to the eight or nine people cross-legged on the floor than the Thai sports which followed.

Sunee's mother always made a more introverted impression out of her own home. She sat facing away from the neighbors' television, with her great, gnarled working fingers spread out and down against the floor like aerial tree-roots. Vimonrat had already changed out of her school uniform. In her grey checked shorts she looked very clean, quiet and polite, bowing over her bowl of rice, then raising a meaty bone to her mouth. She was ten years old.

What do you like to do for fun? I asked her.

Play with friends at Grandma's house.

She had never visited the northeast where her mother was born. On the other hand, she had already seen the center of her mother's world, which she considered "not so bad"; there she helped her mother, pushing a broom, scrubbing, or even making coffee for the boss, who was a young Chinese ladyboy. Whenever he saw her, he'd shout out: *Baby, where's the fat girl?* meaning her mother. That was how he joked.

The girl carefully squashed a mosquito on her arm, then cleaned her hand on a floor rag. Meanwhile the neighbors' fat little eight-year-old, dripping wet and naked but for a towel around his waist, passed behind the television to go upstairs. —These people not so poor, the interpreter informed me resolutely.

Vimonrat took the rag she'd cleaned her hand with and began to use it to scrub the floor where she'd sat. She wasn't sure how often her mother stayed home. If she felt drunk in the morning, she couldn't go to work. Did that happen once a month, I asked, once a week, twice a week? Vimonrat could not say. There were more significant topics about which she appeared to be equally uninformed. For instance, she believed that her mother had only three children.

Now the neighbors had been imposed on sufficiently, and so Vimonrat, her grandmother, the interpreter and I departed into a warm mosquito-infested night like any other night, descending a sloping sidewalk as narrow as one of the shack-studded piers in the Thai fishing towns; indeed, I never got over the fact, already mentioned, that one could practically stretch an arm out the window to touch a neighbor's house across this sidewalk; in short, there could be no privacy here; neighbors made no bones about peering through each other's naked windows. The lady who'd yelled at Sunee: *You talk so much!* had heard every word even though she was three houses down. She stared out her window at us now.

Passing Sunee's mother's house, we walked out of that slum and into Klong Toey's night-glows, lit televisions in corrugated shacks, motorbike drivers, starving cats, warehouses crammed with jute bags, street stalls offering fruits and cassettes, incandescent light tubes in doorways, loud music, drawn steel gratings, green sugarcane juice for sale in plastic bags; three rotisserie chickens all lit up in their stand like some sacred assemblage; a crowd of happy addicts dancing like those grimacing guardian deities all in a cordon at Thai temples, arm to arm around a golden stupa; and then we turned into the next slum, where Sunee had rented her personal hellhole—a five-minute walk from Sunee's mother's house, which is to say nearly a quarter of an hour the way Sunee's mother walked, in part because, the electricity being out at Sunee's, the old lady had to take the neighbor's battery-powered **AUTOMATIC EMERGENCY LIGHT,** which was the size of a ghetto blaster and looked quite heavy; she insisted on carrying it without help. As soon as we arrived, I was reminded of Sunee's customary gasping-for-air gesture, the little room at the top of the rotten pitch-dark stairs being literally stifling; even Sunee's mother had begun to sweat, and the interpreter for once could not deny that the occupant of this place was *poor.*

(Sunee, why don't you live with your mother since you love her so much? —Because I'm a drunk! —According to Vimonrat, the real reason was that Sunee refused to speak to her younger sister, who visited the old lady at Sunee-less hours. I for my part wondered how three people could have slept there; it must have been crowded enough on Saturday and Sunday nights when Vimonrat stretched out beside her grandmother on the concrete floor.)

The girl hastily swept the filthy floor for us to sit on, while her grandmother activated both bulbs of the **AUTOMATIC EMER-GENCY LIGHT,** by whose luminescence I now saw the true hideousness of this place.* Vimonrat had seated herself beneath the two clotheslines (it was her mother who did the washing), and with decent Thai modesty folded her legs beneath her so that the soles of her feet pointed behind and away.

Have you lived here very long?

My mother is always moving.

It turned out that they'd been here for about two months.

What do you think about this house?

I prefer my sister's house, because it's bigger.

Is Klong Toey dangerous for you?

Many drug addicts. I had a bad dream: I was playing with my friend, and a man wanted to kidnap us. I'm afraid here. One time I thought a ghost had come. I was taking a shower, and somebody knocked on the door, but when I opened it, nobody was there, so it must have been a bad thing. I'm afraid of ghosts.

The grandmother, sitting in the darkness, didn't believe in ghosts.

And Mother doesn't believe either, the girl said.

She went to school in a "big *tuktuk*," which probably meant a bus. I asked her which subject she enjoyed most; English, she replied politely in her soft shy voice; she wanted to be a teacher. A beetle, great and glossy on the floor, kept crawling in angles around the pond of

---

* Readers of *Crime and Punishment* are invited to remember Raskolnikov's flat.

light and then behind the mosquito netting where Vimonrat and her mother slept.

Both Sunee's mother and the interpreter had impressed on her that she must be strictly truthful with me, no matter how embarrassing this might be; I was paying for these interviews* because I wanted to learn something which might help others, and Vimonrat understood that, so when I asked about her family life she replied, her face wider-eyed in that poor light which gleamed with cruel randomness upon her sweaty forehead and cheeks: I don't like it when my mother's drunk. Sometimes when she's drunk we have a problem with the people nearby, since she talks too loud . . .

But then, lapsing into her mother's defensiveness, she began to worry that I might disapprove, and said: Sometimes my mother asks me if I want to eat something nice, and she buys chicken for me after work.

(Tonight there was no chicken.)

Sometimes I ask my mother to stop being drunk. My mother says she cannot. She says: Even when you were in my stomach I was drunk!

How do you feel about that?

Up to her, the child murmured. No problem.

Why are some people poor and some people rich?

From the life before. If you do a good thing you won't be poor.

(Is this ideology cruel or not? On the one hand, it makes one hopeless, self-hating. On the other hand, in a society without full employment, poor people might as well be resigned.)[†]

---

* That's right! I was paying for them; I was rich! Didn't that give my invasiveness carte blanche? In *Let Us Now Praise Famous Men*, Evans and Agee inspected every inch of their subjects' houses while the latter were away at church. Only you, the reader, can decide whether such knowledge as you gain from reading that long passage of the book justifies its means.

† And not only life becomes more bearable. The great Chinese writer Lu Xun opined that "the general belief in a posthumous existence further strengthens the casual attitude towards death." But what about the poor? If they were born into a bad existence this time, why not next time? Here again Lu Xun conveyed an optimistic attitude: "They firmly believe that they have not committed sins frightful

Then did you do something bad in your previous life?

No, said the girl slowly, her knees politely folded, supporting herself on her palms.

In that case, why are you poor?

She smiled and cocked her head, scratching at her mosquito bites. —Maybe last time I was very rich and so this time I must be poor.

5

I gave her a hundred baht, and she was very happy because that meant she could go see a film with the other schoolchildren and also eat something. I wanted to give more, but the interpreter warned that if I did, Sunee would take it all. I obeyed the interpreter that time.

It was getting late, the girl now sitting with her head on her chin. Whenever her mother was drunk they went to bed at nine, sleeping together behind that mosquito net. Otherwise they turned in at eight. Soon it would be nine. All four of us were as limp and damp as the clothes which hung on the wall of that grim room. At last Sunee came in, drunk and loud . . .

6

The next time we visited Sunee's house, bucket-water splashed, then the girl came out from the darkness, wet, wearing only a white towel, and she clasped her hands together in a polite *wai*. On this occasion I spied two slits of light high up near the ceiling through which one could see into another tenement, and a human eye was gazing at us through one of them. I remembered how Vimonrat had said that the

---

enough to condemn them to becoming beasts: they have not had the position or the power of money to commit such sins."

neighbors were not so friendly; many people kept talking together about Sunee's loud voice. Was the drunken woman a freak to them, or a mere annoyance? Did that eye like to spy on the girl when she washed? How much could it see? Now she was standing in the darkest corner she could, dressing, while the rest of us looked away.

Sunee sat in lotus position by the mosquito net, a silhouette only. She was very tired today, she said. But she had cleaned the house in our honor. —I never thought anyone would come to visit, she explained. I'm not an important person. So I went to work and came back at six o'clock . . .

This broke my heart.

She hadn't started drinking yet. She was trying so hard to be a good hostess.

Usually she woke up before six, and by seven was out of the house. She took a thirty-minute bus ride, trying to arrive by seven-thirty, since after eight, when the work started, the ladyboy would begin to deduct her salary, and from the way Sunee lived, I suspect he deducted it often. He reigned over forty-five workers. First Sunee cleaned his office; then she entered her territory, namely the eleventh floor of a certain office tower, where she vacuumed, swept and mopped, after which came the part she dreaded: watering the roof garden, which entailed carrying the water up a steep ladder, twin buckets on a pole across her shoulders; for although she was proud of her health and had never been to the hospital except to give birth to her five children—she used to be so strong that after her first husband, the construction worker, divorced her, she'd become a porter in the harbor—still, by Thai standards Sunee was no longer a young woman;* and the buckets were heavy and the ladder less than safe. She showed me the sores on her calves and thighs from

* When I turned thirty, I began to notice that in poor countries most people my age looked five years older. Now that I am over forty, they look at least ten years older.

scraping against the roof day after day. Then she began feebly complaining about the Chinese ladyboy again. She was too afraid to be photographed wearing her blue uniform with the company's three initials on it, since "something might happen," but she showed it to me; in fact, she decided to model it, wearing a strange half-smile. I wondered whether she might thinking of her bargirl days, when she must have worn a pretty bathing suit or one of those beautiful pastel gowns as did the girls of **YOUR'S HOUSE.** But this garment could have been a jail suit; visiting various womenfriends in my country's minimum security prisons, I'd found them wearing something similar; often even the color was the same as Sunee's, but of course her uniform, whose cost had been deducted from her wages, was flimsier; that was why I always felt sad when I saw her and her sisters in their blue or orange livery so much like prison jumpsuits as they flitted slowly along the facets and crevices of Bangkok's great Western-style towers, sliding a broom across a terrace.

Her salary was a hundred and sixty baht per eight hours—about three dollars and fifty cents.* The average household income for Bangkok was three times higher than this. Sometimes she got overtime. The bus cost her five baht and she bought lunch on the street for ten baht more: rice in a plastic bag. As for her most privileged expenditure, that played itself out as follows: If no work, I spend fifteen baht. Just half the bottle for fifteen. If I clean a little bit, then thirty. I

---

* This seemed to be the going rate for this type of work. Moreover, it was approximately the national wage for daily employees, although for Bangkok it remained a little low. Nor did it matter whether the employer might be a legal or an illegal company. For example, I met another cleaning woman from the northeast, slightly younger than Sunee (she was thirty-nine) whose name meant, literally translated, "Beautiful Golden." The poor woman was not beautiful at all, which was why unlike some of the girls from her village she had not become a prostitute. For five thousand baht per month, she worked every day from seven in the morning until five in the evening, with one hour for lunch. In short, she got the same wage as Sunee, but had to work an hour more each day. It may be worth mentioning that in 2001 the provincial minimum wage was 165 baht per day.

don't have addiction, but I want to sleep well! If I don't drink, I feel crabby, unhappy.

(I remembered her drunken crying the first time I met her. Hadn't that been an expression of unhappiness? But maybe crying's catharsis made her happy . . .)

What's the name of your whiskey?

No name. Just 28 or 40 percent.

Is it like Mekong?

Mekong is a long drunk, and makes you lazy. This whiskey, if you drink it, then you'll sleep well. (I couldn't help thinking: *the opiate of the masses.*) And all your pain is *gone*, she said, her arms rising like wings into the darkness.

She always bought it from one particular shop, so that they knew her; on desperate days she could get her half-bottle on credit. Sometimes, not often, she drank methamphetamine for fifteen baht, "to do a good job at work."

And your colleagues also drink?

Some people work hard or they have problems with their husband—for example, drunken husband—and then they drink—

In your experience, are men often bad to women?

Mostly, she answered, nodding emphatically.

Sunee, do you feel that your parents made a wrong plan for your life?

My father died when I was seven, and I had so many sisters and brothers. There was no money for study. So my mother said, stop studying at primary school, just come to help me with your sisters and brothers. I had three brothers. One died from paralysis of an unknown kind (I don't believe this, interjected the interpreter; maybe he died from addiction). When I was fifteen I had three months in a free government school, but it was a two-year course, so I didn't learn that much. After that, I tried to read the cartoons . . .

Can you read now?

Not much.

Can you write?

Only my name.

And your daughter's?

That's very difficult.

If you took a class now and tried to read and write . . . ?

She shrugged and recited with polite insincerity: It's never too late to study . . .

And you want to?

A little bit . . .

Bending, slender, longlegged, clutching the towel around her breasts with one hand, Vimonrat shyly sought something in a crackling tangle of mostly empty plastic bags.

Do you have any hope for her? I asked Sunee.

I hope she can be a teacher. I hope her life will be easier than mine. Sometimes she just plays alone with one book, pretending to teach many students . . .

That was why the next time I came, I brought the girl pens, pads and even a couple of books, calculating that her mother wouldn't be able to turn those into whiskey. Vimonrat was very happy then; does that mean I did her good? That was next time. Meanwhile she sat, trying to draw a picture in the darkness, her head almost on the floor. It was a school assignment: PICTURE FROM MY DREAMS, then NAME AND CLASS. Vimonrat drew an angel holding an umbrella; the angel was afraid of oncoming rain. It wasn't really from her dreams; she'd just made it up. And Sunee, whom I'd seen lovingly helping her into her school uniform, sat drinking happiness in order to gain sadness's release.

What's the best way to help poor people?

If we're poor and don't have money, we can't do anything, only think about doing. Give us lots of money!

And she made another one of her gestures, just as the winged, hairy-legged brown beetle called *mangsab* slowly flexes its long, long feelers with graceful seaweed motions when it dies.

7

I couldn't help Sunee since she was drunk—not *wouldn't* but truly *couldn't*. Nor could I much help Vimonrat, since Sunee harvested money from her; I could help only by giving small funds to be immediately spent on treats, or by giving money to the grandmother to share with her fifty-fifty (no more than five hundred baht, advised the interpreter, who felt fond of Vimonrat). Wanting to do more, I secretly gave the grandmother a thousand baht for Vimonrat, and Sunee heard about it and drank it all up so that she was absent from work for three days. Ten thousand baht might have killed her. As for the two hundred dollars I would have given, well . . .

In Madagascar I once paid somebody's rent for a year. The landlord was happy; his family had a party that night; I think they even killed a chicken. They all got drunk and slept late the next morning in their stinking hut; in the afternoon I finally saw the landlord; he was about thirty, and smiled at me toothlessly, scratching at his lice. As for the one I'd done it for, she was happy, too; she benefited, I think. And as for Sunee, if I'd paid her rent for her, she'd only have gotten evicted anyway.

More books for the child, maybe I could have done that—

Why arc some people so doomed?

I got the eternal answer from a broken-toothed, quarter-demented hotel maid and laundress: *destiny!* (but she promptly amended this to: *half destiny and half character*). She'd paid one thousand seven hundred baht to a marriage service, because she hoped to marry a rich *farang* (foreigner), from Australia maybe. But she couldn't get over her terror of being photographed, lest she or her daughter might end up naked on the Internet. So she wouldn't permit the marriage bureau to take her portrait, and no foreign millionaire ever wrote to her. Why charge her with false consciousness? A single life must have been her destiny.

8

The last time I visited (maybe I should have kept coming, but Sunee always looked so tired when she wasn't drunk, which was most of the time, that I felt guilty about interrupting, and I could not think of anything else to ask her; what else could there be to know?), she brought filtered water from the office for me: *Dlink, dlink!*

Sitting in the hot darkness, Vimonrat had already stuck a candle into the floor to do her homework by, her face an inch away from the flame. She was still in her uniform, and the sweat on her skin was glistening like the lamplight on the Emerald Buddha, the Emerald Buddha clothed in gold.

How was your day, Sunee?

Every day the same.

And the boss?

Boss doesn't come so often. Come or not, we always work—

There was whiskey in her bag, evidently from the money I'd given Vimonrat the day before. And lest you think that I share my interpreter's judgment of this woman's drinking, let me say this: the tale of Sunee is by no means as ghastly as the stories collected by Marx in *Das Kapital*—the eighteen-hour working days, the lacemakers dying of overwork, the use of women to haul barges *because the labor required to produce horses and machines is an accurately known quantity, while that required to maintain the women of the surplus population is beneath all calculation.* And yet when I think about Sunee's life I can't help but feel that it too has been and is being spent on nothing beyond its own animal maintenance and reproduction. No doubt I would still be, in some sense, the person I am if I had to live in that hot, dark, filthy room, with the substance of my days outside that room devoted to monotonous labor which harmed my body, and if I couldn't read or write; but I doubt that I would have been much able to *develop and express* that person who I am. Sunee's drunkenness thus seems to me to be an entirely natural rebellion — therefore, a beneficial one, to her if not to her daughter.

What's your plan for tonight? I asked, just to ask something; really I couldn't think of much reason to disturb her further; she looked so very tired.

Sunee smiled. — Just have dinner. My daughter already ate at her grandmother's. Sometimes she likes to drink milk . . . — and her hands made that little gesture of suffocation.

Meanwhile the girl was bustling about, lighting three more candles for our sake. Not every baht I'd given her the time before last had gone for her mother's whiskey, because she'd actually seen that movie with her schoolmates, a historical film which was very popular.

Would you have liked to live in the time of that film?

She nodded, so happy to think about the movie that she was very near to crying. The movie had been her whiskey. — Old times are better, she opined, because people took the simple way! No bad thing, not much stealing.

She was sitting sidesaddle on a mat beside her mother now, the three candles in the cup; she kept anxiously bustling and fiddling with them, trying to make their home as bright for us as she could. I worried that she'd set the place on fire.

Sunee, what will you do when you're too old to work?

The daughter looked at her sidelong.

If no big money, just work until I get old. No choice. Just try to help myself until the end of time.

Do you have any dream for yourself? I asked her for the last time.

And now Vimonrat had become very alert, inquisitively leaning on her hand.

Just for my daughter, the drunken woman replied. Nothing for me.

Did she hate herself? How could she hate anyone else? She was a drunk, divinely predestined to poverty—what a neat trick!

She often said: My mother taught me, always work hard and never beg. — This adored old mother who now nurtured her was the one who'd kept her illiterate, and Sunee didn't hate *her*; after all, what else could the mother have done? It wasn't her fault that she'd needed a daughter to help at home. Now where did Sunee's aspirations stretch? She wasn't childlike enough to be entertained by a cinematic romance of a perfect past; her darkness didn't wish to be disturbed by any Klong Toey fantasy of pink and green incandescent tubes; nor did she gaze longingly, in Vimonrat's fashion, at some ice cream stand crawling with a Thai brand name. — I wish that I'd thought to ask her: Sunee, since you believe in predestination, does religion give you anything better than resignation? How many times in your life have you stared into the green-and-scarlet dewlapped grimace of a temple's guardian statue? Maybe before your first pregnancy, you didn't have to work so miserably; you weren't drinking then. Did any temple's five-faced golden angel-snake ever twine about you in a dream of otherness or at least of coolness? Or even when you were young, was the only thing you ever wanted *sleep?*

Just for my daughter, she muttered again, and Vimonrat smiled lovingly at her over her shoulder.

9

Who says that Sunee couldn't have been rich? On the back steps of the Central Railroad Station (which also happened to be where she slept because when she slept on the front steps, people would come and push her away) sat a dark brown, very, very skinny beggar-girl whose hands were as small as a ten-year-old's; perhaps she was fully grown, perhaps not **[photograph 24]**. She wore a once-white blouse which was much too big for her, even the giant white buttons an insult to her, a sort of domination.

Her name was Wan. She existed alone; her mother lived in Ubun Rachitani, which again is far away in the northeast. She'd come to Bangkok two or three years ago to seek a job but there had been no job. Unlike the cleaning women, she couldn't begin to estimate how much money she made in a day. She seemed to be crazy. She'd found no food today, so she had no energy, which naturally meant that no one gave her anything; the first requirement of beggary is to stalk and intercept the rich, however tactfully or aggressively, so that they notice the beggar. Wan failed in that, so people didn't see her.

She said that she wanted to go back home (but I think she never go back, remarked the interpreter). Already missing as many teeth as a middle-aged woman, she sat struggling to keep her sad, dull little-girl eyes on my face. She was twenty-three.

Life slowly entered her face as she ate a meal I bought in one of the station restaurants; she drank a stranger's half-used water, gulping and coughing, shivering in the fan-breeze, anxious about her possessions, the sarong and clothes in the small white plastic bag outside on the station steps; I never learned why she dared not bring them inside with her.

What's the most money you ever made begging in one day? I asked, and she didn't know.

I asked about those strange white patches on her cheeks and arms, and she said: Some disease. I don't know.

She didn't know anything.

Do you have some dream for your future?

Yawning, head now listless on her little fist, she said: I just want to go back home.

I gave her what she said she needed to go back home on, guessing that tomorrow and the next day she'd still be there, and then I asked her: In your idea, why are some people rich and some poor?

I think I am rich, she said dully.

She was already slipping into death, and perhaps had never been alive; by which I don't mean that she might not somehow eke out another twenty or fifty semiconscious years. The last I saw of her, she was sitting sideways in her place just outside the railroad station entrance, clutching her white plastic bag of belongings beside her, not looking anybody in the face.

TWO

I THINK THEY ARE POOR

(Yemen, 2002; USA, 1846, 2001–05; Colombia, 1999; Mexico, 2005; Japan, 2004–05; Vietnam, 2003; Afghanistan and Pakistan, 2000)

I

A sweat-sheened tuna fisherman in the Shabwa governorate of Yemen used the word "good" to describe his material life, because in a day he earned between two and three thousand ryals. The upper boundary of that range is not quite equivalent to eighteen American dollars. Of course he hated Americans and Jews, but we'll leave that part of the interview out of this book, which is about poverty, and poverty is never political.

And how much do you need each day to live?

One thousand, one thousand five hundred . . .

What do you spend the excess on?

The motor of my boat.

Are you rich, poor, or in the middle?

Good. Not rich or poor, but I am happy.

In your idea, why did Allah make some people rich and some people poor?

Allah does the right thing for us, he replied. Everybody can work. Everybody can get work if we have Allah-luck.

In the village of Maifa'a, which was not far away, I asked the men and boys the same question, and they replied: It is not for us to answer this question. Allah gives and He takes.

An old beggar-lady named Annah who sat on the street in Al-araf, Lahij governorate, informed me that her children were *far away* and *always needed money* [photograph 27].

Where do you sleep? I asked her.

Outside.

Why did Allah allow some people to be poor?

Allah chose. For me it's no problem. And I am happy.

If you became rich what would you do?

Allah knows! I don't know.

How old are you?

Allah knows.

What do you think about politics?

Allah knows.

She needed four to five hundred a day to live—half the requirement of the tuna fisherman in Shabwa—but sometimes got only three hundred, which was "no problem." (A beggar-man near Ta'izz needed five hundred, because he chewed qat.) As for me, I needed a hundred dollars a day to do my job in Yemen. My requirements were about thirty-two times greater than hers.

Such were the replies I invariably received in Yemen. Were they sincere, or did they simply express stoical pride in the presence of an outsider? Either way, I consider them exemplary. *Narrated Imran bin Husain: The Prophet said, "I looked into Paradise and found that the majority of its dwellers were poor people"*—a sentiment which rings true, although I decline to subscribe to what the Prophet is supposed to have said next: *"And I looked into the Hellfire and found that the majority of its dwellers were women."*

2

I say I consider their replies exemplary, but when diseased and listless Wan whispered: *I think I am rich*, I'd simply pitied her.

What is the difference between *I think I am rich* and *Allah does the right thing for us?*

Tautology: The possibility of false consciousness diminishes as consciousness grows truer—which is to say, as its acceptance of a situation expresses knowledge of that situation.

I think I am rich. But what could she have been rich in? Her poverty was ghastly, her awareness maimed.

It remains possible that my own understanding was of the mutilated sort; and one could suppose that many a rich man, spying Buddha sitting beneath the Tree of Enlightenment, pitied him; but Buddha's silence was not confusion, his stillness not weakness, his propertylessness not pauperdom. Buddha had flowered; Wan had decayed. I do pity her with all my heart.

I think I am rich because . . . would at least indicate the presence of a mind within a reality. *Because* links the speaker with something.

Allah does the right thing for us implies that *because*, namely: *I accept my situation because I trust that Allah has ordained it to me appropriately.*

The logic of a *because* remains vulnerable to various subjective judgments. *I accept the reality in which I discover myself because I am resigned to my bad karma from a previous existence* raised my hackles at first, due to the difficulty I felt in distinguishing it from the following obvious, pathetic and common example of false consciousness: *If Mommy and Daddy divorce, it will be my fault.* We pity the young child who believes this, and endeavor to persuade him otherwise, first of all because it is indeed false—the child bears no responsibility for the failings of the parents—secondly because believing it can only harm his emotional health. But in various Greek tragedies and books of the Bible, the sins of the fathers get visited upon the sons, sometimes for generations, in what must be an attempt by the writers to bring meaning to the fact that innocents do suffer. How consoling it must be to believe that *they suffer because their ancestors were guilty!* After all, who hasn't heard people reassuring themselves about the punitive verdict of a doubtful trial, *well, he must have been guilty of something?*

Do all of the examples in the previous paragraph exemplify false consciousness? If so, could it still be possible that they are superior to their particular alternatives? Might it be that *Mommy and Daddy divorced because they hate each other* threatens the integration of a young personality more than the notion that it is actually powerful enough to cause this catastrophe? One psychoanalytic truism for adults in conflict is: *I need to take responsibility for the problem, because if I simply blame the other person, I depend on him to change his behavior, which he might not do, whereas if I blame myself, I can change my own behavior.* And there seems to be an activist validity for this formulation. Here is Gandhi in 1947, speaking about the atrocious Hindu-Muslim violence accompanying India's partition: *It is I who am to be blamed. There has been some flaw somewhere in my* ahimsa, his nonviolence. *And this was bound to have its effect on the people.* Not only was this self-castigation strategic (how angry can we be at someone who blames himself?), but morally appealing. Consider Dostoyevsky's crazed and magnificent plea in *The Brothers Karamazov* to take upon ourselves the guilt incurred by a murderer on the other side of the world, because we are all brothers and sisters, responsible for one another!

Is *I accept the reality in which I discover myself because I am resigned to my bad karma from a previous existence* equivalent to *I am satisfied*, or does it better equate with *I consider myself bad?*

No matter which of those choices gets asserted, if I become comfortable with a poor person's acceptance of responsibility for his poverty, either because (most likely) that comfort is convenient for me, or else because I respect the right of his consciousness to become what some might call false, then should I live out the Dostoyevskian equivalent, and accept my own responsibility as a rich man for Wan's life and every poor life, in which case I become in some intrinsic fashion guilty?

This would be no more absurd and no less true than Sunee's doctrine.

3

A United Nations report assures us that *a quarter of the world's people remain in severe poverty* but *in the past 50 years poverty has fallen more than in the previous 500*. Meanwhile, a Pulitzer Prize winner opines that *billions of Third World citizens, constituting about 80% of the world's population, still live in poverty, near or below the starvation level*, and that any number of societies risk outright collapse. Who is right? What sorting and counting algorithms shall we adopt to make up our minds? You may remember that my interpreter did not consider Sunee's mother as poor, given the appliances which the old woman owned. Would you agree? And would you define Vimonrat, who attended school and sometimes ate and slept at her grandmother's, as less poor than Sunee? Compared to Wan, *none of them* were poor. Should I simply say, as a good Christian or Communist would, that anyone poorer than I is poor? Is that tuna fisherman in Yemen safely out of poverty because he is happy? If he stopped being happy but his other circumstances did not alter, would he be poor then? If he became physically unable to fish, should charity treat him differently than if he simply decided not to fish? This moral-flavored question is partially out of fashion in my local setting.* In other places at other times, it has been positively paradigmatic: My 1911 *Britannica* worries that any census of unemployed persons would be forced *of necessity to*

---

* I myself admit to distinguishing between woebegone beggars and belligerent drunks. I tend to give when they ask, not when they demand.

include the shiftless and unemployable sections of the population, as well as those on the borderland of employment. (Who is *shiftless*? A *vagabond*, I believe. According to the Vagrancy Act, *offences characteristic of vagrancy are begging, sleeping out*, etcetera. So Wan is a vagabond; Sunee and Vimonrat are not. The Act's stipulated punishment for being caught living Wan's mode of life: two to four weeks' imprisonment with or without hard labor. *A second conviction makes a person a "rogue and vagabond."*) My city's homeless shelter makes no distinction between the deserving poor and the shiftless; from its big warm kitchen with its stainless steel sinks and dishwater smell, it feeds them all. Whenever I drop by, the nice lady at the window hands me a meal ticket. Does my acceptance qualify me as poor? I suppose that she tallies how many meal tickets she gave away, which translates in somebody's calculus into how many needy souls were served . . .

At the beginning of this book I made the best income table I could, in hopes of comparing the self-reported subsistence earnings of the various people whose profiles you are now reading. My best is not very good, as that table's footnotes show. How could I dare to quantify the difference between one person's "living normally" and another's unqualified "need" *versus* his "rock bottom" need? And supposing that I could establish provisional equivalencies, what then? Some intellects define a poor person as one who subsists on less than four U.S. dollars a day.* Another intellect bitterly counters that the half-real entity he refers to as *the market* replaces resource poverty with money poverty, thereby making poverty impossible to measure.† This is indisputable. A nomadic hunter could live well enough without ever seeing a dollar. Thoreau was by his own standards extremely well off at Walden Pond; and his notion of benevolence to the poor families he met was to

---

* See the footnote on p. 56.
† He adds: "The benefits of the Western way of wealth are not in doubt, although they remain out of reach for the majority of humanity."

counsel them to give up their coffee and other luxuries, subsisting on beans as he did. (No one ever followed his advice.) He lists his total expenditures in *Walden*. In today's dollars I am sure that although his income was four times greater than Sunee's he would still qualify as poor,* at least in *the market's* terms. *(Philippine Economics,* 1949: *Standard of living is defined as the amount and quality of commodities and services that an individual or group habitually consumes.)* Never mind; exclude Thoreau and nomadic hunters.

A certain government employee in Hanoi earned only enough for *cinemas, coffee, vegetables.* She survived on black market income (probably supplemented by graft, although she did not say so). But she considered herself adequately compensated at the office, remarking: Maybe I work eight hours or ten hours in the government. The official salary is only small for me. But we can have tea and play cards, be happy. — Even if we exclude her, too, our quantifications will continue to compare apples and oranges.[†] *It is often forgotten,* writes Samir Amin, *that the income of the traditional peasant corresponds to a hundred working days per annum, whereas that of a town worker corresponds to three hundred working days. If we allow for all these factors . . . the difference between recorded incomes, which is sometimes on the order 1:10, often loses its dramatic character.*[‡]

---

* As the income table on pp. xix–xx shows, Sunee made in 2001 dollars $3.56 per day; Thoreau, $14.36 (my numerical precision is surely spurious). The American panhandler Reverend Steele had to have about five 2005 dollars a day to survive; the American-based Guatemalan housecleaner Carmen Morales required $66.66; I needed about $100.

† Most considerations of poverty in our time bear our time's particular blemish: they seek to convey a state of being only at a given moment, employing statistics and proportions worried down to preposterous distinctions: 84 percent of the poor in Burundi fall into this or that category, which was invented twelve years ago and has altered in this or that way in the past four years. Such a depiction, no matter with what quantitative and perhaps even replicable thoroughness it has been conceived, may become as irrelevant as it was once unimagined.

‡ Thanks specifically to this passage, I had originally intended to incorporate a snapshot of rural poverty into this book. In particular, I had planned to visit the

In short, definitions of poverty vary so widely that one might well say: *Allah knows! I don't know.* But I do know that Sunee is poor, and Wan is poorer. I know this because of the dull distress I feel in remembering the one, and the anguish when I recall the other. For me, poverty is not mere deprivation; for people may possess fewer things than I and be richer; poverty is *wretchedness.* It must then be an experience more than an economic state. It therefore remains somewhat immeasurable. If statisticians assured us that so many percent of human beings were unhappy, we would doubt their exactitude. Lacking telepathy (or perfect empathy), I do associate economic factors with emotional ones, in hopes of making *some* comparisons between people, however vague and loose; but I can best conceive of poverty as a series of perceptual categories.

4

Nina Leonigovna Sokolova, aged fifty-eight, will be properly introduced to you in the next chapter **[photograph 34]**. For now, consider the following incarnation of perceptual categories:

I wanted to know whether Nina had once been better off, and she replied: We never had normal conditions. All our money went for living expenses and raising the two daughters. Everyone lived that way but at that time we thought that it was okay. As long as we can remember, we have been in line for housing, but we never got it. My mother had housing at Tchkalovsky. We exchanged it for housing at Volgograd, but it was tiny. There were six of us then; the old woman was still alive . . .

---

coffee plantations of Guatemala. Coffee is, so I've read, one of the dirtiest products on earth in terms of the chemicals employed; and the plantations are supposed to be both cruel and closed. In the end, I decided that brevity was more important than inclusiveness.

We never had normal conditions. Everyone lived that way but at that time we thought that it was okay. In other words, *we never lived under what we now consider normal conditions; but we used to consider our sub-normal conditions as normal.*

Six people in a tiny flat, and in Soviet times that was *normal.* In a refugee camp in Pakistan, I met twelve people in one mud house, all surviving on the earnings of the paterfamilias's brother, an engineer. For them, that had become *normal.*

A few paces away, a paper recyclery paid one thousand rupees for a giant sack, so my Pakistani friends thought that the inmates of those mud houses were not poor at all. One said: In Afghanistan people are very bad life. They come here, buying and selling! —his jealous implication being that because they could buy and sell their *normality* must have improved. Remembering my glimpse of Afghanistan in wartime, I cannot disagree. Nor can I admit to envying their wares. Along the horizon-touching canal by Jinnah Model High School (WORK AS IF YOU WERE TO LIVE FOREVER, ACT AS IF YOU WERE TO DIE TOMORROW), people were vending just one bunch of bananas or a single fish . . . And beyond the canal, there came to me a glimpse of tents like sleeping white birds, that panorama more or less the way it had been when I saw it twenty years before. *We never had normal conditions.* In other words, conditions had become *normal.* Does that mean that these poor people had ceased being poor?

5

That fascinating, appalling and at intervals illuminating work *The Great Soviet Encyclopedia* makes a distinction between absolute and relative deterioration of the proletariat's situation: decrease in quality of life *versus* decrease in share of national income. The concept may be simplified down to absolute versus relative poverty at a given time, let's say in our time.

Consider these cases:

1. In a hypothetical Hmong village in northwestern Thailand, everyone lives more or less the same socioeconomic life: illiterate agrarianism,* high child mortality, endemic parasitic disease. Imagine that it is three hundred years ago. With the very distant, not to say unreal, exception of the royal family, all outsiders of whom these villagers are aware live at a similar level.

2. We now move this village, with its qualities unchanged, to 1960. Some people in Thailand are getting very rich, and it might be that the villagers hear tales of flush toilets, air conditioning, etcetera. I would expect that such devices remain too fabulous for them to covet; after all, a quarter-century later, when my friend K. married a prostitute from this region, the mother-in-law accompanied the newlyweds to Bangkok, and upon entering the first elevator of her life wet herself in terror. No call for elevators, then! But it may be that mosquito coils and toothpaste successfully introduce themselves as enrichments.

3. Finally, we set this village, still almost unaltered in character, in the year 2000. Many villagers now own televisions, and their poorer neighbors drop by to admire these items. Scratching their insect bites, they watch American soap operas about millionaires. (A novelist of post-Soviet Poland describes the phenomenon thus:

---

* The transition from nomadism to agrarianism might be considered an example of absolute impoverishment, being in the judgment of anthropologists "a shift from generally high-quality to low-quality nourishments," due to the indigestible cellulose content and scarcity of essential amino acids in plant foods. Wheat, for example, is inadequate in lysine and isoleucine, thereby stunting children's growth; rice lacks protein and thereby inhibits vitamin A metabolization; hence one prevalent form of blindness.

The concrete, wood, sagging roofs, relics of fences, and iron balustrades produced a fallen cake of poverty and a yearning for the world as seen on TV.) Affluent tourists occasionally come to photograph them, then get chauffeured away in Land Rovers.

Are these people relatively poorer than when they had no one to envy? Do their appliances render them absolutely richer? What about the ones who go to Bangkok and follow in Sunee's path? Do they become richer for living as she does? Would they be better off if their village *normality* lacked that alternative?

Of eighteenth-century Cantonese poor families who live in fishing boats we read: *The subsistence which they find there is so scanty that they are eager to fish up the nastiest garbage thrown overboard from any European ship*, even bloated and reeking dead cats. Call them absolutely poor. Would they remain relatively poor as well if *eager* truly did mean *eager*, not desperate? If they got pickier, and rejected the *nastiest* garbage for choicer offal, for instance freshly dead cats, how relatively or absolutely enriched would you call them?

6

In Hanoi at half-past six in the morning, a plump lady in a conical hat dumps a bike basket full of refuse very carefully into the street, straightens, half smiles at me with her hands on her hips and then thoughtfully spits; and the glob, which is as large and white as a cocoon, tumbles end over end into her garbage. It is because of her and people like her that within an hour the street has begun to stink. Here a stinking street is *normal*. In the California city where I live, it is *normal* only in districts whose inhabitants would never think of half smiling at strangers. Does that mean that in my city, speaking generally, stinking streets are not *normal*? There do seem to be more stinking streets in Hanoi than in Sacramento; but in Sacramento it is far from *normal* to find the long purple blazes in the drooping *bang lang* trees at the edge of the lake, these flowers are what the school-boys give the schoolgirls when they graduate. If ugliness is a kind of poverty, then Sacramento must be poorer than Hanoi in that respect. (But what if only I think so?) More ladies in conical hats are carrying lychees in paired baskets connected by bamboo shoulder-pole which flex as they walk. Their shoulders must get tired, bruised or chafed on occasion. For them, is that *normal?* (Aristotle: *The use . . . of slaves hardly differs at all from that of domestic animals; from both we derive that which is essential for our bodily needs.* In other words, brute labor is *normal.*) Is it complacency or realism on my part to suppose that they would trade places with me if they could? (What if I demean them by supposing that what they do is "brute labor"?) How enriched and impoverished would they become by entering my *normality?* Would I grow as wretched as I imagine, were I trans-formed into one of them? Actually, the bright, humid slowness of their lives gives me hope that I could "adjust." But when my imagina-tion departs the city by Choung Dung Bridge, constrained amidst the raincoated people who ride motorcycles in double file, tan and grey in the rain; when I negotiate the crowds of Lung Bien Bridge, whose *normalcy* is presided over by a half-silhouetted skinny police-man beneath an umbrella; when past many awnings and gratings I see a grimacing woman whose flimsy rainslicker half tears away when she rubs her streaming forehead against her husband's back as they go home on their scooter, the patience of everyone with what to me would be weary discomfort unnerves me; and now past the final pagodalike apartments I come into rural Vietnam: banana leaves in the rain, then people in conical hats stooping in rainy ricefields, oh, those women in conical hats, their faces veiled by white or dark cloth; and it rains and rains upon their bent backs; no doubt their lives are *normal* with ringworm in their armpits and other parasites in their feet; and horror explodes in me like tall, tapering hummocks of greenswarded limestone bursting above the wet flatness of the ricefields; in the richness of my ignorance I fear that even a day of that toil would be unendurable; it would not be, of course, nor would a week; but how would I feel if I were condemned to it until I died? Montaigne opined that those who are afraid of becoming poor often live in greater anguish than the poor themselves. If this is in fact the case, the reason must be: fear of a possible contraction of *normality*. I recall the women snowshovelers in Kazakhstan who used to be teachers **[photograph 91]**;* likewise that Mexican cleaning lady of illegal status who had once upon a time taught elementary school in her country;† the former were exhausted, the latter sufficiently bitter to leave dirt in the corners, so that one housewife after the next fired her. I am she; I am what Mao called a *stinking intellectual*. How much happier to be born into ricefield work than to first live a richer life and then degrade! —But that line of thinking implies the following: How much better never to have been born!

It goes without saying that I consider the woman who spends her days behind a water buffalo to be as worthy as I. I can easily suppose her to be as happy as I, or happier. Why then do I fear to become her? It can only be because I judge her situation inferior to mine. — Again, the situation is not the person; it's not she who's inferior—but most pleasures I prize—reading, writing, appreciating reality's variety in my own way—all these require *money*. (Naturally Thoreau would disagree. Set him aside again.) — I possess Thanksgiving (my parents peeling chestnuts at the dining room table, with no boss or tax collector to hound them). What does a rice farmer own that I lack? A strong body, I hope, and perhaps a joy in the familiar. Who am I to say? What can I know? But her countryman, the street vendor

* See p. 9
† See pp. 179ff.

Hong, who will appear before us with appropriate brevity in the chapter on invisibility **[photograph 64]**, refrained from opining that I should envy his particular *normalcy*. — Sometimes we wonder why we've been born in a poor country, he said to me quietly. We don't have enough to travel around like you.

7

In 1272, a dying Japanese emperor was reassured by high priests: *Through virtue in past lives you have risen to the rank of emperor . . . Have hope that you will be reborn in paradise.*

In 1999, a poor Colombian told me that his eighty-two years had finally dulled his fear of violence, which had tormented him because he had been robbed many times; once they'd cut his belly open. — I requested his opinion of the rich. — He clenched his fists and said: Oh, they don't do *nothing* for the poor people!

The ones who had harmed him were poorer than he—and still he hated the rich.

Beside him at that dried-up fountain sat a younger shabby man in greasy clothes, lank, white hair, dirt-stained trousers, dusty shoes.

Have you been attacked? I asked.

Too many times, and I'm a poor guy. They take everything I have: papers, jewelry, everything, so many times. They take it with a knife. I never resist.

Are they more rich or more poor than you?

More poor.

Do the thieves hate rich people?

The rich take advantage of the poor, and the poor hate them. *I* hate them.

And then there was Sunee, who was not rich because she had not been good. Did that make her less or more poor than those two men who were good because they were not rich? That question impels another, which may be a disguised repetition of it, and which already shouted itself at me in front of that paper recyclery in Pakistan: If poverty becomes normalized, as it partially did for Sunee (since she accepted her predestined place) and did not for the Colombians (who expressed less than complete satisfaction with their lot), does the normalized person become less poor? A third version of the inquiry: What *is* false consciousness?

8

The Mexicali street prostitute Angelica, who came into my room at the end of a night's work, stinking of urine and sweat, assured me: I'm not poor because I can work.

Why are some people poor and some people rich?

There are no rich and there are no poor, she said.

Then what are there?

We're just humans.

Why do some people have more money than others?

Because there are people who know how to take care of their money, work hard and take advantage of opportunities that come their way; and then some of us, we don't know that.

Beneath the veneer of individualism and self-reliance, Mexico's class hatred can be easily pricked, as I was expecting to do when I said to her: I understand that there are many poor people in the south, who come north to work in the *maquiladoras*.*

But Angelica, instead of following the Colombian example and denouncing the rich, turned on the poor, saying: In the south the government gives the people a lot of money to take care of their children, but they give them too much! If they give them a piece of land,

---

* Foreign-owned manufacturing plants. The factory owners are usually American, Japanese or Chinese.

instead of working, they go and sit in the sun. I lived in the south, so I know. I'm from Zacatecas.

Her remarks telescope two very common statements about poverty, both of which were more gently repeated by the near-saint of Imperial County, California, Leonard Knight, who had lived in Thoreauvian austerity for twenty years while building Salvation Mountain with his own hands in a climate where a hundred and fifteen degrees was unremarkable. When I asked Leonard why some of us are rich and the others poor, he replied: I think the love of money has a lot to do with it. Not to criticize anybody, I think a lot of people are poor because they want to be poor. There are people here, the state gives 'em fifteen hundred dollars a month 'cause they got two kids, and they can't get by! It's a matter of attitude. If you're starving here in the United States it's your own state of mind. I'm not insulting the poor or the rich; I've got love in my heart for both . . .

To Leonard, then, poor people, in America, at least, had convinced themselves that *they couldn't get by* when they really could have done quite well. After all, hadn't he? And he told me about a panhandler who kept wanting more money the more Leonard gave him, so finally he stopped giving him anything. But there were times when a poor family came to Salvation Mountain and Leonard would give them money. He never knew what was right in this matter, and he wished that he did.

9

The poor fail despite or even because of the fact that we help them. I have seen this for myself. These are the twin assertions which their neighbors so frequently make.

In the early twentieth century, the critic I. A. Richards passed out unidentified verses and asked his English undergraduates to write brief critical appraisals of them. Some poems derived from the canon; others were sentimentally or platitudinously ephemeral. Richards wrote a book about the resulting misreadings he'd collected, remarking: *I see no reason whatever to think that a higher standard of critical discernment can easily be found under our present cultural conditions.* Prominent in his catalogue of indictments was stereotyped thinking, which he readily conceded to be necessary in ordinary social situations but which damaged the reading (perception and analytical understanding) of unfamiliarities. Mediocre poems whose hackneyed words carelessly expressed shallow thoughts (and here I should add that Richards would have pled innocent to the charge of elitism; his deconstructions of the good and bad poems remain impressively logical) received accolades for their nobility, profundity, et cetera. Great poems whose complexity could never be plumbed without repeated rigorous readings risked denunciation. One of the most revealing complaints was that a given snatch of verse broke its readers' rules — in other words, it was tainted by originality. *The chief cause of ill-appropriate, stereotyped reactions,* Richards persuasively postulates, *is withdrawal from experience.* And it is precisely that withdrawal which the stereotyping mind seeks to deny. *I lived in the south, so I know. I'm from Zacatecas.*

So in some cases the rich are to blame for my poverty, and in others I am not poor at all, and poorer people are not poor, either. Either one of these assertions may well be true. Either one may also be a conveniently numbing manifestation of false consciousness.

10

We never had normal conditions. The rich take advantage of the poor, and the poor hate them. The government gives them too much! It is almost certain that in all these three statements the crucial terms *normal, rich, poor* and *too much* come into play implicitly when not explicitly, that the sense of them varies in each statement, and that my own understanding of them falls into some equally isolated fourth category. (*Handbook of Income Distribution*, 2000: *Depending on how resources, poverty lines and equivalence scales are defined, . . . poverty in Ireland increased a lot, a little, did not change or decreased a lot using the same data set between two years.*)

Who then am I, to call Wan poor if she thinks, or at least claims, that she is rich?

But she is poor all the same.

How do I know it? —Her dull-eyed, blotchy scrawniness tells me. Would I bet my own life that she is dead now? Not quite; few doctors would be so rash with their own terminal patients. All the same . . .

Poverty is wretched subnormality of opportunity and circumstances. This definition can be applied by any observer who understands the external realities of his own normality. It makes a useful first approximation; and the United Nations' shorthand of *poverty is an income of less than four dollars a day* is a *practical* approximation of the approximation. Some difficulties with this materialist conception have already been discussed. Here is a more fundamental one: It addresses merely the physical, measurable aspects of being human. Such a person might as well be Rousseau's savage: *The only goods he recognizes in the universe are food, a female, and sleep; the only evils he fears are pain and hunger.* Of course the thoughtfullest policymakers of governments and relief organizations will supplement Rousseau's catalogue of goods with such treats of civil society as education, gender equality and the like; the more they add, the more disagreements they will suffer as to which should be funded to what degree—in short, the further they fall into the subjectivity to which this book has already abandoned itself. *Poverty is wretched subnormality* . . . But what is wretchedness? As long as those two Colombians have their food, their sleep and their females, who are they to pull at our hearts? The question's very offensiveness proves that we* know they deserve more. Yes, they *deserve* it.

Poverty is deservingness of a portion of what I have. This is charity's definition. *Deservingness* need not be tainted by the Victorian ethos which, deficient in charity, excludes vagabonds and habitual rogues.

I may not be as educated as I would like; all the same, my life more or less suits me. That beggar over there has food, sleep and a female, but he's illiterate. How much education does he "need"? Why not answer, *as much as I have?* Why not even *as much as I wish I had?*

What if he wants less? Once I rescued a child from coerced prostitution. I paid for her school for a year. She chose to learn to sew, not to read. Should I have insisted that she do otherwise? The last I heard of her, she was married, illiterate, self-supporting and not unhappy.

If someone owns less than I, and is unhappy about it, I'll call him poor. If he claims to be rich, but I see him *failing to thrive* as medical textbooks put it, best to call him poor. When there is any doubt in the matter, why not call him poor? Charity demands it.

But if based on my perceptions of his reality and my judgment of his logical coherence I call him sane (for this is where the Marxist notion of false consciousness went wrong: it failed in that sort of charity which requires us to respect the self-awareness and self-judgments of others wherever possible), and if this sane person, no matter how much or how little he possesses, insists that he is rich, charity requires me to believe him.

---

* Who is this "we"? My Chinese interpreter Michelle (pp. 84ff) firmly excludes herself, for she says: "Everything you should do by yourself. You should not complain life is unfair to you."

II

So the tuna fisherman in Shabwa is not poor. Nina Sokolova is poor. I remember from Madagascar the gaping mouth and sad black eyes of the old beggar-lady who clutched with spiderboned hands at the skin that sagged from her bony face; she said that she could never remember filling her belly [photograph 79]; it would have been an insulting taunt to ask her if she were poor; her belly had answered me. — What about Annah the Yemeni beggar-lady? She says she is happy, and she says she is poor, so she is poor. And the ladies in the Vietnamese ricefields? My honest answer is that I do not know, because I have not yet asked them.

Are you poor? That question can be answered easily enough by most of us. — *Why are you poor?* In appropriate contradiction of this book's hopes and pretenses, poor people's answers are frequently as impoverished as their lives:

A withered Japanese sat on his bicycle in the encampment along the river's edge, with his feet on the cement. I asked him:

Why are some people rich and others poor?

He leaned on his bike to think about it, then said: Because some have jobs and some don't.

And that's from luck or from some other reason?

As you get older, he said, when you want to work you can't. Most of us here are working at construction. I clean up at the park.

Is it a difficult job?

Yes, it is hard . . .

We gazed at each other, and there was nothing more to say.

THREE

NATALIA'S CHILDREN

(Russia, 2005)

I

Indicting the season of her birth — why does it matter when she was born? she could have been bitten by that tick in any autumn!— convicting the gypsy who doomed the marriage, carried off the children and perhaps murdered the husband with magic poison, Natalia told a poor person's tale: specifically, a tale whose dates fail to add up, particularly in the all-important matter of the children [**photograph 32**]. She begged by silently nodding, whether in prayer, greeting or spasms of pseudo-Parkinsonism I never inquired; in any case, the jittering of her head made a striking contrast to the immobility of the rest of her as she sat there on cardboard on the sidewalk beside the Cathedral of the Spilled Blood, with her legs tucked beneath her.

Unlike Sunee, she related her autobiography in narrative form, complete with foreshadowings, narrative complications and a climax; and although the children played extraordinarily mutable parts, at least their presences, however tragic, remained more consistent than those of Sunee's offspring, who numbered either three or five depending on whether Sunee or Vimonrat told the tale. After all, Sunee's occupation was cleaning offices, while Natalia's was winning rich people's pity, a project which could not but be furthered by a polished story.

Painfully rising, she accompanied me to a bench in the Mikhailovsky Garden and said (her formal phraseology partially hers and partially the interpreter's): I am the child of a second marriage, born when my mother was forty-nine. I was unfortunate to be born in eastern Siberia, and in May, which set me up to be bitten by a tick in the fall, when the ticks are especially poisonous. When they pulled it out, it was already *this* big, and she made a grandiose emptiness between her thumb and forefinger. —I think she feels it was destiny, interjected the interpreter.

I was bitten on the soft spot on the top of the head, Natalia continued. My sister from my mother's first marriage, who didn't live with her husband because he was an alcoholic, extracted the tick since she had long fingernails. My sister was seventeen then. In eastern Siberia you can't call an ambulance; there aren't any. The tick had been inside me for forty minutes. If it had remained any longer I would have been dead. When she took it out, I cried. Of course I have no memory of this, but my mother told me. My sister, who had bad relations with the family, used to say she wished she had never saved me. She eventually died from jealousy and wickedness.

My first epileptic seizure occurred when the tick was extracted. The seizures returned in 1983. They now happen more and more frequently, and they last four to six hours.

How would your life have been different if the tick hadn't bitten you?

Probably I would have finished university. Probably I would have married the same way; my husband is now dead. But I wouldn't have been a beggar on the street the way I am now, said Natalia, her arms folded across her heart on this cool day, her coat buttoned down to her ankles, nodding knowingly.

And how did your marriage go?

My husband died from tuberculosis of the spine. He and I had good relations until he had an affair with a gypsy who wanted legal title to our house.* She may have done something to him, since when my mother-in-law died there were signs of poison. People said she was a gypsy although she had a Ukrainian last name. She was older than my husband, not in actual years but in experience.

Did he have tuberculosis of the spine before he met her?

He had problems even then, because he worked at the Lomo camera factory, where lots of people got sick from the chemicals.

Were your parents poor, in the middle, or well off?

Not bad. Mother worked at a printing press, but after she got heart problems they downgraded her to selling newspapers. Then a heart attack paralyzed her but she received a pension.

Why did you leave Siberia?

My father was a geodesist and his work permitted him to live here. My mother was a war veteran. She went into combat only a few kilometers from her village. We lived in Father's room until Mother was able to file for her military pension. Father died in 1998. Then Mother lost her job and benefits because she missed so many days taking me to the hospital.

So I think she feels guilty, like she ruined her mother's life, remarked the interpreter.

2

The sea-green eyes in that pale, doughy Russian face, that blue-green coat one shade darker than her eyes, the way one always found her sitting on cardboard on the sidewalk with her legs tucked under

---

* My interpreter glosses this: "*Propiska*—legal right to be registered and occupy housing in that city, for which she would need to get 'written in' as a member of the family, by marrying Natalia's husband, for example."

her and the Cathedral of the Spilled Blood diminishing her beneath its candy-colored grandeur — these were the facts concerning Natalia, facts to which other data could be appended: born in 1956, brought to Petersburg in 1958, spent much time in various sanitaria, married in 1985, and gave birth to her first child that same year. Her husband's affair with the gypsy began in 1990, and he died (she had to think) in 1993.

When I asked her to continue the story of her life, Natalia said: From the time I was two, my right side was partially paralyzed. I've always had the shakes. I've regularly undergone various medical treatments throughout my life.

That was what defined her; she never escaped from it.

We all lived together, she said; there were six of us including my mother-in-law. But Father wasn't getting along with Mother, so he lived with my sister. My future husband lived next door. He too was the child of a war veteran. I was working in a hospital then; we met at a hospital reception in the fall of 1983. In 1984 we married. When my seizures came back he was extremely understanding and said: I will live with you and take care of you. I gave birth to a healthy daughter for him, so I showed him that my blood was healthy and it was only an acquired disease. He died when my daughter was six years old.

In that case (so I calculated), he must have died in about 1991, not 1993 as Natalia had first stated. Never mind. She told me the names and birthdates of all her children. Elena was born on 22 June 1985 (an unhappy day: the anniversary of the Nazi invasion), Nadezhda on 17 February 1989, Alexander on 20 August 1991.

My children were put in an orphanage, she then said. I was told that the two youngest had committed suicide and the eldest had run away. I went to look for her; I tried; but I was in the hospital with severe seizures and Elena was never found.

How did it happen that your children were committed?

My husband did it, said Natalia.

Why?

He was on an alcoholic binge, and I was in the hospital, so the children were by themselves. The other woman intensified the situation by saying publicly that I shouldn't have had children. She persuaded my husband to take them to the orphanage. I was in Kuibyshev at the time, in the hospital.

This happened in the early nineties, Natalia had originally asserted. So Alexander would have killed himself at no later than age three. But if her husband had been responsible for institutionalizing the children, and had he died in 1991 instead of 1993, the precocious Alexander would have committed suicide around the time of his first birthday.

When did you say this happened? I asked.

In 1998 or 1999. I wanted to run to Moscow Station to retrieve my children, but my friend (here the interpreter said: I think he's more than a friend) talked me out of it. Also, I found out that to get them back I'd need to get a letter from the hospital stating that I would have no more seizures, and I couldn't get that.

All right, I said. And how is your life right now?

I cohabit with a man with whom I have very good communication. We both live with similar medical conditions. He has cognitive difficulties and seizures. He also drinks a lot. His mother was fifty when she gave birth. Before she died two years ago she signed over her apartment to me and said: Take care of him for me.

Was your economic situation ever good?

In the eighties, between 1984 and 1989, actually, when I worked at the clinic before I was married. I was very excited about my work. I was in Hospital Number 98. Then I lost my job since I was taking care of three kids.

Later she said: My seizures returned and that is how I lost my job at that clinic.

So when did you become poor?

1993 was when my relations with my husband went bad. Later he tried to reconcile, I think to get the property, but I said no. So he lost his housing. And I ended up here . . .

3

Natalia, why are you poor?

Epilepsy. Here in this neighborhood everyone knows me and has seen me fall down. Police know me and give me my medical shot. They know I don't drink.

That pitiful woman of nearly my own age, whose head was so much greyer than mine, who could not even tell her own story straight, much less that of her children, made meaning out of her poverty, not by invoking karma as Sunee had done, but by holding *circumstance* accountable. But I remembered the way her autobiography had begun: *I was unfortunate to be born in eastern Siberia . . .* — and I had not forgotten the interpreter's gloss: *I think she feels it was destiny.*

I absolutely believe in destiny, agreed Natalia when I asked her. I have been to several churches where I have been comforted with my lot. I have gone into a church and prayed to God to relieve me of my disease, I know it is a sin to ask for such things but I have done it.

Why was it your destiny to be bitten by a tick when you were little?

The tick bite was just a coincidence. I was born at a bad time. There is much tick poison in the fall . . .

4

A few steps around the cathedral, and right up against the railing which encircled it, Natalia's rival, the spry babushka Oksana, who disdained her because "she surrounds herself with alcoholics," told her own tale with greater rationality and intelligence and wore even now the more cheerful self-confidence that clothes those who've experienced stretches of success (by which I think that I mean security), nonetheless expressed an outright magical conception of destiny, which I found shocking in this product of the Communist era **[photograph 33]**. A circumstantial accident more gruesome than Natalia's had extruded her here; all the same, she believed in what for want of a better term I will call folk superstition.

Oksana was eighty-one years old.

In '41 when I finished seventh grade I was sent directly to war to dig antitank trenches, she began. There was an auto factory and we were digging the trenches to make sure that the enemy couldn't get there. They tapered down nine meters deep so that a tank would fall in. That's what we did for the entire summer of '41. I was eighteen. After that I was sent to dig turf and fill containers with it; it was used in electric stations. The next two years I got hired as a clerk at a state organization, and in the nighttime I washed hospital floors. I lived with my mother. My father had been killed at the front. He was mobilized at the end of '41. We heard that once he came down with dysentery and was sent to the hospital at Novosibirsk, then back to the front. At the end of the war we received a letter stating that he was killed.

My family was definitely not rich, but also not the poorest of the poor. Mama was a kolkhoz* brigade leader. Papa was a chauffeur at the kolkhoz. I worked at a statistical bureau which kept track of the kolkozy. Then I got sent to a factory which gathered statistical data on all the kolkhozes in the *rayon.*† Every *rayon* had one of these counting factories. Everything would be counted and weighed, all produce, grain, linen, animals. I was in charge of the factory; I was chief statistical inspector of Tchkalovsky Rayon, near Gorky . . .

Oksana said this with a *certainty* surpassing mere pride. Evidently

---

* Collective farm.
† Administrative district.

she had done well in this important position; it had befitted her; she
had been entitled to it.

I was living with my husband at that time, she continued. Mama
remained in her original village. I met my husband in '45. He died
of alcoholism in '49. In '47 our daughter was born. It was a varied
marriage, not that great. Afterward I had no desire to start another
family.

When you were married did you feel financially secure?

We were not making enough to feel secure. Everyone we knew
was struggling. Before the war, things were better. My father worked
hard, so we had some goods, a lot of farm animals. During the war
we were still young and full of energy, so when we were sent to dig
trenches we didn't even notice what we were missing. Then after the
war life got worse. 'Forty-seven was the worst, since the bread ration
dropped to only two hundred grams.

Did you blame Stalin for that?

At that time we did not think about politics like that. We accepted
the decisions that came from above.

And now?

She wept, then said: And now life is at its absolute worst.*

This deeply religious woman had never been inside the Cathedral
of the Spilled Blood, since that would have cost money. But who knew
its outside better than she?

I asked her the necessary question which I always hated to ask:
Would you describe yourself as poor now?

Absolutely. I have no housing. I cannot get my passport exchanged
so I cannot get a job. This problem has been going on since '93. My

---

* According to the United Nations, "Eastern Europe and the countries of the
Commonwealth of Independent States . . . ," which of course comprise the former
USSR, "have seen the greatest deterioration in the past decade. Income poverty
has spread from a small part of their population to about a third—120 million
people below a poverty line of $4 a day."

son-in-law's father gets no pension and our documents have never been processed since we came here.

Why are you poor?

I don't know. Maybe we did something wrong at some point. We are the kind of people who are unaccustomed to begging, so we are simply where the river of life has carried us. I have four dependents . . .

Do you believe in destiny?

I believe in God. Therefore I believe in destiny. The reason why, I was in the Metro, having been hassled out of my spot, and a beautiful tall blonde in black gave me a *pirozhok*.* A policeman came and tried to hassle me, but she stood up for me.

So was it your destiny to beg? Could you have done anything different?

I do believe in destiny. But some people can adjust better than others. We just had poor luck adjusting. We were approached by a church worker who promised to help me and photocopied my documents, which he sent to England. We were supposed to get financial aid. My daughter was in the hospital for stomach surgery; we asked the church workers for help; they said they needed to renovate the church. I still believe they got the money for me but used it to renovate the church.

Well then, did Oksana believe in destiny? Oh, yes! Once upon a time, when she was a little girl, she was approached by *a woman tall and beautiful* who studied her hand, then announced: When you are old, you will be begging. —I believe that that woman was a spirit, said Oksana.

Imagine this: to be born into a realm whose official creed is militant atheism, to live most of one's life in the shadow of that creed,

---

* A type of meat-filled pastry. The English-speaking reader may be more familiar with the plural form: "piroshki."

and achieve material success in one of the institutions of the land, and still be haunted by a supernatural vision! Who else could that spirit woman have been, but a reification of causality, like the gypsy woman who'd ruined Natalia's life?

So why are some people poor and others rich? I asked.

Oksana smiled and shook her head; opening her hands, she smiled with her head tilted back. —Because there is no justice in the world, she said, and because people who are richer have taken from the rest. It's the order of things; God must permit it.

(Subtract cultural differences and self-blame; then we find ourselves very near to Sunee's answer: It's karma.)

Was it that way under Communism?

Then it was better since I could always complain and the state would put the offending party back in his place. Now I have no one to complain to.

Why does God permit this?

It is not just a single God. There are also unclean spirits, the ones which wouldn't let Jesus live on earth either. But I refuse to acknowledge them, because I believe only in one God. So I get no help from them.

5

And so, even though Natalia insisted that *the tick bite was just a coincidence*, I took note of the way the lethal gypsy haunted her explanations as ubiquitously as gull screams echoing through Petersburg. Superficially her fatalism appeared to be much weaker than Sunee's. For instance, when I asked her why there are rich and poor in this world, she replied much as Oksana had: I believe it is a matter of how well a person is able to adjust in life. If I weren't sick I would gladly get a job . . .

The notion of differences in our ability to "adjust" to the situation in which we find ourselves may indeed be linked to attitude and individual choice. But for Natalia it might just as well have been the case that "adjustment" is an inborn quantity. I never heard her blaming herself for failure to "adjust." *If I weren't sick I would gladly get a job.* In this context, illness scarcely sounds like a character deficiency.

6

The next time I saw her, it was a warm day and so she wasn't wearing her heavy coat. Without it she seemed frailer, slenderer, more twisted and wretched. She said that she was in great pain. She spoke to the woman whom I was with and seemed not to recognize me. After the third or fourth time she took the trouble to learn my name, but soon forgot it. The fifth time, she had just suffered two seizures. She spoke much more slowly on that occasion. She said that her head felt funny and she suspected that she was *stressed*.

She lived in a two-room flat which had belonged to her boyfriend's mother, a war veteran who for killing several Germans had received a special dispensation. —She was a battalion commander; her chest was covered in medals! proclaimed Natalia slowly, gravely nodding. Then she remembered her own lineage and said: Before my father died, he received the status of general.*

---

* Grandiosity is an unremarkably ubiquitous human trait. But when the poor magnify themselves, their poverty reins them in, either by exposing their lies about experiences they obviously never had or else by compressing those lies into credible and pathetic meagerness. Might the tales be true? Their meagerness remains. I recently met a homeless man in Sacramento who proudly boasted that he was from everywhere: West Germany, Roseville, North Highlands, Carmichael! All but the first are suburbs of Sacramento. As for West Germany, his military unit had been stationed there. He was very proud of the fact that because his service involved nuclear matters, he had been investigated and cleared by the FBI. This person, the self-styled Reverend Steele, who whether or not he took his medication heard devilish voices urging him to kill, rob, bomb the Capitol, had been jailed on occasion, and while he was panhandling me the police drove by and warned him away, so I

Her boyfriend worked at the Krupskaya Air Compressor Works, cleaning the compressors. This red-bricked building had since the fall of Leninism been named away from honoring Lenin's wife; now it was the Progress Factory.

Nodding and grimacing, Natalia said: I would be on the street if he hadn't taken me in.

When you gave birth to your first child, were you and your husband happy?

I well perceived the absolute weariness that came into her eyes when this subject was mentioned—should I have desisted? But she was the one who had literally solicited my pity from the very first with these dead children of hers. And I was paying her to teach me, for my sake and yours, the particulars of her misery. Had our conversations borne no consequences, I could easily enough have respected her changes of rules. As it was, because I was rich and she was poor, I was, if you like, cruel; or you might simply say that whenever I put my money down I am accustomed to getting my way; or perhaps you'd award me the kinder labels of thoroughness and sincerity. There were two or three moments during these interviews with Natalia when the interpreter expressed a posture of reproach. She thought that I should let the children go. I suppose I could simply have told you that they were dead; then when fact itself began to melt I could have stricken them from this record altogether, thereby showing tact; but wouldn't this have deprived Natalia of one of her best claims to your sympathy? Moreover, when I asked to visit her at home as I had already done with her competitor Oksana, she refused on the grounds that she had bad relations with her boyfriend's father. So what was I left with to try and know her by, but her account of herself, whose mercurial details, like

---

would hardly have expected him to be thrilled with law enforcement; but the fact of his FBI investigation remained glorious in his mind. He boasted of it in the same self-important tone that Natalia took on when she asserted her father's generalship.

her nodding head, continually altered place in my attention? I am not asserting that every aspect of her autobiography was false, merely that every aspect bore as little repeated examination as a sticky spiderweb.

One morning Oksana, who as I said disliked her, let it be slyly known that Natalia had had a spectacular take yesterday; some tourist had given her thirty euros.* When I asked Natalia how yesterday had been, she took on this same exhausted look. Perhaps it wasn't weariness so much as wariness. Was she now trolling her damaged brain for true memories of her children, or was she simply trying to remember which fable she had told me before?

I was overjoyed when my child was born, she finally replied. My husband and I were surprised when she was so healthy. We had a really good relationship, until the other woman destroyed everything.

Were they planned children or unexpected?

She was smiling. —My husband really wanted a son, so we kept trying. So we had two girls and one boy.

This was the part of the tale she preferred to dwell on, the sweet beginning when she gave birth to wholesome babies, enjoying her own remission into health and the affection of her husband, who had not yet met the fatal gypsy; it must have been thanks to these factors that the tale of her children dazzled her and me together like the sun's white sphere of painfulness on the golden dome, the ice-cream-candy domes of swirls, domes of squares, all rendered meaningless in tortured green wriggles on the dark brown water of the canal. How many domes, faces, angles and pictures did that cathedral possess? As many as the world! But the canal flattened and distorted them, dimming them down into rags of themselves.

Natalia lowered her voice, the interpreter tilting her head to hear her in the clattering cafeteria where we had brought her this time. — The boy grew up confused, she continued. I told him one thing, my

---

* Then about U.S. $25.50.

husband told him another, and the gypsy woman told him a third. Conflict began as soon as my husband decided to cheat on me. The other woman only wanted to get our housing and to worm her two children into it. She treated them very coldly, actually. She was married to a naval officer who got sent on long voyages. She kept cheating on her husband. She was part gypsy, so that explains it,* Natalia said, slamming one pinkish undersized fist into the other palm.

Did your seizures come back before or after your husband began his affair?

I am telling you the truth: Definitely my health would have better if this hadn't happened. In '85 a doctor told me my condition was improving, and I kept getting better until '89.

Did your husband still love you and the children or did he only care about the gypsy woman?

Natalia, hardly moving, hunched forward, her hands in her crotch. She never took off her coat. Speaking ever more unwillingly, she said: My husband had a falling out with her at one point and when he heard I was doing better he wanted to come back to me. I said no. Two days later he died. I was in Kuibyshev Hospital in the nerve unit. He never visited me. I was trying to minimize our contact. But our children wanted to see me.

This contradicted her earlier assertion that they had been taken away when he was in a drunken binge.

And what happened to the children? I asked as if for the first time.

My younger daughter was in the orphanage for a while and then she ran away, aged six.

Could you tell me more about how the children ended up in the orphanage?

---

* Here I cannot resist quoting from one of Turgenev's heroines, ca. 1850: "Don't you know us gypsy girls? It's our way, it's how we are. Once the longing to be off comes over us, and calls our hearts away to somewhere far off, how can we stay where we are?"

It was after he died that they took away the children, she now insisted. He never would have allowed it. The other woman was afraid of losing her chance of getting housing . . .

So what exactly happened?

I was in the hospital and I had a falling out with the children and the gypsy woman made use of it. When I have seizures I experience partial memory loss. And I get a condition called indifference.

So you felt indifferent to them at that moment?

Yes.

How long were they home by themselves?

Her eyes squinted, and she mumbled slowly and sleepily: Mostly they were with my mother-in-law, with whom I had also had a falling out.

How long were you away from the children?

I passed three months in the hospital, maybe two and a half. After a couple of days they signed me out because I didn't have good housing . . .

Her gestures wandered. She looked confused.

What was your first indication that they had been taken away?

My husband's friend liked to drink. He was an alcoholic. He died in a park. They found him in a pool of blood and crows were working at his eyes. He had gangrene of the leg. He was the one who told me. He was afraid of the gypsy woman. He and I used to meet either on the Nevsky or at a Metro station, and one of those times he told me. They wouldn't allow him into certain Metro stations due to the gangrene. They were afraid that he was contagious.

In your opinion, was he also more than a friend to Natalia? I asked the interpreter.

I think so.

Natalia, what did your mother-in-law say when they came for the children?

She was dead already, actually.

So the children were by themselves?

It was word of mouth, Natalia mumbled. I never received my documents . . .

How did you feel when you heard the news?

I was in a state that I wouldn't wish on my enemies. I was agitated!

What was the next thing you heard?

I had no news, but the gypsy woman kept teasing me, saying: You can't have children and anyway I will take them. My friend with gangrene told me that my youngest daughter had been taken away. Spirkin was his name. He went and visited my children and took them for walks.

Why didn't you go to see them?

Natalia, slowly turning away and seeking secrets in her bag without looking down into it, said: I wasn't allowed to see them, because of the conflict I had had with my husband and also because the gypsy woman was always there, so I couldn't imagine visiting.

(Why was the gypsy woman always there? To help the children or to keep Natalia away? What was she?)

7

What has happened with your children? I asked her.

Suddenly her head lowered forward and her eyes looked blue-green again. She was hardly moving.

The reason I need money is to buy a ticket to look for my children. I know a man who might be able to find them.

Natalia was very grim and straight now, her arms folded. Shaking her head, she refused to be photographed anymore. Perhaps at that moment she hated me for having been caught in all her lies, if they *were* lies; it might also have been that each version of the tale was true for her when she uttered it. Anxious not to agitate her into another seizure, I decided to let her go, which restored her to such cheerfulness as she possessed.

I had a lot of milk when I breastfed, she confided.

And when the interpreter took a few steps ahead, she touched me lewdly.

8

Unlike Natalia, Oksana had kept her children, and nourished them to this day. Only one had come from her womb; namely, her daughter Nina Leonigovna, who was now fifty-eight years old. Nina's husband Nikolai Vasilyevich Sokolov was one year younger than she. They had two girls whom Oksana described as being *over twenty* (they were actually thirty); their names were Elena and Marina. All of them stayed home while Oksana went out begging **[photographs 34–37]**.

What a hardy old babushka she was! Come to think of it, I should not have claimed that she was actually *cheery:* whenever she recollected how she had been taken advantage of by the church workers she began to cry; and there were other occasions when she was reminded either by herself or by me that beyond this moment lay other moments very much like it—in short, she was reminded that she was poor—at which point she began wiping her old eyes, her trembling mouth turning down as she lifted her spectacles over and over to dab herself with her forefinger. All the same, she remained proud and, in a way, even optimistic. She once said: I worked until '93. I was born in '24 and am still working now, as you see. I never drank or smoked; that's why I can still work. I used to go to labor at the kolkhoz by skis; I never took a ride. I was a great swimmer; I swam across the Volga. I used to go to an island to gather berries and mushrooms; now I wouldn't even put my toe in a river! I was the kind of person who always had hope and never begged, and even though I spent my life as a factory boss I don't feel humiliated by begging now. When I feel low, I pray to God and the Holy Spirit and then I feel better.

The most I take in is a hundred to a hundred and twenty rubles a day.* We live on bread and tea, no sausage or cheese, sometimes a carton of juice. The rent is six thousand a month. Luckily, I have a cousin near the Volga who pays it.

My daughter's husband was sent to clean up Chernobyl. He got radiation poisoning. So we came here, because the only hospital for this illness is in Petersburg. His symptoms are bad headache, high blood pressure. They took X-rays of his entire body. He was in the hospital for many months. He has problems with his heart. He would be happy to get an assignment as a streetsweeper.

When my daughter got ill, no hospital would take her due to her lack of documents. I fought for her life! Finally I found one doctor. I believe in God, so when she was in the hospital for her surgery, all that I collected begging I gave to the church. Now Nina's health is better. I believe that my prayers helped.

My grandchildren do not work due to their health problems. Perhaps it is related to radiation. Mostly they stay at home and read.

9

They lived far from the center of Petersburg, of course, in one of those developments whose vast once-white apartment blocks went all the way to the horizon. It took Oksana at least an hour and a half each way: an hour on the Metro, where on certain days a certain policeman robbed her of her earnings, then up to thirty minutes more to wait for a bus that took another half hour to bring her home.

---

* Her daughter later told me that the family needed two hundred per day for family to survive, plus three hundred per day to set aside for the rent. She did not state how they made up the shortfall. Perhaps Oksana's cousin took care of it.

Those latter two transits were telescoped by Nina, the interpreter and me into a ten-minute walk; Oksana was too ancient to make it. Not wishing to tire her (not to mention the fact of the interpreter's hourly fee), I elected to go by taxi. When we entered her neighborhood by this unusual method, Oksana grew confused and could not tell one block from another; all of us, including the surprisingly patient taxi driver, agreed that they looked alike.

And so I met the family, about whom the interpreter later remarked that once she had gotten to know them they seemed more ordinary to her; she remembered visiting the homes of friends who at grade school seemed not in the least marginal and finding that because the father was alcoholic there was nothing to eat and they were boiling cheese* in water to make soup.

(Despite her worn tennis shoes and stained jacket, Natalia did not look poor, either.)

Oksana had said that she learned about the unclean spirits from a book which Nina had lent her, so I looked around the flat seeking signs of religion and I found them: Jesus pictures on the walls. There were also wind chimes, little masks and coils. Everything was clean; the place did not look "transient" except that there were suitcases everywhere, suitcases stacked up against the wall, a clock, a table, many things in back where one girl, Marina, had fallen into herself, hiding her head in her arms, her long hair spilling down, her knees drawn up. She never said a word. I did not commit the cruelty of photographing her; as for my portraits of the other members of that family, my immigrant friends in America who worked in the so-called menial professions, opined, just as had my Thai interpreter in the case of Sunee's mother, that these people did not look poor at all!

------

* She adds here: "Processed cheese, not regular cheese . . . otherwise it doesn't come across how poor they were, because regular cheese was expensive. There were these little briquettes of processed cheese packaged in tinfoil that you could buy for a few copecs each."

IO

Nina, who had been the family's agent of verification twice in my case (first she telephoned the interpreter to inquire about our motives and resources, and then when I had invited myself into their home she had been the one who emerged from the doorway graffiti'd KISS MY ASS to inspect me), who calmed her husband whenever he got overly worked up against the government, and who seemed to be closest to the two daughters, had originally seemed to me, even taking into consideration Oksana, who in spite of being the breadwinner was after all eighty-one years old and who so frequently wept, the most capable physically, mentally, and emotionally. Nina was a handsome, careful woman who was aging well.

I had no idea that things would turn out this badly, she said. They promised us an apartment in Petersburg. We had no idea; we were actually lied to. We were told that my husband was sent there for construction, not to clean up. We heard about it on the radio, but they told him that he would be a safe distance from the contamination. He was away for three months. He wrote letters. He was forbidden to let us know that anything was wrong. So I took him at face value; I thought that my husband would never deceive me. His health problems began immediately. He could no longer complete an eight-hour workday, so they proposed to fire him.

And what did you do?

I sat with the children a lot and also taught grade school.

II

In front of the cathedral Oksana had said: He doesn't like to talk about it much, but he was right at the epicenter. One of his comrades stole a piece of metal that looked gold and put it under his pillow. He never woke up. But my son-in-law followed all the rules. He was in the main compartment. At the end of each day they incinerated his suit and gave him a new one.

Like the spirit who had foretold her beggardom, the evil-working gold bore a fairytale character; and by this I do not mean to imply that Oksana was fantasizing. Could radiation have killed in such a way? An oncologist reminds me that people usually perish from acute radiation exposure when their gut-linings slough off. A massive dose of gamma-rays to the head, for instance through a pillow, might cause death through cranial swelling, but this would, she thinks, take two or three days minimum. Never mind. There is no reason why an ignorant worker could not have hidden something radioactive beneath his pillow and died from it; in 1971 several Japanese won nausea, lesions and anemia from hoarding another tainted treasure: a mislaid rod of iridium-192, whose unearthliness tricked somebody into taking it home. What a dangerous world this is, speckled with wickednesses whose inexplicability might as well be called supernatural! Should I have asked Oksana's son-in-law to verify the story of the poisonous gold? He never repeated it of his own accord. Beside him in the tiny flat stood Oksana (there being not enough chairs for everybody), and I forbore to humiliate her.

12

When Natalia wore her slightly stained camel's-hair coat, her eyes became the same grey as her hair. Although I most often saw her at the edge of the Cathedral of the Spilled Blood, curled upon her piece of cardboard like a desiccated spider, when she enters my inner eye she is sitting beside the interpreter and me on a bench in the park with the trees green and the air grey and birds coolly singing, because that is where she first introduced me to the ghosts of her children, not to mention the tick and the gypsy, the fatal gypsy.

As for Oksana, when I think of her, I remember her saying: I want to thank the kind people of this world. If it weren't for them, this world would turn upside down!

Do I think that the world would alter in any way if only evildoers remained? Not really. But Oksana believed in miracles. —Well, even Natalia had her benefactor, a man who came by in a car and gave her a thousand rubles at a time, but most of Natalia's miracles were of the malignant kind.

Oksana's miracles did occasionally bear a wicked character, as in the case of that radiation-poisoned gold; but mostly they were as sweet as the elongated wooden horses, pigs and birds of nineteenth-century Russian toys. Here is one of her memories from the Great Patriotic War:* Once we were transporting a trainload of turf and an enemy plane dropped several bombs that fell onto the car without exploding. They were filled with sand and contained notes saying in a mixture of Russian and German: *We will try to help you.* —I can believe that this happened, for the Nazis used slave labor in their munitions factories, frequently working the slaves to death; thus testimonies of sabotage are abundant. All the same, I doubt that Oksana's war was shortened by those kindly bombs. To her, however, the messages themselves constituted help. I think that like Natalia—or for that matter Sunee—she believed in providential intervention.

13

When did you know that something was wrong? I asked.

I knew exactly when they measured me, the man replied. My exposure was nine point four.

And what did you know before they sent you to Chernobyl?

I *didn't* know, he said. On my official military ticket they put down that I would only build houses, nothing else.

---

* Known to us as World War II.

I had always thought that the USSR was fair to the workers, I said.

That is absolutely not true, he insisted, raising his voice. Fairness to workers is only what they scream about in the newspapers. I have written a letter to Putin. The reply told me to contact the regional authorities who have already ignored me.

The man had lost some of his hair. He was very lanky in his old blue suit, and sported a strangely pale and bony face.

He showed us his card which bore the date 1986, an incorrect year, which meant that he couldn't prove that he had been at Chernobyl and therefore remained ineligible for compensation.*

Have you stayed in touch with the other workers?

No, he said.

His wife thought the date to be merely an error. But he was sure that the government wanted all personnel in the cleanup crews to die.

I think that Moscow is responsible, he said. The whole point was to change the situation so that no one is responsible for what they have done to the people.

How are you today?

Unwell, he replied.

His wife said: When he was in the hospital, he got treatment. Then, when he had no more housing, that meant no more treatment . . .

I produced more radiation than the X-ray machine used to measure my lungs! he cried in proud horror. It was a four and I was a ten, so the X-ray was unsuccessful.

Was your presence dangerous to your family?

The lady who works the machine has to wear a lead apron against level four and I am a level ten, so absolutely. The situation was caused intentionally . . .

---

* Here something must have been lost in translation or else Nikolai Sokolov was confused, for the date of explosion was in fact April 1986. Perhaps his part of the cleanup took place in 1987, for he later said: "From '88 to '94 we lived in Volgograd trying to get housing."

How was your life before Chernobyl?

He stood there folding his arms, thought, then said: My life was stable and very simple. I put in ten hours at the factory. Now I get the shakes and my joints ache. I am a house builder. I build from the bottom up. That is how I was trained, but I branched out into different types of work. Work is work everywhere. I started branching out into factory work and office work but then I started being discriminated against. I wasn't making the same rate as others—

As I said, there were no more chairs in the Sokolovs' flat, so he stood. I, the guest, observer and rich man, sat. By now he'd begun to exert a weird effect upon me with his lank hair and bald forehead, his heavy greying eyebrows.

When you went to Chernobyl what did it look like?

Very regulated. We would get on a particular bus, travel to an intermediate area, put on our suits, then go to the main reactor compartment. We would carry armatures and concrete, and pour the concrete. Japan sent robots inside the reactor, but the radiation was so high that those new, shiny robots became useless. They just stood there.

What did it look like inside?

The reactor was already capped with concrete when we got there. But there was a machine tunnel next to it, the mechanical chamber. What had blown out of the reactor in the explosion landed there: walls, pencils, whatever. In the beginning we had to run, not walk, because the radiation was so high. We were in there with shovels wearing masks. We were only there for several seconds at a time. Five seconds per *day* was what we worked. We would run in, shovel one load into a trench, then run out. The trench was six to eight meters deep. Once the tunnel had been cleared out we were told that it was all right to walk. When the trench had been filled, we pumped concrete over it. Downstairs where we worked, we wore fabric suits. On the roof they wore lead suits. They were better protected.

How many workers did you see?

There were several busloads of people every day, just for our shift.

Why didn't they just fly over it in an airplane and drop sheets of lead?

Elena, sitting in her chair, brushed her pale hands together and said something bitter in Russian. Meanwhile the man grew more and more loud, leaning forward ever closer. —I've asked myself that many times. The reason is that they were too cheap to spend the money and chose instead to expend people.

Elena echoed bitterly: *Just people.*

It's war, but people basically end up dead. Our veins are clogged, so they just tell us to drink more vodka, which makes it worse.

How many people have died?

I don't know. I don't listen to the radio. I'm tired of listening to fables.

If you hadn't gone to Chernobyl, what would your life be like to-day?

I would continue building houses, he shrugged. I would be able to have a decent job, and enough money.

14

So these were his symptoms: headache, hair loss, weight loss and *clogged veins*, which might have equaled what Oksana called *high blood pressure*. He was also or had been for a time contagiously radioactive, so he believed.

As for their children, Marina had been in a mental hospital, was often suicidal, and today felt too nervous to talk; Nina would later express resentment at my visit, which had agitated the girl. —Elena said of her sister: Possibly her problems were related to radiation. I always had a strange ability to contact static electricity. They used to make fun of me. I have high blood pressure. I can't go out in the sun or I get dizzy and my blood pressure shoots up.

We all have nausea problems, said Nina.

The hair loss, weight loss, headaches and nausea were certainly textbook manifestations of radiation poisoning. What about the rest?

According to the Swiss Agency for Development and Cooperation, *to date there is no broad scientific consensus as to what diseases, other than cancer, may be caused by low-level radiation.* Reports of respiratory difficulties, and cardiovascular troubles, perhaps including Nikolai Sokolov's complaint of clogged veins, are *not based on statistical evidence but on subjectively perceived trends.*

Low-level radiation poisoning, continued the Swiss Agency, seemed to be caused by ingestion of contaminated food. There was no mention of infection through interpersonal contact. But I remembered that a certain followup study of American women who had painted radium dials prior to 1930* drew its conclusions by the radon in their exhalations. Wouldn't this imply that their breath was radioactive? If so, could Nikolai's presence in a tiny flat have harmed his family? I don't know; and perhaps neither does anyone else.

A "Psychological effects" subsection of that Swiss Agency report added two relevant symptoms: *Dependence, victimization.*

15

On a related subject, how serious was the Chernobyl accident? The Swiss Agency document asserted that *about 25,000 of the 800,000 liquidators,* meaning cleanup workers such as Nikolai Sokolov, *have so far*

---

* One detail could have been nicely worked into Oksana's supernatural stories: Some of these fun-loving factory girls used to paint their teeth with radioluminescent paint, then go out kissing.

died as a result of their exposure to radiation. According to the Liquidators'
Committee, the total number of deaths is 100,000. These figures are how-
ever disputed. By the time I visited the Sokolovs, eighteen hundred
children and adolescents had gotten thyroid cancer in Belarus *because*
of the reactor. This figure was projected by the World Health Organization to increase to eight thousand; by the United Nations Development Programme to reach fifty thousand; and one German radiation
specialist held out for a round hundred thousand. In 2002, the Ukrainian government agency Chernobyl Interinform said that eighty percent of the three million Ukrainians exposed to radiation in the
disaster were *sick.* However, the sickness rate of uncontaminated people was not known.

Two months after I met Oksana and her dependents, a panel of a
hundred-odd experts appointed by the United Nations concluded
(as summarized by *The New York Times*) that a mere fifty fatalities
can be directly attributed to acute radiation exposure, while four thousand more *will probably be attributable to the accident ultimately—*
compared with the tens of thousands predicted . . . Of the four thousand
pediatric thyroid cancers, ninety-nine percent had turned out to be
curable; only fifty children died. In short, Nikolai Sokolov's radiation sickness was as much a phantom as Natalia's children! Next
came this insignificant footnote: *The report acknowledged that there*
was a core of people, probably 100,000 to 200,000, who continued to be
severely affected . . . Of course it's hardly worth our while to care
about such trifling numbers; nonetheless, who might they be? Inhabitants of contaminated areas, it would seem (call them poor
people); thyroid cancer sufferers, and—here at last we find the
Sokolovs—*those who were resettled after the disaster but had never found*
a new life or employment . . . The report's recommendations sounds
as if bankers dreamed them up: Reduce payments; restore economic
progress, stamp out the culture of entitlement.

16

Elena, lanky like her father, longhaired yet masculine, tended the row of plants on the windowsill.

If the Soviet Union were still here, I asked her, would your life be better or worse?

I feel very negatively toward the Soviet state, she said in her deep hard voice. It was just a bunch of lies. I would have gotten a job but it would have just been breaking my back for the state all my life.*

Then as now you had to give on the side, her mother put in. Then you had to do it secretly. Now you do it openly. Recently we offered the regional director six thousand to straighten out our housing situation and he said: Six thousand *what?* For six thousand *dollars* I could help you!† Everything has to do with lack of money. If we had been able to buy a house, we would have documents immediately.

How much would you need to buy a house?

I would need enough to buy an apartment: eight hundred dollars per square meter. To count it all up we can't even imagine.

And what would happen if you returned to Volgograd?

The same. We lost our housing there.

---

* As for Natalia, when I asked her whether life had been better or worse under Communism, she simply replied: "Those six years between 1983 and 1989 were the best, because I found my husband and was married and had children." She might have been more self-absorbed than Elena; or, having lived more of her life when rule by police state was stringently effective, she might simply have been habituated to avoid overt political discussion.

† In short, the director was upping the ante by a factor of twenty-eight.

17

Why are some people rich and some poor? I asked the family.

Some people are faster thinkers and some are slower thinkers. The fastest make the most money, yawned Elena, scratching her ankle.

Her father said: The Bible says that it's easier to squeeze a camel through the eye of a needle than to get a rich man to part with his money.* The rich always want to become richer, and squeeze the last bit from the poor. They don't understand the natural equilibrium: If they make everyone poorer, the economy gets poorer and they get poorer, no matter how many mansions they build, no matter how many guns they keep.

Nina's answer was this: The Soviet Union programmed people to live poorly, and think that that was normal. So now most people are not able to escape this conditioning. This was done because the government was trying to save money.

I asked her husband his opinion of Marx and Lenin. Folding his arms and leaning forward, he said: Karl Marx and Lenin had the right ideas, but the masses are so out of touch, their ideas got misinterpreted.

18

Do you have dreams for your future?

Hope dies last, said Elena bitterly.

Hope is that we can get a janitorial job and after that get housing, said her mother. They've offered us nothing . . .

----

* Of course the actual verse (Matt. 19.4; Mark. 10.25; Luke 18.25) runs: "It is easier for a camel to go through the eye of a needle than for a rich man to enter the kingdom of God."

Elena said: I would go back to the university and study. I would work first. I am interested in English.

What's your favorite American expression?

Fuck you.

Her enunciation was almost incomprehensible.

That expression, said her mother, is commensurate with the life we lead.

19

Everyone in the family was pale.

(They wrote their names for me as follows:

Sokolov, Nikolai Vasilyevich, 57 years
Sokolova, Nina Leonigovna, 58
Sokolova, Elena Nikolayevna, 30
Sokolov, Marina Nikolayevna, 30
Geramilieva, Oksana, 81.)

20

Nina, who walked the interpreter and me to the Metro station, said she felt comfortable going out only at night in the winter. During the white nights she felt very exposed. She had no television, no radio or newspaper. She wanted nothing to do with the world. And in these few moments when we were alone with her I began to realize how far away from me she was, as I had already known her husband to be; I can't say they were *lost*, because they knew where they were; where they were was *gone*; they were poor; they were the living dead.

I kissed her pale cold hand goodbye.

21

Neither Sunee nor Oksana nor Natalia expressed optimism that their lives would improve. *Hope dies last,* said Elena, and they were already in the category of last things. But Sunee's karmic situation of hopelessness contrasted with the other two women's if-onlys. The tick, the gypsy mistress, Chernobyl, the unhelpfulness and possible dishonesty of Oksana's church workers, the collapse of the Soviet pension system remained eternally available to be blamed. Meanwhile, Oksana and Natalia's reiterations of powerlessness, reinforced by their belief in destiny, rendered their outlook nearly the same as Sunee's. And so I came to wonder whether one characteristic of poverty might be *surrender to defeat.*

FOUR

EVERYTHING YOU SHOULD DO BY YOURSELF

(China, 2002)

I

I remember long shady afternoons in the almost empty park, where young couples, not many of them, walked together, their sandals softly clasping and unclasping the sidewalks beneath the "dragon's eye" trees, whose round fruit was still too hard to eat this early in the season; and the funhouse mirrors reflected eerie sleepiness in the old chambers that ringed round the old fort's crown jewel, an artillery piece; meanwhile birds and cicadas sang ever more urgently with the increasing heat until they too fell overwhelmed. This enervation, perfumed with drowsiness, was precisely what gave Nan Ning ("Southern Tranquility") its paradisiacal character. Here in People's Park the old ladies fanned themselves and smiled as they played mah-jongg beneath umbrellas and palm trees, with the hot, aromatic breeze from the botanical garden blowing in their faces. Leaning forward, waving their woven-leaf fans as slowly and gracefully as catfish move their flippers in restaurant aquariums, they clashed down their tiles to win or lose; at intervals they formed their games anew on that faded green table, building what appeared to be green-roofed double rows of white tofu or coconut slices. Each lady peered behind her own secret wall, awaiting her turn to slam a tile down. Maybe she would get doubles, which they called *the eyes*. Time hung in the air like the hot perfume from the lotus pond, whose dark leaves were almost as coarse as cabbages. Sleepiness sublimed from their wide-open pink flowers like a gas. Soon the temperature would rise even more. People's clothes would stick to their bodies; the parasol-carrying women would dab at their foreheads. And then the haze of heat, plant-breath and motor-breath would press down upon the white skyscrapers, tree-lined streets, whitish-grubbyish roof-tiles, gridlocked traffic and construction skeletons of Nan Ning, which boasted more towers every month. One interpreter proudly announced that the population of Greater Nan Ning was now two million four hundred thousand. Nan Ning itself comprised one million people. So the building continued as it did all across China; many of the construction workers I interviewed in Beijing labored only for food and a place to sleep; they came from the countryside, where they'd had nothing. Whether this was the case with the builders of Nan Ning I cannot tell you. The main point on which you will desire reassurance is that soon that city's citizens would have more air-conditioned hotels; and more of them would be able to watch soap operas in their impressively spacious white-walled, white-floored apartments. In one of these, a sick pigtailed baby was eating a bun, and on the coffee table lay a bag of dragon's eye fruits, which I would have called lychees. A fan turned almost as slowly as a sunflower, while the guests drank chrysanthemum tea. On television, the divorced couple had just met again in the rain, possibly to reunite forever in the next installment. The baby, who for coolness wore a filmy white dress not unlike a wedding gown, cried for Mama to shuck another dragon's eye.

Outside it remained so hot that many men walked half-naked and sweating, with their shirts wrapped over their heads. In the main street, traffic sometimes choked itself for ten minutes or more. Cyclists lowered their sandaled feet to the pavement then, waiting and waiting.

Some of these bicycles hauled trailers of metal or wood; here, for instance, I saw a lady whose not quite translucent conical hat was strapped under her chin and whose job it was to gather garbage and haul it away, for which she received three hundred yuan each month, or around thirty-five dollars **[photograph 38]**. (I paid half her salary for the four hours on the computer on which I entered these notes in Beijing.) According to a retired railroad worker, whose pension was four hundred yuan, three hundred yuan was insufficient for survival in Nan Ning. The garbage woman for her part, who still kept herself pretty and clean, told me that her wages were not bad; she got enough to eat. It was her second month of this work. Her dream was to do some business for her family, to change her life and her family's life, she wasn't sure how. She was married, with one son. Unfortunately, she possessed *no ability to be rich* because *I cannot read books too much.* She was not jealous of anyone, she said with a faraway half-smile. (Why are some people rich and others poor? I asked. —She believe everyone has his own life in this world, the interpreter explained. She cannot understand why. She work hard same as the other people but not understand why.) Then she passed on, and so did the other cyclists, for the signal had changed at last. Sometimes people rode two to a bike here in Nan Ning as they did everywhere in China. Crowds wiped their dripping faces. Sungoggled motorbike drivers shouted into their cell phones, and the air was spiced almost pleasantly with exhaust.

Now it was night time, which meant merely warm time, and the barbershops came alive with longhaired Chinese girls in translucent outfits who laughed and beckoned; usually the only one who could actually wield a straight razor was the madam. Sometimes the stairs led to rooms with narrow massage tables where for thirty yuan they would lay you down, mentholate your skull with stinging cream and inquire what else you wanted to do; sometimes they led more directly to rooms of tired double beds, toilet paper on the windowsill. And next door lay another barbershop with more slinky girls laughing, smoking cigarettes, all gathered around on low stools, shoulder to shoulder with their legs widely spread, watching the soap opera while one of them washed my head. The mirrors were ornamented with little pumpkin-balls of crimson velvet strung on brass chains. In the back room, girls made the deliciously skeletal clitterclacking sounds of mah-jongg; two of them blew me a kiss.

The madam took me to a door behind which were stairs which I expected would lead into another brothel. Instead, they turned right, and after passing through another short corridor I suddenly found myself, like Alice in Wonderland, at the threshold of my own hotel's immense lobby, my conductress standing wistfully by my side; when I took my leave of her, she continued to peer sadly at me from the doorway. Activated only by the highest scientific motives, I gave her my room number, and late into the night the phone rang and rang with this girl or that girl offering me a "massagee."

Maybe next year if you come to Nan Ning you will find it even more beautiful, said one of my interpreters, a young hotel administrator who was too busy for boyfriends; she delightedly copied out of my spicy phrase book the following pattern sentence: *How can you make a fortune based on the disgusting nature of your company?* —In Hanoi the interpreter kept saying: No, please don't pay me, I'm just your friend. —I had to physically force the twenty dollars into her hand. —But Wei Xiao Min, who spelled her chosen English name as she pronounced it, *Mishal*, commenced negotiations thus: From 8:00 to 6:00 twenty dollars is okay, but if you want me to show you Nan Ning by night you must pay me more. —When she signed my receipt book, I told her that for using my pen she must pay me twenty dollars, and she laughed: No way!

This slender efficiency expert and hard banterer (most of whose jokes, like mine, wilted in translation), who was exceptionally good at boring her way to the head of a queue on my behalf, showed outright genius at buying sold out train tickets, bargaining down taxi drivers, taming strange charges on the hotel bill, guiding me busily amidst Nan Ning's white skyscrapers and matching white apartment towers; for me she came to symbolize Nan Ning's unswerving pride in its development. In other Asian countries that I have visited, Chinese get stereotyped, often negatively, as commercialists. There was indeed a brusqueness about China; it was not as consistent or extreme as the Korean kind, but it definitely made itself known, as in the trains when the blue-and-white-striped attendants pushed their way indifferently through clumps of passengers, or when in the observation lounge of the long, fancy, air-conditioned hotel where Michelle brought me for a morning coffee accompanied by prerecorded music, I finished my snack, and the waitress, instead of bowing and softly thanking me as she would have done in Japan, crabbily pointed instead, making me hand the plate to her. There was nothing personal in this; Chinese are in a hurry, that's all.* Chinese mothers sternly slap their children for almost nothing, then just as quickly comfort them. Well, sometimes it does get personal, like the pouting of the Hunanese child-singers when you won't hire them; they rap you sharply with their songsheets, then spitefully pinch your arm black and blue. By and large, however, the Chinese character, like the American, remains more admiring than jealous of fortune. In Nan Ning one says goodbye to storekeepers by wishing them *how mai*, good business. And fortune has certainly come to Nan Ning these days; it permeates the city's hot grey air.

Michelle told me that most of these wide pale streets and white-tiled apartments were but one or two years old. Concrete streets, concrete walks, everything was new! —I think Nan Ning is a green city, a green pearl, she said proudly.

---

* My next interpreter, Mai, said: "In China, so many young people don't have time to love. You want to live in a city, you must have money. You want to live in a city to protect you. Too many people, so difficult to find a job . . ."

Why are some people rich and others poor?

The rich want to invest and become richer and richer, and the poor people are lazy.

What do you want to do in your life, Michelle?

I want to be a good manager and manage the people because that's the best way for the human resources, to do business. If I have child, I will get vacation to travel in China. I plan to go to Tibet.

The young bride in the white-walled apartment with the sick baby was Michelle's friend. She said to me: The roads arc getting wider and larger, and buildings higher and higher. And more clean. All is good! —As for the retired road-mender, who had cared for the same stretch of pavement for thirty years and who now stood smiling in his straw hat and worn blue shirt, sometimes touching the white stubble on his chin, he gazed into the tarry foulness of the Chao Yang River and said: Now it is better and better. All this grass, all the trees, they are new. There are no more wooden buildings like before. This river is becoming clean. Before, at home we had to cover our noses all day, but not anymore. —He was plausible, the smell today being no worse than that of burned rubber. With every millimeter of his happily whirling, squint-wrapped eyeballs the old man beamed and said: Communists have helped the Chinese people to the right way. They help us better and better. I thank Chairman Mao and Deng Xiao Ping very much.

He agreed with the retired railroad worker that *just three hundred yuan is not enough.* He thought one needed six or seven hundred a month to manage. He himself received four hundred.

Why are there rich and poor in this world? I asked him.

There are all kinds of people in this world, he said. Too many people are in the government, so the workers' salary is low.

All the same, his life was getting better, of course. That was what they all said. But on Wangzhou Road, in the dreary district called "Africa" on account of its poverty, there was a hillside of clinking rubble, largely made up of bricks and brickshards, upon whose shifting surface men and women in sandals slowly gleaned **[photographs 39–41]**. These houses had been demolished six weeks ago, for the sake of a forthcoming road. Other homes would get knocked down any day now. Through the men's open shirts I saw that some of them were almost skeletally thin. They said that the government had recompensed them for their houses to the tune of a hundred and seventy yuan per square meter*, but the IOUs had not yet been honored; it was up to the road developer to do that. Anyhow, a new house would cost twelve hundred yuan per square meter.†

It is safe to say that they were not happy. They had lived in those houses for thirty years. Seven hundred families had been thus dispossessed.

A figure in dark clothes and a pale hat crept in sandals along the edge of a rubble-pile, with a long pale bag slung over its shoulder and its face so shadowed that for me and certainly for Michelle it had no face at all; others, such as the man in the yellow hard hat, clambered right across that shifting clinking shatterscape as if they were already "used to it," but this human being contented itself with kissing the skirts of desolation, so to speak, slowly seeking for I knew not what fragments of wretchedness lay within reach. Perhaps it was not a former homeowner, but a neighbor, in which case why not call it rich? Oh, you other human beings!

The man in the yellow hard hat and the bareheaded man in sandals were trying to tell me that they had had *eight areas*, but I never learned what they meant, because Michelle said that it was time to go.

Seven hundred families! One of them, not yet as poor as the others, took me into the high-roofed grungy-white corridor that lay

---

* About $6.32 per square foot.
† About $44.61 per square foot. In central Nan Ning the cost was 1,600 yuan per square meter. My friend Ben, who is a real estate appraiser in San Francisco, informed me that the comparable figure in his city was 30 times greater than in Nan Ning.

behind his storefront, which would be bulldozed very soon; they had not told him when. It had been in business since 1972.* He was sixty-six years old. Michelle later assessed him for me as *between poor and rich*. He showed me the property deeds which the Maoist government had given these people; they were now worthless, and to stay in the game one had to purchase a new certificate of ownership, which few of the people in "Africa" could afford. Still, even he granted that everyone in Nan Ning was better off than in the old days of grass houses. —Before was very poor, he said. —Sitting barefooted and wrinkled beneath the long narrow calendar and the two clocks in that cool hall he'd built with his own hands, his eyes burning with sadness (and beside him a woman shouted hysterically at me, holding up a photograph of her pretty two-storey house now smashed under), he spread on the floor a map of the land once given by the government and he said: Everything is better and better, but . . .

Will there always be poor people in China?

Now is becoming better, Michelle interpreted. In future he have no idea.

Grimacing, he said: They want to develop, but without spending enough money . . .

By now there were fifteen people in his shop, and they were all shouting angrily.

Another man held up two photographs of his destroyed house with a strange calm smile as if the former reality proven by that picture remained so powerful that he still possessed a home to be proud

---

* He said that during the Cultural Revolution of 1966 to 1978, city people had been sent to the villages to work; when that period was finished, "the government did not arrange where to go." This was how he had ended up in Nan Ning. "— Was the Cultural Revolution good or bad?" I asked him. —"This is a political question," he said, spreading his hands. "There has been change in China."

of; his eyes were wide as he fixed his partial smile upon me, and two children stood neutrally behind him. I later showed his portrait [photograph 40] to several of my countrymen, none of whom could detect any indication of trouble on his face. If you look at it you will see the title deed behind the photographs.

Why are people rich and poor? I asked him.

In this village, he said, some people are rich and some are poor.

The man with the receipts elaborated: Some people do business, so they become rich. Others, they don't do work.

Then he fell silent, perhaps remembering that they were all about to be poor now.

I wanted to stay longer, but Michelle grew anxious that the police might come. I did not wish to bring upon these people any more grief. So, thanking them for their trouble, I left behind that sea of white and red brick with a few mournful figures picking it over, and skyscrapers far below.

The way out of "Africa" was a wide road. Probably the new road would be like this. As Michelle explained: The government try to do everything to let the people live better and better. So it's more convenient.

Now the sun-beiged and sun-bleached rags on laundry lines, not to mention the other broken streets and that hillside of rubble, seemed almost impossible. We passed the Flower and Bird Market, on whose upraised steps lay little cages of dogs for sale, and I asked Michelle whether she had liked the people of "Africa." She replied: So-so.

The daughter of professionals, a settled believer in the wisdom of Chairman Mao (she also thought that the Tibetans were basically contented under Chinese rule because they were *simple people, so if they can eat enough, that's okay;* they had no use for music; if any of them had negative feelings, that was the result of outside agitation), Michelle had long since accepted the notion that *in China every state and every country must be united for the sake of a strong China. If everyone had independence, there could be no development.*

When you see those houses being broken, do you feel sad?

The government must attract the company somehow. I think for the sake of development they must give up something. If they do not give up the old thing, they cannot be developed.

What if they don't want to give up the old thing?

Smiling, Michelle said to me: The little party must obey the great party.

2

When these families in Nan Ning received title deeds to their homes, they could scarcely have foreseen the accident of futurity which would undo so much of Maoism, including Maoism's promises. Even had they foreseen it, who could have imagined that the de-Communization of China meant the betrayal of poor people on *all* fronts, even in that most un-Communist sphere of all, private property? Surely the new capitalists ought to have upheld *that*. A title deed is a title deed, valid forever. Death is inevitable, but we all like to believe in the immortality of our freeholds. Property means something or else it does not. Eminent domain is incomprehensible.

What about those demolished houses? I asked Michelle again.

Everything you should do by yourself, she replied sternly. You should not complain life is unfair to you. The history is the history!

3

The hour-long glimpse I had of the rubble-hill and the destitute people stooping and wandering upon it haunts me more and more. As I think upon its sickening implications (one of which is detailed in the chapter on invisibility,* another in the chapter on accident-prone-ness†), my mind swings back on Michelle, who was a likable enough person. *You should not complain life is unfair to you,* and she never did. If she lacked compassion, well, just what was she supposed to do for those people? For that matter, what had I done? I threw a little money and some attention at a random few, then departed the premises. One man in a tall hat stood in a little dimple in the rubble, gazing down at something which I could not see, perhaps an indication of his former house, and I wanted to walk over the bricks to him and tell him that I was sorry, but Michelle did not care to go; and I considered wordlessly handing him something, but feared to insult him, especially in open view of all the other dispossessed, and so I did nothing, and in my memory he is still standing there.

Everything you should do by yourself. This was Michelle's credo, and from what I came to know of her, she lived by it. What a little whirl-wind she was! Who better exemplified the booming new incarnation of Nan Ning than she? I would be surprised if by now as I finish this book she is not indeed *a good manager, because that's the best way for the human resources, to do business.* All the same, I would rather not be her employee.

Everything you should do by yourself. But hadn't those seven hundred families done everything by themselves? As the other interpreter had paraphrased the garbage lady, *she work hard same as the other people but not understand why.* As for those seven hundred families, they had committed the sin of being unlucky, so that the new road unrolled itself through their houses; accordingly, they became poor; and, as we know, *the rich want to invest and become richer and richer, and the poor people are lazy.*

---

* See pp. 111ff.
† See pp. 136ff.

They were not rich enough to keep what they had by purchasing new title deeds; so they lost what they had, as a result of which people like Michelle blamed them.

Meanwhile the barbershop girls mentholated rich men's skulls, and new white-tiled apartments for rich people bloomed on white tower-stalks, and Nan Ning got more cars which required more roads, and *they help us better and better.*

FIVE

THE TWO MOUNTAINS

(Japan, 2004–05)

I

This last portrait must be more true than the previous three, because it conveys and claims less; after all, if I ever met Big Mountain or Little Mountain away from their bridge, I might not recognize them; nor would they remember me. Isn't this fundamental to the situation? If it amused me, I, a rich man, could choose a few poor people to be my pets, and then I could feed them in the most joyously self-congratulatory manner; but it remains incumbent on me to avoid entanglements with the millions of others who live in the rain **[photographs 42–49]**.

2

They dwelled, as I said, under the Shijo-dori Bridge on the Kamogawa River in Kyoto, in a blue-tarped box house. Big Mountain was short and Little Mountain was tall. In their front yard, so to speak, they kept chairs around a little table. A teapot was boiling over a fire in a blackened bucket in the river.

How long have you lived outside? I asked them.

A year, said the man in the germ mask. That was Little Mountain. —I lost my job. I was a salaryman. The company restructured.

Now that you have been here so long, will it be difficult to become a salaryman again?

Of course I want to, but because of age restrictions they don't accept me. There are many people living like this.

Even younger people can't get jobs, said the other man, so it's utterly hopeless.

This is the first time I have been homeless, Little Mountain remarked.

What did you do when it happened?

The first day there was no plan, but at least we had to secure something to eat. We got cardboards and sheets. That first place was here.

He's from Kyoto, said his friend. I'm from Hokkaido. We met each other just by meeting each other.

He had also been a salaryman. I used to work for a major pharmaceutical company, he said proudly,* and then I *quit!* I had been in the company for thirteen years. Now I've been here for three years.

Why are you poor?

Big Mountain leaned back and said: I don't regard us as poor. *We are not poor.* If we have a place to live, we go there; if we have a job to do, we do it.

He said these words in that same tone of proud insistence, and the other man laughed, in embarrassment, I thought.

How do you get your food now?

We collect empty cans and we sell them for recycling. In one day, we make three thousand yen.† Then we go to the convenience store. The best food for the price is ramen, rice, vegetables.

When people walk by, are they nice to you?

---

* Here I remembered Natalia's boast: "Before my father died, he received the status of general."

† Around US $28.00.

They nodded.

How do you stay warm?

Well, I used to have a girlfriend, said Big Mountain with a sad smile. I miss girls.

What is your dream for the future?

Corporation president! cried Big Mountain.

Little Mountain said: I'd like to work.

What would be the best way to help people like you?

Little Mountain smiled sadly at me, his head cocked one way, his dark polyester cap canted another, and he said: Make a society that is easier to live in.

They shared an aquarium with thirty goldfish in it, *just for fun*, they said. It sat out on a pedestal in the middle of the water. Birds used to get their pets, so they put a lid on it.

3

Once I had drunk the tea they poured me they gazed at me almost hopefully, I thought, or perhaps their expressions were sad or simply patient; another word might be *submissive*; they might not have wanted anything to do with me, but business required them to be welcoming just as it does for bar hostesses—and yet many of the homeless men I met in Tokyo were gruff with me; perhaps the two mountains truly didn't mind me; looking into their eyes, I began to experience a nasty kind of sorrow which was in equal parts useless to them and to me, so I felt shy before them, as I had not in, say, Madagascar, when, encountering a baby's wool cap peeking like an onion-top from its swaddling-rags, which were nested in the rags of its beggar-mother who waited against a paint-scabbed wall by night, her eyes half-closed **[photograph 80]**, I had but to pass through the iron grating (whose purpose was to safeguard my richness) a few banknotes to send the mother straight to joy; or again, when I met that small beggar-boy on the empty dirt street in Kinshasa — his ragged shirt was too big for him and kept falling off him as he looked into my lens for money [photograph 28] — I believed and still believe that I was doing him a substantial good, the *normality* of the Congo being so unbearably poor that one could quite cheaply enrich almost anybody there, from the women of all ages who would desperately call to me from across the street, *Make love with me, white man!* to the hungry people who squabbled over rotten fruits in the marketplace, to the half-starved, stinking policemen who shook me down; but Big Mountain and Little Mountain, while I might succeed in *gratifying* them with, say, fifty dollars (which is what I gave them), remembered a *normality* closer to mine, aspired at least in theory to return to it, and lived like cysts within the immensely refined wealth of Kyoto itself; so, granted that altruism equals self-gratification, it was really in my interest to give up on them.

4

A year later they were still there.

 I'll tell you how I returned to them: Walking out across Choraku-ji Temple's wide white tatami mats, I descended the ancient stone-walled channels of summer; I walked down wide steps, past ornate lamps and across a park's boardwalk, couples on benches and packs of tourists in floppy white hats who were weighed down by their video cameras; I passed through another wide temple complex of vermilion arches and lamps with many immaculate courtyards, concession stands, tapering gable roofs whose images were half-hidden in darkness like Little Mountain's already dark gloves beneath the bridge on that dreary day the year before; steles tucked away behind vermilion fences—and I remember that a rich young couple strode the flagstones, he with his arm around her, she waving an official leaflet as they passed into the sun-rays down at the end of the next set of stairs beyond which began Kyoto's expensive shopping district: windows of ice cream sundaes, calligraphy sets, kimonos, lamps; and after numberless grand items and reflections, after throngs of uniformed high school students, old couples and businessmen in subtle suits, pretty salesgirls in doorways, waiting to bow, after all the glowing shelves within the beverage vending machines, stationery shops and hotels, bookstores, purses, pay telephones, cigarette machines, contented evening crowds, at last I reached the river and, gazing at the summer view, I crossed the bridge, then very near the elegant eel restaurant where I would spend a hundred dollars for dinner for two, I descended the final set of stairs to the quay. And here, with the lovely summer evening shining on the river underneath the bridge, hulked uncouth blue-tarped objects like packing sheds all in a row; bicycles awaited their owners; cagelike crates contained additional belongings; folded chairs sat mostly vacant; and beyond them all, another rich young couple sat with his arm around her waist, admiring the reflection of the evening sun on the water.

Yes, they were still there, but their goldfish had been washed away, along with their bicycles and house, in the big typhoon. They had a new house now, blue-tarped just as the old had been.

Why are you poor? I questioned Little Mountain, for I had not asked him that last year.

Because I have no job, he said.

That was when I first noticed his toothlessness.

Oksana wept about the lost church money; that was when she came to life by acknowledging her death; as for Little Mountain, he and I never saw the life in each other. Perhaps he was tired or hungry just then; my own perception, that I was keeping him from something more important than answering my questions, namely, surviving, might have been a mere projection of a guilty impulse to escape his life, but to me he seemed to have been infected by numbness, not to the same extent as Wan in Bangkok, but more so than he had been a year ago; well, the truth is that I knew and know nothing about this man.

He now wore a pastel jacket; he oversaw a cage of cats. All around him, ladies with nice purses photographed each other.

5

That first time, when I had given them money, Big Mountain, wrinkling his forehead, had sought to refuse, but I implored him until he finally agreed to take it. He was proud, which is the same as being ashamed.

The second time I was weary and Little Mountain was busy, so we left him alone beneath the bridge because he was someone we hardly knew and he had forgotten us; we were rich and he was poor . . .

PHENOMENA

The United Nations lists the following "dimensions of poverty": *short life, illiteracy, exclusion, lack of material means.*

My own list, easily deducible from the first, would include the following:

- Invisibility

- Deformity

- Unwantedness

- Dependence

- Accident-Prone-ness

- Pain

- Numbness

- Estrangement

I do not pretend to know (and this is a very twenty-first-century issue to even wish to discover) how many of the phenomena I cite are experienced by what proportion of the poor. I can merely state that I have noticed them "in connection with" poor people, who, like other people feeling other things, feel them according to the caprices of existence. And these categories are themselves capricious, not to mention at times mutually exclusive (pain and numbness, invisibility and deformity). Communication being, like other skills, a skill of the rich, the poor people in this book sometimes failed to tell me what I longed to know. Natalia's dates did not add up, and their memories, like mine, were inconsistent—one reason why this book cannot be simply a collection of oral histories.

At any rate, here follows one more sad and probably useless categorization of the "dimensions of poverty."

SIX

INVISIBILITY

*(Afghanistan, 2000; Yemen, 2002; Burma, 1994; USA, 2005
and 2000; Vietnam, 2003; Hungary, 1998; Pakistan, 2000)*

I

Through the mesh of the blue burqa,* a level gaze *sees* me, but I cannot see. How sad I felt at a Yemeni wedding to be dancing in the streets with men, doomed never to meet the bride! But I might have been the only sad one. And at this instant I am less melancholy than apprehensive; for here in Taliban Afghanistan the man whose glance declines to skitter away from a strange woman's, no matter how invisible her counterglance, affronts custom, approaches illegality, and endangers both parties.

First, consider custom, personified just across the border by my driver from Peshawar, who gleefully enjoyed a lunch in an Islamabad restaurant where several pretty ladies sat eating with their hair uncovered; he thought that they must be Shia to behave so wantonly; he

---

* Three kinds of female modesty garments will be mentioned in this chapter. A *burqa* covers the woman's entire body, including her face. Not even the hands show. A *hijab* is a headscarf, which usually wraps around the entire head to conceal the hair, and ties under the chin. However, some women wear the hijab only over the top of the head. A *chador* covers the shoulders. In Afghanistan and Pakistan the chador is likely to be black, the burqa either black or pale blue (although I remember the Hazara ladies in their tattered yellow burqas), and the hijab black or occasionally some other hue such as green or gold.

said that Peshawar women would never believe such a place! I asked what Peshawar women would think of these ladies, and he replied: They would think of them as rubbish.

His wife was precious. In the presence of third parties, including her own mother, she always forbore to sit beside him on a bed; and although he was a very earthy man who loved to look strange women up and down (I showed him my wife's photograph, and he grinned as if I had allowed him to see her sitting naked on the toilet), when it came to his marriage he was proud to feel her modesty in his heart. A Pathan bride is certain to be a virgin, and the bridegroom will be probably the same. So it had been for Reza and his wife. They lived in a mud house; call them poor if you like, or simply refer to their lives as *normal*. Reza honored his wife; indeed, he informed me with considered explicitness that he *respected* her—not least for the invisibility she expressed toward all men, himself tenderly excepted. He did the shopping for her burqas, underpants, and menstrual pads; after all, storekeepers need to be out in the world, so they are men; how could he want his wife to chaffer for intimate items with another man? Protecting her from that was one of his ways of adoring her.

In the same vein, a Yemeni who called me brother told me how grateful to God he was for his two wives, who stayed forever at home, eating dates, watching videos, wandering amidst the lemon trees of the walled roof garden; his greatest joy was to pamper them, because unlike Christian women they had given the beauty of their faces to him alone. It is possible that his wives saw matters differently; they had cooking, scrubbing and tub-laundering to do, and it must have been a chore to haul buckets of water to the roof for the sake of those lemon trees (remember that this task Sunee dreaded above all); all the same, while his conception of their lives might have been complacently idealized, an American interpretation of those lives as impoverished by confinement could be still more off the mark. As a outsider to this secret world—which is to say, as a male who does not profess Islam—I run the extreme risk of fallibility; that being said, my opinion, reinforced by my temperamental inclination to see the good in other ways of life, is that traditional Muslim women expect to be kept safe from the inimical realm outside the home, and so to the extent that they must deal with that realm unassisted, they grow fearful, resentful; the paterfamilias has failed them. Bereft of their seclusion, they wilt.

My shopworn parallel with Sunee's case now resurrects itself: That Thai woman blames karma (at least nominally) for her poverty; she keeps herself down. But if she must stay down anyhow, isn't she better off? Cultures, like poems, shape by restricting. A negative space, an incurve of the bottle, is also a positive boundary. In short, what you or I might interpret as institutionalized dependence (as indeed it is) a Muslim sees as *cherishing*, as expressions of *respect*.

In the time and place of my writing, this must unfortunately be repeated: Muslim women are not impoverished for being Muslim women **[photographs 50–61]**. Segregationalist strictures to enforce respect may on occasion invite the same cynicism as the *separate but equal* policy through which a hypocritical white America pretended to solve its "Negro problem." In that context, *separate but equal* meant *invisible and unequal*. It meant continued impoverishment. —*Separate but equal* meant something very different when expressed by General N., a man for whom I feel the gratefulest affection. Twenty years before visiting the Taliban, I entered the Muslim world for the first time, and was treated by him as one of his own sons. Thanks in large measure to him, I respect Islam and offer my brotherhood to any of its adherents who extend me the same courtesy, as so many do: I have not always been liked, but almost without exception I have been protected, treated with sincerity, and, yes, *respected*. As for General N., he possessed a combination of power, wealth and benevolence, so that he accomplished more practical good than most souls I have known. It was at his word that on that hot summer so long ago the Mujahideen took me into Afghanistan to see a little of their jihad against the Soviet occupation. I literally trusted him with my life, and he preserved it. As his guest and debtor, particularly as a young man whose main virtue was a sense of his own ignorance, I had not dared to risk offending him by requesting a justification of female seclusion. But now that I was middle-aged and he was ancient and it grew improbable that I would meet him again, I realized how much I still longed for guidance from him on this question, which I put as tactfully as I could on that coolish night in Peshawar, a year before the events of September eleventh.

The General replied: It is just self-respect. For example, you wear long trousers or you cover your face. Either way, you are a human being. The point is, you must respect the ladies. Now a lady in a house, she *runs* the house. So you have to respect her. And bringing up the child is the responsibility of the mother. Can you bring up a child without her? So you must respect her.

In one of the religious schools, or *madrassahs*, a certain Mohammed Ismail, who had been to America, spelled out the matter more bluntly: American girls are nice, but innocent. They need education. Men just use them like tissue paper.* I am so sorry for them.

In short, Pakistani and Afghan girls received respect, American girls did not; and that might have been why at Kachagari Camp, whose low, tattered tents crowded together, smoke arising from them into the dusty sky, a refugee woman, speaking through the veil which her lips fluttered, assured me: Taliban is *good, good people.* —She must have borne memories of the bad old days in Afghanistan, when every few kilometers there would be a barrier so that local Mujahids could extort

---

* General N. frequently employed the same simile. He had been to my country in an international delegation and one of his memories was this: "In America they use a girl just like kleenex, then throw her away and get another one! Poor girls!"

money and pull women off the bus to rape. Afghan women were much safer from that now; the Taliban did respect them.

2

In the foggy mornings along the border I so often saw horse-drawn carts full of snow-white shrouds* packed as tightly together as geese in a cage; from each shroud a pair of eyes peered out just above the shroud-sleeve, which hid the mouth, and I was willing to suppose that they possessed the locality's *respect;* moreover, it might even be the case that unbeknownst to themselves American girls needed more education in being respected than they; but in the evenings, the reception clerk in my hotel in Peshawar, whose innocent sincerity grew ever more likable, discussed this question in accordance with his own opinions, which I explored for signs of respect for the other sex. The spoor I found was equivocal. This boy believed that women should not even show their hands outside the house. Only their eyes should be on view; and, of course, he'd like it better if those too could be hidden. Within the house, a woman could expose her hands for housework, but her burqa must not come off. I showed him a photograph in that day's *Khyber Mail* of two Peshawar ladies in a "women's entrepreneurship" event; one wore only a headscarf, and the other's head was entirely uncovered. I asked whether this made him sad. He said: Yes, but now we are modernized; we are changed. We are not same Muslim as before. Our hearts are empty. —He was looking for something to make his heart full. That was why the Taliban pleased him.

I thought it onerous to be required to wear the burqa in one's own home. And in this connection let me introduce to you the family of

---

* A white veil over the face is "Pakistani," I was told, while black is the Punjabi hallmark. Punjabis, of course may be either Pakistanis or Indians. Green and other colors over the face signifies Afghan-ness. A white chador in combination with a black burqa is Afghan.

Afghans who slept in a one-room mud-house in Kachagari Camp—
well, actually, two rooms. —Other room is toilet, sir, said the father.
But the lady, since you are here she is hiding. —I thought: Perhaps
respect for the guest wins out. Otherwise, why shouldn't respect for
the lady require *us* to converse in the toilet room?

3

How can you respect a woman by not seeing her?

The same way, I suppose, as you can respect her by not seeing her
vulva.

4

Why do you wear the hijab, Amel? I asked an Algerian woman.

I wear it because it's a part of me, a part of my culture and religion
and everything. Like, when I go pray I have to wear it. When I was a
child we grow up with modesty and then it gets easy to wear the hijab.

How would you feel if you didn't wear it?

Oh, my God! Well, Bill, how I would feel? I would feel okay, because I'm not gonna judge you because what do you wear; I'm going
to judge you because of what you *do*. There's a lot of people who wear
hijabs and they don't respect their parents, they steal . . .

Would you ever choose to wear the burqa?

Never.

Why is the hijab good and the burqa bad?

I respect the people they wear that, because each one has a different interpretation. If I'm going to talk to this lady, she's going to say
mine is the right and I'm going to say mine is the right. I mean, it's
the same thing, just like cover your hair, but I don't agree cover your
whole body, because if I work as a babysitter I think I need some

freedom so I can see more, see better, hurry to my job, do more stuff. I just feel like more free. I don't say *bad, bad, burqa is bad.* Whatever the lady want to do! If she's happy and proud, what the problem is? Just, you can't force me to wear the burqa. She feels like secure, she feels like this is the correct way to wear it. But if she wear it and complain, it mean that she's not happy with it. Maybe she can't see the money or she trip sometimes or . . .

5

The woman who chooses to show her vulva in a strip club has my respect, because, as Amel said, *you can't force me to wear the burqa.* The woman on the bus who covers her private parts, whether she defines those to include only her breasts and groin or whether her face also enters that category, I respect her likewise. Because I guard my own privacy, I must respect that of others.* It is our right to withhold ourselves.

6

But the invisible face behind that blue burqa, the face of a poor woman, does it suffer for not distinguishing money, does it feel secure not to be seen, or both? *Whatever the lady want to do!* cried Amel,

---

* On a Japanese subway, crowded between strangers, I struggle to sit down between two women who pretend to take no notice of me but who furl their skirts at my approach. Then they lose their eyes again. They pretend to be sleeping. But they get off when their stop is called. A man sleeps. Even the pack of cigarettes in his breast pocket seems tired. It leans and sags like his lower lip. And yet I have no doubt that he too will leap up at his stop: Yotsuya or Ginza or Nishi-Shinjuku . . . Some might claim that these behaviors manifest respect. I say that they signify shyness or even shame. But I can respect the shame of others; they can respect my preoccupations; and I prefer the beggar who gazes at me silently to the one who hounds me down the street.

but choice appears irrelevant in this setting for that face's gendered life: female in Taliban Afghanistan.*

7

Mrs. Fatana Gellani, head of Afghan Women's Council, said: After Taliban has come, the first time they took many places in Afghanistan, they not talk too much about the very strong fanatic ideology that they have. In '96 they give a promise to the people: *We came for the peace.* Then one day they give order to the womans to stay at home: Don't move, don't go out. And now it is four years, and they are using the Islam name in a wrong way. They womans inside of Afghanistan stay too much! They stay like a jail!

Now is all in the street, she continued with a sad smile. The majority woman is become the beggar. Life is too hard for them. Every woman is four children, six children, nine children—very hard for them.

They have very strong law by the name of Allah, by the name of Islam, but maybe not nice to use name of Allah, because Allah is very *kind,* she said, her voice breaking.

She was headscarfed, of course, but her patrician, middle-aged, classic face was visible to me. I could see her gaze as she could see mine. Accordingly, I could see some of her feelings and thoughts.

Why does a Muslim woman wear the hijab? I asked her.

It is for the *safety* of the woman, she insisted, her voice rising. It is very *kindly* for the womans! We are so happy we are a Muslim

---

* This generalization must be qualified. At Torkham one saw many ladies in black chadors or grimy blankets with their faces exposed; in the fields around Jalalabad, many female harvesters left their entire heads uncovered. Taliban rule, like the other kinds Afghanistan had borne, was most effective in cities. In an attempt to counter stereotypes, in the next few pages I will drive this point home several times.

woman. But this people is not understand. Islam is not say to the woman, go to the street to become a beggar. Islam is listening to the people. But Taliban is never listening to them.

8

The majority woman is become the beggar. This was an exaggeration. The *majority woman* stayed invisibly at home, or went out invisibly, which is to say in the burqa and with relatives. *It is very kindly for the womans.* For some invisible women, that might have been the case. But the case altered if they became destitute.

Poverty equals invisibility to begin with, and in this connection I remember the destroyed houses of those seven hundred families in Nan Ning whom nobody cared about, not to mention Rangoon's night sidewalk where the street kids were already lying down on dirty cardboard, smoking cigarettes: dirty faces, long dirty shirts, barefoot, four boys and a girl. One boy had the white *thanaka* paste smeared on his forehead, nose, and cheeks. By the glowing firepots under the tall sidewalk kettles, others children strutted in shirts and sandals too large for them; then ladies in Chinese skirts walked two abreast; young men with their arms about each other's shoulders strolled past the sidewalk tables which were set out with coffee cups, condensed milk, garlands to Buddha. A boy took the steaming tea kettle and carried it to a tableful of customers who sat on low stools in the street. A boy in a sarong was shadowboxing with no one, a baby cried, and three blue curtains glowed in the upper storey of an apartment building. Was the continuous low rush of noise I heard the sound of poverty? The children who had to sleep on the sidewalk were poor, weren't they? What about the customers who had to sit in the street? That arrangement would never have been allowed in my rich American city; the cafe's proprietor would have been fined; but these street-sitters in plain view of the sidewalk-sleepers were perfectly well off, thank you; their situation was *normal*.* And just as in the course of this paragraph I have moved from street children to street tea drinkers, so in very few steps one can leave that poor boy with the white *thanaka* paste behind even while seeing him. He is invisible because nobody wants to feed him or give him a place to sleep, while nobody wants to feel guilty about his existence, either.

When his poverty becomes metabolically intolerable, or more probably some time before that, it calls attention to itself: He begs.

He shows himself; he's free to wheedle or extort; if he sickens or starves, his face will show that distress. This constitutes, as any poor person will tell you, no guarantee of succor—but imagine if he were legally required to shroud himself in blue or black and refrain from approaching anyone. Not only would his imminent need become unknown, but so would the very fact of his poverty.

Do you remember Natalia? Why should you? She's one of several indistinguishable Russian beggars. She told me that unless the ambulance attendants *knew* her, by which she meant recognizing her and being aware of her condition, when she suffered her next epileptic fit they might fail to give her the appropriate injection, supposing her to be just one more passed-out alcoholic. What if she were forbidden to teach them to know her? How can we tell one horizontal bundle of human invisibility from another?

A teacher becomes a beggar, clutching her teaching certificate within the burqa. She approaches a man, whispering: *I am your teacher. Why don't you help me?*

Her former pupil did help her. He was the one who told me that

---

* Compare their *normality*, if you would, with that of the shack-sized teahouse in a little Kazakh town between Atyrau and Sarykamys: The walls within had been painted Dutch blue. Everybody was in caps and parkas, crowded around rickety tables, eating boiled potatoes and drinking vodka. My Burmese acquaintances would have felt miserable there, not only because there was no coffee, no condensed milk, no Buddhist garland, but because it was extremely cold.

tale. Who knows what some Talib might have done to them both, had he seen that transaction?

To restate the obvious: It was not the fact that women begged that was specifically rather than generally egregious (in Afghanistan I saw a university lecturer, a man, selling bananas for no salary); it was the fact that their begging had been made illegal in the name of respect.

9

Recently I happened to be walking the train tracks of Salinas, California. Within sight of the passenger station began a zone of drugs and prostitution whose separate deals were secluded in part by trees and in part by the urgent wavings-away of the participants. That was on the south side of the station. An equally small distance to the north, a woman was fellating a man on the gravel. The worldly thing to do was to walk past that happy couple without seeing them—the same service one performs for the poor Burmese boy with the white *thanaka* paste on his face, or Big Mountain and Little Mountain in their box house amidst the promenaders of Kyoto. My two companions, both of whom were successful businessmen, remarked on how useful it was for them to be reminded of the existence of this mode of life, which I found somewhat sad and they found much sadder. How could it be that these open-minded, adventurous-hearted men who had already passed near about a half-century on this earth perceived these all too ordinary scenes as anything but ordinary? What rendered the gap-toothed crack whores and meth peddlers mostly invisible to them was that convenient social subdelineation variously called the Jewish ghetto, the red light district, Niggertown, the combat zone, the *zona de tolerancia*, the bad side of town, or (here's one that fits) the wrong side of the tracks. Willed blindness was accordingly not needed for well-off seekers of tranquility: the poor kept themselves physically out of sight! (*You're out of your area*, a policewoman once scolded a streetwalker friend of mine.)

If one had no business on the wrong side of the tracks, why go there, especially when going there increased one's risk of being robbed, assaulted, or annoyed? The Oakland freight train yard stinks of excrement, so why go there? Everything militates toward separation of the classes.* The places where we never go are the invisible places, and it is the business of police authority, economic pressure, self-preservation and simple habit to place aliens there, so that they become invisible.

It works both ways. How often have you seen a panhandler inside a gated community? Anyone unbalanced enough to play such a visible part would immediately get rapidly neutralized by uniformed antibodies, flushed out of the social body.

We are speaking here of that coldblooded system of mutual class invisibility called *segregation*. What I saw in Taliban Afghanistan was not the effect of such a system. It was an accidental result of fanatical literalism. This is why I feel more sympathetically toward the Taliban than toward the architects of South African apartheid. Most of the Talibs I met did not wish women any ill. They assured me that they *respected* them! Once they'd won the civil war (as they surely would have in the absence of the events, more catastrophic to them than to us, of September eleventh, 2001), they meant to build separate female schools; they simply lacked the resources right now, they said. (Gradually they are going to make some policies, a man explained grandly.) They were, in short, poor, not only in means, but also in education, in understanding and in that first casualty of war, empathy. Many of them honestly could not comprehend why women should feel inconvenienced to be removed from public life. One man remarked that he

---

* While writing a book about poor people, I sit on a terrace in a hotel in Hawaii, and my little girl exclaims with wonder that a man is climbing a palm tree! He's pruning it; fronds come sizzling down. To her he's entertainment; to me he's first picturesque, then uneasy making as I wonder whether he finds that work exhilarating, perilous, painful, hateful. I remember how some *palmeros* in the Imperial Valley used to complain about the hundred-foot date-bearers they scaled. . . . He descends. Out of sight, out of mind.

had kept his daughter at home here in Jalalabad *because I did not want her to be kidnapped.* Now Jalalabad was under Taliban rule and women were safe. Meanwhile, his daughter remained home.

10

The girl sat with her bare feet touching, her hands clasped in her lap. She wore trousers, a black and white plaid shirt, a black chador with a green hijab framing her soft young face.

Before, I was in medical college. Now I am jobless. I stay at home with my uneducated father and brother, she said in a singsong.

This interview took place in a flat in Kabul; this family was friends with my interpreter from the old times. We were safe here; no one could spy on us. As the girl remarked with her only hint of mirth: *Afghan men may not always know what happens behind closed doors.*

The Taliban they destroy our education, she said. No one can go to the outside. So there are a lot of problems, especially for widows. They are very cruel.

How do you pass your day?

From morning I pray. Then I teach my brothers and sisters. I teach English and mathematics. I wash the clothes, study for medical.

What is your greatest hope?

Sir, this has become my big wish, to become a medical doctor. I hope to go to Pakistan to continue my education.

How many ladies do you know who like the Taliban?

A lot of Afghan women are uneducated. They are working on the mountains like a slave. *They* like them. But the educated ones, they hate the Taliban a hundred percent!

Although the Taliban made her more invisible than before, it would be a mistake to blame them entirely for impoverishing her, for, as she remarked: Actually I don't have good memories from even before Taliban. When I go to school, many rockets is coming and my classmates is killed. How can I get education? Refugees they are crying. They are hungry. How can I feel when I see these people?

All the same, however miserable Afghanistan's situation had been, at one time this young woman could have been a member of the professional class.

In a low and dreary voice she told me: Sometimes when the Taliban see me alone, they say some bad things, like why do you go outside alone? They have hit the woman many times, near my house, and women are crying. And also they are joke on the woman, like, *ha! ha! It's not human!* They never have good manners.

And then she added venomously: *They are very poor.*

11

Who were these Talibs? They sat on the porches of their checkpoints and forts, black turbaned usually but not always,* waving traffic down in a lordly way. I remember men in green turbans, wrapped in blankets. They extended to me their hands, offering brotherhood. I remember a terrified, ignorant boy who smelled of hunger. Another Talib showed me his bullet-ruined legs.

12

What is the emblem of a woman? Like the reason someone is poor, that varies regionally.

The emblem of a Thai woman is almost impossibly slender. She shows her face. She shows her grace (I remember, for instance, dancers in glittering, towering, sparkling headgear. I remember their anklets, inky or green, and the ornamental scales of their dresses. Thai tourist organizations often depict these ladies in their travel posters.) She is

---

* They assured me that the color of the turban made no difference.

the one who is meant to be gazed at. —Who then is invisible? —Why, Sunee, of course, thick-waisted, sweaty, drunk, drab, Sunee—the merest object, in short, a forgettable thing muttering to itself at twilight between the snow-white noodles in a wheeled street-shrine and the roaring freeway. No one notices when she gasps for air.

The emblem of an Afghan woman is a burqa'd ghost.

13

In Hanoi there was a cafe by the lake where early every morning amidst the red *jiong vi* flowers, famous symbols of summer, a certain waitress, smiling, lovely and young, served me coffee and flirted. I remember that she wanted to finish school and possibly go to America. Giggling, she asked whether I would marry her. I was not much younger than I am now and certainly no handsomer, so I might as well consider the possibility that to the extent that it truly attracted her to become my wife, financial calculations operated. I enjoyed her company so much at first that I overlooked Hong, the man in the hat and grubby bluish-grey shirt who stood trying to sell Vietnamese phrasebooks and postcards for a hundred to a hundred and fifty Vietnamese dong **[photograph 64]**. He too was there every day, but his business, like his life, was poor. Indeed, I later learned that he sometimes made nothing from morning to night.

Once I discovered that the waitress refused to see him, I enjoyed her company less; and when I invited him to breakfast, I myself lost considerable matrimonial appeal in her eyes. Perhaps it humiliated her (not that that had been my intention) to be inexplicably compelled to serve this being who had already stood in sight of her for three years the hours of which trolled by like the slowish columns of motorcycle riders, this entity whom she resolutely *refused* to see except when he came too close, at which point she sternly gestured him back into invisibility. Wrinkling her nose, she brought my menu, and when I requested one for Hong as well, her pretty face grew hideous with hatred.

Why are you poor? I asked him.

He rubbed his sweaty, stubbled lip, clutching at his wares: maps, postcards, Vietnamese phrasebooks for tourists. He gave me the same reply which I so often hear in Mexico: People don't have enough to go to school. And we don't have good clothes, so we cannot get jobs. That's how it is in the rural areas.

There were five brothers in the family. He could not read, but knew to orient his books right side up. These sold for ten thousand dong in a large bookshop; he could buy them for eight thousand in a small one. There was his profit margin: two thousand dong.

He needed six thousand per day to make the guesthouse charges for two persons, the other being his younger brother who cleaned suits for a living. (He did not tell me how much his brother brought in.) Two thousand was *rock bottom*. Six thousand allowed the two of them a hot-water shower and tea. There remained another minor matter: thirty to forty thousand per day for food, this being again calculated for two people.

In 2002, one dollar was fifteen thousand dong. Dividing his expenses by two to obtain a per capita figure, we find that Hong's survival required sixteen to twenty-three thousand dong, or an average of a dollar and thirty cents a day. If you like, he could get by if he sold one book every twenty-four hours. We know that he could not count on that.

In his photograph he smiles a trifle, lowering his eyes at the fan-shaped spread of wares in his hand. He has a very gentle look. I remember that beneath this gentleness, a bitterness concealed itself so well that one could hardly tell whether it was vicious or merely resigned, like Sunee's. I think I would have trusted myself to him.

He believed that he someday he might be *recommended*, either to an employer or to Buddha, for not cheating people. As for reincarnation, he did not know.

I requested his views on Marxist-Leninism, and was answered by a flash of teeth. He said: The King's children will be kings and the poor children will be farmers. It's not easy. You don't ask the King to help you; you don't have enough food in your stomach to think about it.

He finished his meal and then rose from the table, took twenty steps and resumed invisibility, with his blue cap pulled down tight over his sweaty black hair. When I departed, he was gazing everywhere, but not at the waitress, with his reddish eyes.

14

On the M7 line of the Metro in Budapest, deep, deep underground, two policewomen had a gypsy thief up against the wall. They were shrieking at him. One woman had her hand in the man's hair and was mashing his face against the wall. Everyone flowed past; he was invisible. It would have been unpleasant and potentially dangerous to involve ourselves with this; his tormentors would have turned on us.

And in Taliban Afghanistan, a man told me that one month before, he'd seen a woman being beaten with a whip. Who was she? How could he know? She was invisible; she wore the burqa.

And if Hong occasionally got mistreated, who would see? That waitress, who must initially have been no more than passively blind, was now actively, maliciously so; although I had meant well and hopefully eased his existence for a day or two, I might well have earned him an ill turn at her hands, merely by seeing him . . .

15

Invisibility has compensations, as we see from the three drunken Eskimos in Nome, Alaska **[photograph 65]**, who are sitting on a side street on a sunny summer midnight, bottles in their hands, the woman in the middle cradling hers with both swollen hands, her eyes shut, her lower lip hanging down to show her teeth, her pallid block of a head sinking forward between her pudgy shoulders, upon one of which the other woman, who is slenderer and whose eyes remain beatifically half-open, rests her head, gripping the other shoulder, snuggling her with an open bottle tucked neatly in between the two of them; meanwhile the man cocks his gaze and drunken mouth at me in a cheerful half-stupor, his eyes the widest of the three of them, but if his teeth weren't attached to his jawbone, they would definitely have come tumbling out before now; his hands rest on his thighs and his head sinks sideways toward the woman in the middle.

Everybody who passed could see them, and nobody saw them. They were beyond the pale. I took a stroll with one of them and people might have been disgusted, but they said nothing to us and we said nothing to them; we went our invisible ways; we might as well have been in the bushes in Salinas and they might as well have been on the passenger track looking blindly out at us through the picture windows.

16

To the man in Peshawar who ultimately helped me to gain my visa to Taliban Afghanistan I must always be grateful; he was good to me; meanwhile, in his turban and smoked glasses, lounging on rolled carpets, he watched me drink the tea his servant-boy brought, and he smiled with a quick, wounded hostility; he was acidly intelligent, seeking any pretext to hate me as a person.

You westerners want to see our women through your own glasses, he said. All right, you have democracy, but why should we have to be like you?

How would you like your women to be? I asked.

They can be in the house, go to the bazaar, work—but men and women should be separate. In your country, can a woman—or a man—do everything the heart desires? Of course not. There are always limits.

A father brings to a teashop his daughter dressed in loose magenta trousers, a long magenta skirt, and a scarlet headscarf which makes a half-diamond down her back. Her face is entirely visible, only her hair covered. Outside, a woman draped head to heels in a dark, pleated shroud carries a pot on her head. And in the Smugglers' Bazaar at Kachagari I readily see many female faces reddish-brown against the reddish-brown mud houses: mothers in doorways, only covering their mouths if they see a stranger's glance; other women in blue from head to toe flicker among their menfolk who are fixing bicycles or making boxes. To me this is life; this is culture; and, to employ an oft-used word, I *respect* it.

One sunny afternoon in Peshawar when I set out in company of a veteran Afghan journalist on the daunting project of *talking with a woman*, we failed even with a beggar-lady who took my twenty-rupee donation with silent thanks but then pleaded not to comment on anything.* We couldn't have taken her for a soda somewhere because the act of walking beside us could only have given rise to suppositions of sexual purpose. This was not Taliban extremism, merely conservative Islam. I respect that also. It saddens me that I could not have understood her poverty better, but, as the man on the rolled carpets said, *there are always limits.*

One Pakistani Pathan of my age (naturally, being poor, he looked

---

* To show you how Afghan women look, I sometimes paid poor ladies to take their portraits, which felt to them and to me like the most sordid kind of prostitution, and sometimes from behind or from a distance, so that I'd not be seen, photographed burqa'd ladies walking down the street. In Afghanistan, to take a photograph of a woman was as illegal as photographing a secret defense installation. In Pakistan, it merely brought crowds of disgusted and enraged men.

ten years older than I) said that if a Pathan were to make a window in his house facing the neighbor's window, the neighbor must shoot him. I not only respect that, I applaud it. My privacy is my treasure.

In the Afghan countryside, wherever men stop to pray they may easily find a Russian tank-round in the greyish pebbles around them; and almost as easily I have discovered ladies in bright chadors bending in the terraced wheatfields, many of their faces utterly uncovered even to the hair, in their bright red and green dresses, they look not unlike Romanian peasant women and I respect them from my alien distance just as through friendliness I respect the men sitting crosslegged on a tan-blanketed table against a tan wall, their tanned, creased faces elongated by their beards; I am as happy in their company as I am to see the river shining over its stones as it eats deeper into its broad basin, sheep grazing in scree, rich grasses in river-islands, the cold white foothills of the Hindu Kush rising above everything; I feel inexpressibly privileged to be a guest in their world where the boy with the ewer pours water over one's hands before and after dinner, the men of the household all outside with the guests. I respect them all; I admire them; I will never stop feeling gratitude to them.

There are always limits; that is true. I cannot see every veiled woman. But I swear never to become blind to the poor woman, the veiled woman who dies alone.

SEVEN

DEFORMITY

(Japan, 2004; Russia, 2005; Thailand, 2001)

I

The day before yesterday, wrote Montaigne, *I saw a child that two men and a nurse, who said that they were the father, uncle, and aunt, were leading about to get a penny or so from showing him, on account of his strangeness.* Four centuries and a decade later, in the reddish dirt and mud a few steps west of the Cambodian border, I met a girl whose face earned my pity and money **[photograph 66]**. Her nose baffled three doctors to whom I showed her portrait; the nostrils were still there, but then the bridge of the nose spread out beneath her eyes like clay carelessly molded by some child; and indeed that was what I kept thinking when I saw her; the religions are correct; flesh *is* clay; she was not so much repulsive as simply unfinished, as if the potter who had made her simply needed one more moment to work her nose between his fingers, moisten it, and smooth it out to be as perfect as the rest of her—what was she? The center of her face was a sort of blur. And yet her smile was formed, her gaze distinctly her own. Were she my lover, I could very easily find her beautiful. But why would I even imagine loving her? I never knew who she was; and although she and I shared lunch, conversing through an interpreter, and met again on another day, all that I now remember of her is her appearance. Deformity is the other face of invisibility—or, if you prefer, the reification of unwantedness. The old Russian beggar-woman in Kazakhstan whose mouth is a black oval within a dead white oval of numbed face whose black eye-slits are less prominent than the black scab on the right cheek, around which, as in some astronomical diagram, smaller black scabs have frozen in mid-orbit—should I mention the black wool cap pulled low and specked with snowflakes, the coarse scarf wrapped around that poor, half-frozen old head?—when I gave her money and took her portrait for you [photograph 67], she seemed *unremarkable* because she stood shivering hopelessly in an icy doorway, ignored by all, with no money in her cup; she was invisible; but when I look at her image now, I'm appalled; her misery is monstrous. Poverty equals invisibility, except when poverty insists on itself, shouting out its loathsomeness. The dead are gone, invisible to us, but that's because we bury them in the ground where we won't have to smell them. —Why is an opened grave a fearful thing? For the same reason that visible poverty is.

2

Indeed, deformity is among other things the stench of unclean flesh, of poor people's clothes dank with old sweat and rain, of badly healed wounds which would have returned to flawlessness upon a rich body. Deformity is the noisiness, the abusiveness, the sniveling or groveling abnormality through which so many beggars seek our help. One of Adam Smith's minimal requirements for richness was the ability to appear in public without shame. The man out of line in the Osaka subway station [photograph 68] fails to meet this standard; he is a shameful entity who gets tittered at by the ordinary rich.

That shame corrodes his belief in himself. I will never forget the old man in Tokyo [photograph 46], who sat on the sidewalk reading a comic book and stinking of urine.

Why do some people have more than others? I asked.

That is because the rich people and the poor people, he said, well, if you compare them, it depends on the ability of the individual. It would be happy if everybody could be rich.

Do you consider yourself poor?

He smiled, hesitated, affirmed the humiliating fact.

Why?

He threw his comic book on the ground and shouted: *It's my fault!* Nobody else's responsibility!

Why is it your fault?

Because I am living outdoors, and once you sleep outside, nobody will know you and you are stuck. I cannot get out of poverty . . .

3

The repulsiveness and outright eeriness of a deformed existence facilitates the isolation of rich and poor from each other. Excepting medieval saints, who cares to kiss a leper's sores? It was on account of her deformity that Natalia, unlike the healthier Oksana, was placed under (or at least claimed to be under) legal constraint.

The police no longer allow me to be here every day, she said.* They allow me to beg every other day. A certain police captain who comes around is afraid of me when I have a seizure. He crosses himself and tells the others not to touch me . . .

4

But deformity is also, as Montaigne and I both observed on our separate occasions, a vendible commodity, both to those who are deformed because they are poor and to those who are poor because

---

* She added: "Also my boyfriend is worried about me and I don't want to upset him by dying here in the park."

they are deformed. Consider **[photograph 69]** the armless man who knelt beside the topmost step of a pedestrian overpass in Bangkok; day after day I saw him, using his teeth for hands, begging submissively. Should I have felt defrauded of the few baht I'd given him, when after a week I'd caught on to the clever way he'd contorted his arms behind his back? He leaned against the railing to disguise his enablement. Should I perhaps have admired him for putting on such a good show? I actually felt amused and annoyed, the former being a weak cousin of admiration, since in fact the show had not been so good, the latter deriving itself as follows: I thought he'd needed that money! —Immediately came the next thought: Of course he needs it! —Once that misunderstanding with myself had been cleared up (it lasted for less time than it took the man to rearrange his arms), I continued to pay his tithe, and with a cheerful heart.

EIGHT

UNWANTEDNESS

(India, 1979; USA, 1920s–40s; Thailand, 2001)

1

Industrialisation, being the basis of urbanisation, must be emphasized, advises one of West Bengal's well-wishers. *In order to strengthen the internal economy of the region, however, there should be a directional approach to keep the in-migrants at a low ebb, so that the people of the region . . . can really reap the benefits of employment-generating industries.* Our well-wisher's depiction of in-migrants as a negative quantity in West Bengal is impeccably reasoned; for these wanderers have been polled; their motivations stand visible in his Table 3.6. No wonder that one characteristic of poverty is mutual antagonism! After all, those *employment-generating industries* can hardly support everybody, can they?

To the extent that the poor constitute a supply of something—cheap labor, easy availability for some project (war or prostitution, for instance), convenient obedience—they will be tolerated, even "wanted." To the extent that they constitute a demand for common resources, they will be unwanted. Estrangement, a phenomenon to be considered at the end of this list,* is the natural reaction to unwantedness.

Back to Table 3.6: Almost none of the female in-migrants to West

---

* See p. 153.

Bengal have undergone the journey in order to work; they've come for marriage, to accompany family members who already have or hope to have earnings, or for "other reasons" (which also makes for a significant category of male motivation, by the way). Since they refrain from competing with locals for jobs, would they be less unwanted than their men? I suppose the answer depends on whether or not they enter the welfare rolls. If they dwell secluded at home, emerging only to expend on food, clothes, etcetera, the money earned by their men, West Bengalese storekeepers at least should consider them a positive factor. For a contrary example of the negative, consider again the begging widows in Taliban-governed Kabul who in the name of respect for their gender got condemned to unwantedness. Their presence would not have been an affront—at home. But they had lacked homes, or at best had homes without male relatives; and so they were hungry. The regime washed its hands of them. How then were they supposed to live? The international relief agencies should take care of them, I was coolly informed by the Minister of the Interior.

2

Explaining the increased suicide rate during economic downturns, a lecturer remarks: *A depression is a time . . . when millions of individuals feel they live in a community which has no use for them, which will not afford them a living, in which they cannot find their niche to work.* This well describes the situation of those Taliban-era widows, not to mention (since we often don't) poor people generally. And there is another aspect to unwantedness: self-loathing. An encyclopedia of the Great Depression remarks that *during the 1920s, many Americans had begun to equate self-worth with material possessions. Therefore, when times turned bad, people felt worthless.* It may not have been that simple. But people do as a rule equate self-worth with, or at least partially measure it by, the degree to which they feel included in society. If they possess a subculture of their own, they will hopefully be insulated from some of unwantedness's effects. Since every benefit comes at a cost, to the extent that this subculture of poverty becomes distinct, it will be disdained by the rich culture in sight of it. A history of Italian Americans offers the following generality: *Because native-born Americans mainly saw poor and ill-kempt common laborers who spoke incomprehensible languages,* they stereotyped them as *dagos or kikes or Polacks or Hunkies.* In other words, they opine that *there should be a directional approach to keep the in-migrants at a low ebb,* or at least out of view. In similar terms, a Japanese American remembers the years shortly before World War II: *We were never taught that Caucasians were better than Japanese, but you automatically felt like second-class citizens, because we were all poor because our parents' jobs were not that good. My father had a little clothing store; he sold mainly to Japanese. I think that* feeling inferior *was the reason we stuck in our community.*

3

Unwantedness may be too strong a word.

Beautiful Golden, who in appropriately impoverished fashion got only a footnote in my chapter about Sunee, decided to leave the northeast (Province 101) for Bangkok because she *needed a job, needed money.* At home she had been a rice farmer. Some girls from her village had gone to be prostitutes, but not many. She went into Sunee's line of work; and when I met her, well into her third year in Bangkok, she wore the livery of a cleaning corporation. What can I say about this homely, ordinary person? She had two children, aged eight and thirteen; she herself was thirty-nine. If I met her today, I most likely would not remember her; nor would she recognize me. What if she stood beside Big Mountain and Little Mountain, who have grown nearly as unrecognizable to me? They stand together for a moment, superficially available to my rich man's blind gaze, and then . . .

Beautiful Golden's invisibility was increased by her fear, manifested at the end of the first interview, which accordingly became the last, even though I'd paid her a day's wages for a fifteen-minute chat, that by describing her unexceptionally disheartening working and living conditions she might somehow get in trouble with her employers; and indeed several other cleaning women, in spite of or because of their impoverishment, refused to be interviewed for the same reason.* Sometimes their initial willingness would be undermined by the whispered warnings of their colleagues. I never learned just what it was that they were afraid I would expose. It might well have been that the companies were doing nothing illegal or even by their own standards unethical; all the same, these poor women reasoned that they had less to gain than to lose, should they be reported to the management. Beautiful Golden was proud of having found this job herself. She wanted to keep it. I got the impression that she lived a hair's breadth away from outright unwantedness; in other words, she was *expendable.*

Suppose that she wasn't. Suppose that she was the best cleaning woman in Thailand. Even so, how many rich people would have invited her for dinner?

---

* For instance, see p. 11, interview with cleaning woman in Ratchutori.

NINE

DEPENDENCE

(Colombia, 1999; Virginia and England, 1700s)

I

The master foresees, says Aristotle; the slave works accordingly. *Thus there is a common interest uniting master and slave.* Slavery is natural; slavery is *normal*. After all, *it is out of the association formed by men with those two, women and slaves, that the first household was formed.* (By the way, *nature has distinguished between female and slave; they have different functions.*) In either event, men are naturally fitted to rule them both. Should affection exist among the various parties, that may be *advantageous,* but slaves (and women, I infer) exist to be used; affection therefore equates to guarding the tool against rust.

But what I see as the exploitative instillation of dependence, Aristotle presents as *interdependence.* The slave belongs to the master, he says, just as the foot belongs to the body.

If what I originally interpreted as the exploitative instillation of false consciousness in Sunee's situation might actually be adaptive or even humane, how can I be sure that slavery in Aristotle's epoch was wrong? I turn this question over on my tongue, and decide that I do not care to taste it.

2

All the same, I will not come out against patriarchal Middle Eastern families. Therefore, what right do I have to reject the proposition that authority might theoretically be absolute, personalized and benevolent? Certainly an evil institution can be mitigated or even rendered benign by a sufficiently virtuous master. The Roman father had the right of life and death over his children. We do not thereby deduce that all Roman fathers were evil, or even that the Roman system was necessarily evil.

3

On the other hand, we ourselves, spoiled, emancipated children, might not wish to be children in ancient Rome.

4

How can poverty not entail dependence? Self-reliance is a luxury of the rich. (Thoreau, you'll recall, defined himself as rich.*) A poor person is someone who cannot be sure of gaining or holding the resources to meet his necessities. Therefore, he is unfree, in peril of humiliation and servitude, and certainly dependent on circumstance if not necessarily on any fellow human being.

Montaigne refers to *the common run of men today, stupid, base, servile, unstable, and continually tossed about by the tempest of the diverse*

---

* He insisted that there was always a way out of poverty, through renunciation of perceived needs. Perhaps he was right. For instance, if poor people merely get rid of their integrity, couldn't they stop annoying us rich folks? "If a lady comes begging into the shop and she has soft hands," said an Afghan refugee, "why, maybe someday they must ask her to do like this" — namely to become a whore.

passions that drive them to and fro; depending entirely on others. Doesn't this include most of us? It certainly includes the poor.

In Colombia a street vendor told me: Police took my merchandise, although they gave me a receipt for it. I have to sleep in the street. There's no place for me to stay.

Can the guerrillas help you?

Nobody helps *nobody* today. The guerrillas took everything from my family.

In one sense this man was less dependent than I. He existed without a home and now lacked even his former modest capital—yet he declined to die! Wasn't that a triumph of self-reliance? I for my part have my house; but, as Thoreau remarked, my house also has me. Sometimes I wonder how to pay next month's mortgage.

This being duly noted, the fact remains that this Colombian was a tightrope-walker and I a comfortable spectator. He had put on a good show by not falling yet. What would happen when he got tired? His self-reliance temporarily sustained him on the rope. In and of itself, it showed him no way to dance to safety.

5

The master foresees; without him the poor one must remain *continually tossed about by the tempest of the diverse passions; depending entirely on others.* What if the poor one could foresee quite well? Would he grow any less dependent? He would certainly be less inclined to consider his bondage a good bargain.

An Afghan refugee said to me sorrowfully: Uncle cannot take care of the child of his brother. He doesn't have money for his own children. —If Uncle possessed superior foresight, could he save more dependents?

Foresight is power, to be sure, and it may well encourage such

self-disciplined aids to continued survival as saving, planning, bud-
geting. But if there remains nothing to save, or if one is powerless to
alter some perfectly well foreseen harmful contingency, what then?
As you may remember, Oksana saw and foresaw quite well, explaining her poverty with unarguable simplicity: I have no housing. I
cannot get my passport exchanged so I cannot get a job. This problem has been going on since '93. —She knew quite well that she
needed to exchange her passport in order to work. But she lacked
the power to make that happen. As a result, she was *continually tossed
about by the tempest of the diverse passions; depending entirely on others.*
Would she have been better off had she numbed herself down to
Wan's level and murmured *I think I am rich*?

6

Once upon a time, Adam Smith reassured us that in societies enjoying a complex division of labor, *all are often supplied, and a workman,
even of the lowest and poorest order, if he is frugal and industrious, may
enjoy a greater share of the necessaries and conveniencies of life than it is possible for any savage to acquire.* But for him the Negro slaves in Virginia
were but Aristotelian tools; as for the freeborn workers in his commonwealth, however industrious and frugal they might be, they too
ran the decided risk of getting used up. *A carpenter in London . . .* he
admitted, *is not supposed to last in his utmost vigour above eight years.* All
Smith could think of to help carpenters was to encourage high wages
and discourage piecework. Alas, his economic mechanism was supposed to function perfectly by itself. To be sure, a London carpenter
might sweat and gyrate on the tightrope longer than that homeless
vendor in Colombia, but someday the ninth year would come.

Accordingly, we find dependence closely associated with the next
category, *accident-prone-ness.*

ACCIDENT-PRONE-NESS

(Iraq, 1998; Serbia, 1994; Australia, 1994; USA, 1999;
Colombia, 1999; USA, 1820s; France, 1754; Ireland, 1889;
Republic of Congo, 2001)

I

One evening in sanctioned Iraq, between the first and second American invasions, black-clad women in ones and twos and children playing on the pitted sidewalk rendered quotidian the prayer tent set up for the neighbors and relatives of a seven-year-old who had died in the hospital from a bad heart; this was in the back streets of Saddam City, where garbage was mixed with rubble and sand. Would the seven-year-old have died without sanctions? A bad heart is a bad heart, but perhaps under other circumstances the perfect stent, drug or diagnosis might have lain ready on the shelf. If the family had dwelled in the privileged enclave of Tikrit, where Saddam Hussein's relatives clustered, or if the child's need had announced itself before the first Gulf War, or if any other accident of wealth supervened, why, then, this accident of poverty might not have occurred.

One morning in sanctioned Serbia, with the civil war slipping from stalemate to defeat, a woman in a red coat stood holding a bag and peering through the panes of Beogradski Izlor at a display of lamps and plates; a man hurried, buttoning his coat; most people moved more evenly and steadily, passing through the squares in ones and twos, a few dirty, most clean; I would have thought they had some errand to do and perhaps they did but my eternally sorrowful interpreter remarked that there were too many of them, especially now in the middle of a business day; and presently I saw that almost none of them were buying anything. There was a long line at the bank; people wished to exchange dinars for Deutschemarks and dollars. The people in ones and twos did not approach that line. The day wore on. It was time to eat, but none of them were eating anything. Weren't they poor by accident? Had the succession to Tito been a more orderly affair, had Milosevic, Tudjman and Izetbegovic been feebler nationalists and stronger compromisers, wouldn't these people have been eating?

In unsanctioned Australia, in Sydney, very early on a rainy morning in King's Cross, a bony girl crouched sneezing and coughing in the wet doorway where she had slept. Prostitute, runaway and sister to you and me, she exhaled the stinking breath of poverty. If she had slept the night in a clean warm bed, with dinner in her belly, then very possibly this accident of sickness might have passed her by.

Accident is both cause and effect of poverty. Natalia's tick bite and Oksana's unfortunate son-in-law impoverished those two old women unforeseeably.* As we have seen, the rancorous, alcoholic family of the former, and the decomposition of the Soviet Union might also have played their part, in which case even a distant observer, witnessing their births through a telescope whose only lens was demographic, might have been able to predict a bad end for Natalia, at least, and, if his crystal ball showed him that they were fated to outlive Communism, possibly for Oksana as well: pensioners of a bankrupt system, they both struggled in peril of dying poor.

In any event, once poverty gets hold of a person, further accidents become almost by definition more dangerous, not to mention more

---

* Just as the son-in-law had been himself impoverished. As you remember, when I asked him what his life would be like today had he not been sent to Chernobyl, he replied: "I would continue building houses. I would be able to have a decent job, and enough money."

probable. That girl in King's Cross might have been rendered just sufficiently witless by sleeplessness, drug withdrawal, or even a head cold to be killed by a car that day, or to go with a man whom her more wakeful judgment would have shrilled out against. This is hypothetical, since I knew her only for ten minutes. The following is not.

I once met a man in Imperial County, California, who while driving to his court summons for an act of possibly self-defensive violence was ticketed for having a cracked windshield; when he returned home to his squatter's camp, he found that his dog, whom he'd had to leave alone in the heat, had gotten tangled up in the leash and choked to death. Had he not been poor in both money and friends, he could have found somebody to take care of the dog; if he had possessed the resources to fix the windshield, he would have saved the considerably greater cost of the ticket—for that matter, had he been sufficiently rich not to be a squatter, he and his assailant-victims might never have met, let alone fought (he claimed they ambushed him by night). Perhaps they attacked him unprovoked and he truly would have repaired the windshield and his dog just went crazy in the heat; maybe he attacked them and would have let the windshield go and the dog was as vicious as the other one; in either case, a mansion, a new Mercedes and a professional dogwalker would have almost infallibly prevented these particular ills. What sort of character he had and what he might or should have done grew nearly irrelevant in the light of such considerations.

2

In short, one measure of poverty is *susceptibility to accident* [**photographs 70–78**].

Life is an extended camping trip. With a leaky, inferior tent one runs no more risk of rain than anyone else; but if it does rain, the person in the cheap tent chances soaking his sleeping bag, and possibly dying of hypothermia.

In Colombia the rich could afford to pay a shotgun-wielding guard six hundred dollars per month; every good high school did the same. Rich children got chauffeured home. Of course even they ran the risk of being kidnapped; arguably their risk was higher since kidnappers had a higher ransom to gain. But the poor were more susceptible to the malicious accidents of opportunity. The eight-year-old black schoolgirl in the Colombian shantytown of Nueva Esperanza who got chased home by two boys with knives would not have been vulnerable to precisely that sort of bad luck had her mother been able to afford a chauffeur. What could the mother in fact afford to do? Why, like any citizen she could make a statement to the police, who of course did nothing. When I saw them, the daughter was shaking, the mother grieving, furious and terrified, *powerless*. She knew who the two boys were and they knew where she lived. Perhaps there would be no more rain, but her tent was cheap.

And Nueva Esperanza was but a drop in that sea of poverty called Ciudad Bolívar: a dreary place of rainy potholed streets, people lounging in doorways or trudging through the drizzle, most of them lacking umbrellas, the taillight of a white van sickeningly red. It was there in Ciudad Bolívar that a boy told me how he was in a house at three in the morning *and some guys were raping in the street*; he called the police, who hit one man in the head and shot into the air; and one of the girls who was present when this story was told started laughing and crying until her face was shiny and slick. God! What had that poor girl experienced? She resembled the cigarette salesboy I saw in Albania who was running between cafes with his head down in the rain, trying to protect his stock in the cardboard box whose lid could not close. And it was now getting rainy and dark in Ciudad Bolívar, so that the hour of rapists and murderers was approaching these walls as grey as the sky, this bus's fluttering headlights, that young Virgin decal on the rainy glowing window, those tenement-lights nastily shining, these tottering fences, those ugly old bricks, that ugly dirty plastic, those lights under the bridge, dull rainy lights, and the mountains were blue on blue, bleak as streetlight on a grey winkled puddle. In the morning the morgue would receive the latest naked, stitched corpse wrapped in black bags so that the bullets wouldn't tumble out of them before the investigation. When I saw them, their hands were folded across their groins or locked straining in the air. They were already the color of clay. I remember an immense penis drooping, the mouth wide in agony, teeth showing, eyes open, a bullet wound above the left breast, another in the neck. Most of them were adult men. Many or most were poor men. I would suspect that almost all were victims of poor men. —In my country there is an overwhelming correlation between violent death and alcohol. Specifically, most murdered or suicided corpses contain liquor of one sort or another. —In Ciudad Bolívar there is an equally convincing link between poverty (and who in Ciudad Bolívar is not poor?) and accident-prone-ness.

3

Naturally, accident-prone-ness is exacerbated by unwantedness.

In a similar case to the Afghan widows whose quest to beg their bread had been prohibited were the families in Nan Ning whose homes altered from private monuments to public impediments. Meanwhile, a black American recalls a gang of whites in Tidewater, Virginia, during the late 1820s: *No free person of color within their reach was safe in person or property.* Night riders tied his sisters to a tree and whipped them. *The sound of the whip and the cries of the sufferers rings* [sic] *in my ears at this writing and will as long as I live.* What an inexplicable coincidence, that bad things seem to happen to unvalued people!

4

In 1754, Rousseau catalogues *the multiplicity of unhealthy trades, which shorten men's lives or destroy their bodies, such as working in the mines, and the preparing of metals and minerals, particularly lead, copper, mercury, cobalt, and arsenic: add to these other dangerous trades which are daily fatal to many tilers, carpenters, masons and miners . . .*

In 1889, a physician describes to the House of Lords a room that haunts him, a room *about 12 or 14 feet by 10, and eight feet high,* in which on the only bed the mother of the family lies dying of consumption; *although it was summer, there was a large fire in the room, before which the husband was at his work as a tailor, pressing cloth and so, of course, filling the air with steam;* and here I might remind the reader of the treatment for consumption: a dry climate. *Beside him,* Dr. Squire continues, *there was his son also at work; then there was the daughter with her sewing machine at work; and playing on the floor were two or three small children; all crowded into a room which would properly contain two or three people at the most, with due consideration for health.* Lord Kenry asks him to explain exactly what "infectious" means, and he does, concluding: *The influence of the conditions under which these poor people work is shown chiefly in producing a predisposition.*

The influence of the conditions under which live free blacks in antebellum Tidewater, Virginia, squatters in Nueva Esperanza, and runaways in King's Cross, produces predispositions of a kindred kind. As for my Congolese interpreter Monsieur Franck, he got malaria twice a year; it was just a fact of life for him as for many others in that poor country . . .

ELEVEN

PAIN

(Thailand, 2001; Serbia, 1998; Russia, 2005)

The rich associate poverty with a particular form of pain called *hunger*. Oksana and Natalia certainly worried about getting enough to eat, and Oksana's dependents were skinny and pale. But Sunee and Vimonrat dwelled in a country where food was cheap. A woman from the south who had been both moneyed and unmoneyed once told me that for her there was no such thing as poverty because for less effort than Thoreau spent on getting his living, and for literally no money, she could fill her belly on bananas and fish. Never mind that she regularly requested and accepted money from me. She had faith, as her urban Russian sisters obviously could not, that at worst the jungle would take care of her.

And so I assert that poor people are not necessarily hungry. That is why in this ugly little list of poverty-phenomena I omit *hunger* for the more general if more awkward term *pain*.

Sunee's thigh-sores and calf-sores, incurred, as you may remember, from daily abrasion by the roof-edge while carrying two buckets of water up the ladder to nourish her employer's roof garden, are poverty's wages. I took a photograph of this woman's extended left leg (the right remaining crossed beneath it in deference to Thai modesty), and looking it over now in my rich man's chair I find three rectangular white bandages slapped on crookedly below the knee, the righthand corners of all of them peeling, and then another bandage more neatly applied behind the knee, and one more about an inch above the big toe of the right foot whose seamy sole bespeaks hard work, but less loudly than the striations upon the upper surface of the left foot, although those may be nothing worse than sun-induced premature aging; and above the right knee, in horizontal parallels upon the thigh, I count five superficial or perhaps nearly healed scrapes. Not far beyond them, on the still girlish, almost delicate flesh of the upper thigh (ordinarily shielded from the sun, I presume), an old woman's hands grip each other, and the dark, muscular forearm takes us to the border of the photograph. Sunee's injuries, I must confess, do not appear any worse than those incurred by any American child in the process of learning how to ride a bicycle; but she is no child, and I have not met any American cleaning woman who routinely skins her knees on the job.

The mysterious sicknesses of the Sokolov family, which may or may not all be related to radiation—which moneyed authority cares sufficiently to find out?—were certainly painful. Had this family been richer, it would have been less susceptible to the accident of having one its breadwinners drafted to fight an irresistible supernatural enemy at Chernobyl; and one hot morning in Madagascar I met a woman who stood in the doorway of her shack, grimacing shut-eyed with fever; I photographed her for you [photograph 81]: and her little girl leaned against her side with an expression that might have been a sort of smile except that she looked away from me; the mother suffered from these fevers almost daily, so I would suppose that she had malaria; I gave her some of my aspirin tablets and went about my rich life, wishing her the best—what should I have done? From time to time I entered hospitals and jails on that island, picking out some poor sufferer who caught my human, hence capricious, attention; to the powers that were—the poor doctors who had been doing nothing, the poor jailers who were permitting their charges to starve—I offered to pay all expenses required to ease this or that wretch's agony . . . and then what? I gave commissions, fees and double fees; but for all I know, the only ones who benefited were the uniformed guardians who pocketed my money. Well, as I said, they were poor, too . . . Meanwhile, that woman with malaria or whatever it was, what can I write about her? Fever was her life; pain was her life . . .

I believe that I have already mentioned the premature aging of many poor people. Ten years ago the Serbian hotel clerk Miša, who shares my year of birth, was completely grey and half toothless. He considered himself elderly. I remain in the early stages of greying. Natalia entered the world in 1956, three years before me. She looked middle-aged from a distance but definitely elderly in closeup. Elena and Marina looked older than they were, although Nina looked younger. (Nikolai merely looked ill; he could have passed for older or younger than his real age.) Aging is painful; the rotting teeth, the impotence, the loss of muscle tone and the workplace discrimination are all painful in different ways.

Beyond these observations lies the obvious fact that pain is in and of itself an impoverishment and poverty is pain. The dying and crumbling of what enthusiasts refer to as "human potential" is a particularly horrible cause and effect of pain. If there is any more to say, it is *being* said in the lives of Sunee, Natalia, Oksana, Big Mountain and Little Mountain.

TWELVE

NUMBNESS

(Bosnia, 1994; Scotland, 1700s; Mexico, 2005; USA, 1999;
Thailand, 2001; Pakistan, 2000; Russia, 2005)

I

Equanimity is the goal of many philosophical schools, the ancient Stoics achieving spectacular examples. *Torture me; murder me!* they'd challenge this tyrant and that disease, *I've learned how to endure everything.* Montaigne consoled himself as follows: *Whatever I can bear, I will bear; whatever I cannot will kill me, thereby removing me from the pain.* — This mode of being requires pride, knowledge, acceptance.

When Marx characterized religion as the opiate of the masses, he was referring to a different and to his mind inferior strategy of endurance, a way to which pride is irrelevant (and, indeed, to third parties the partaker of opiates often appears quite simply *degraded*), a way which experiences knowledge as one of the heaviest stones in the hopeless burden and accordingly does what it can to throw it off, either by denying it outright for as long as possible, or else by accepting it *numbly.*

That woman from besieged Sarajevo who told me that because she lost a friend a week she'd grown numb to death, in her phrase *cold to it,* resembled the little girl whose mother compelled her to play the piano for hours and hours, setting back the clock for this failure and that lapse. If one asked her how the practice had been for that day, the child would cheerfully, sincerely say, sometimes with the tears still wet on her cheeks: *Great!* —Well, aside from a few Stoics, don't we all do the same? We believe, for instance, in *saving for the future*, but in the future we'll be skeletons. We *look forward to the weekend*, meaning that we seek to overlook much of the remaining five-sevenths of life. When survival requires drudgery (or, if you prefer, when labor becomes alienated), then experience can be improved by further diminishing consciousness, either selectively or entirely. Does the patient prefer a local or a general anesthetic? As helpful as the Stoic approach may be when anesthetic is absent, wouldn't most of us rather have the choice? The one who refrains, do we admire him or find him freakish?

Numbness is *adaptive*. What good would it have done the little girl to weep over piano practice all night? In Adam Smith's time, a Highland Scotswoman might bear twenty children, and succeed in keeping only two alive. Wasn't it best for her and them if she could consider that situation *normal?* For that matter, wasn't Oksana better off than her rival? As I have already told you, when my questions brought certain realities back into her mind Oksana would burst into tears; but mostly she begged more happily than Natalia, who had more reason to feel sorry for herself, given her bodily and mental afflictions, not that it must have been easy being Oksana, either, which is to say being an eighty-one-year-old mendicant on whom four other people depended. Natalia earned merely my pity; Oksana, both my pity and my admiration. To some extent she had become a Stoic; for she'd said: *I was the kind of person who always had hope and never begged, and even though I spent my life as a factory boss I don't feel humiliated by begging now.* These words reveal full awareness of her altered circumstances, acceptance of them and pride in herself. But then she'd continued: *When I feel low I pray to God and the Holy Spirit and then I feel better.* Who are we, and who was Marx, to deny Oksana that local anesthetic?

Numbness is also *maladaptive.* The morgue pathologist in Bogotá assured me that fifty percent of the corpses her attendants cut open bore evidence of cocaine ingestion. I have already mentioned that in the United States, pathologists cite a similarly powerful relationship between suicide or homicide and alcohol in the dead tissues. These findings comprise not merely a word to the wise, but a scream.

2

In Mexicali, José González **[photograph 82]**, who was twenty-three years of age, sat on the sidewalk on the edge of a pile of garbage, with his accordion beside him, and allowed that he was poor. He needed to earn a hundred pesos a day—less than ten dollars—to *live normally,* as he put it; this he achieved *just sometimes.*

And the other times what do you do?

He smiled vaguely and murmured: In October I'm going back to where I'm from . . .

Why are some people rich and others poor? I asked.

He turned his head and smiled. —I don't know, he said at last.

I inquired again, respectfully requesting him to help me from his experience, and he finally said: It depends on a man's luck.

Is your poverty your fault, the fault of others, or no one's fault?

No one's fault.

Do the rich have any obligations to you?

No.

Why don't they?

I don't know why . . .

Does God have an obligation to you?

I don't know.

It was only when I asked him whether he would sound a chord or two on his squeezebox that he brightened, and he played beautiful music, at much greater length than he needed to have done to satisfy me;

I saw how he lost himself in that music, going joyously blind to me and the garbage around him. I did not envy him, but I was almost happy for him. He'd become the antithesis of the equally numb man I'd seen on the grass in San Francisco, one knee up, hands clasped across his breast as he lay twitching in the sun, sheep-stubbled all the way up to the brim of his shadowy cap. His belly rose and fell. Fresh-drained bottles of port wine lay beside his ankles. — Or was this merely my prejudice, that I perceived a passed-out drunk as worse off than a conscious man sitting in trash? Don't we all need to sleep?

3

As for Sunee's drunkenness, wasn't that likewise both adaptive and maladaptive? Who could grudge it to her? What else did she have to look forward to? (Adam Smith again: *I have seen several boys under twenty years of age who had never exercised any other trade but that of making nails, and who, when they exerted themselves, could make, each of them, upwards of two thousand three hundred nails in a day.* This he thought a good thing. And doubtless when Sunee exerted herself she could clean upwards of a certain number of square meters of office space in a given period, for the greater benefit of us all.) But what if there had once been a faint possibility that she could indeed have won something worth looking forward to, if she'd only refused to numb herself with predestination, if she somehow could have learned to read, if . . . ?

4

In Pakistan I asked a teacher in Kachagari Refugee Camp: Is the Taliban good or bad?

We are poor people, she replied. We can't say if they are good or bad.

What did this mean? Was she saying that because she was poor she, a teacher, lacked the ability to form judgments, or had no knowledge of the wider world, or had no *right* to express an opinion, or would endanger herself by doing so? Let's simply say she'd gone numb.

5

You may remember that Oksana's family did not go out much, thanks to necessities which might at some point have become choice. Nikolai's pallid unhealthiness and desire to avoid the lies of the newspapers, Marina's suicidal withdrawals, Nina's desire to reject the entire world, these were in a way praiseworthy assertions of self; for a soul in impoverished circumstances cannot expand experiences and acquire things in the breezy way that rich people do. A Stoic, Socratic, or even Epicurean consciousness might accept its poor reality calmly and exactly; and there are some sadly beautiful moments in Solzhenitsyn's great novel *One Day in the Life of Ivan Denisovich* when the prisoner-protagonists relish a stolen nail or a swallow of soup; all the same, who are we to ask anyone to follow this standard; why should doing so be in any way superior to the other course of proud negation? Nikolai might have "felt better" if he'd gone out into the sunlight. Perhaps a friend or two would have done Nina good. (For all I know she did have friends.) About Marina, for whom my outsider's presence was harmful in all but the financial sense, I do not know what to say. All the same, the Sokolovs impressed me with their defiant strength. Their flat was clean and tidy; so were their wills. They possessed their poor people's pride.

I had thought to take them out to a restaurant so that they could at least eat well for once, but the interpreter and I quickly concluded that for them this would be a mere ordeal. My next notion was to revisit their home with some groceries and other things, but when the interpreter telephoned Nina, she was informed that Marina still had not recovered from her previous encounter with us, most of which time she had passed either in the kitchen with Oksana or else alone in the bathroom. So that would not have been a straightforward kindness, either.

I could simply have given Oksana more money; she was easy enough to find; but the person for whom I felt the greatest concern was Elena. She reminded me of Sunee's daughter Vimonrat in Bangkok, except that she happened to be a quarter-century older. Her cloistered dependence was childlike; like Vimonrat she had her drawings, her shyness and her hopes. Vimonrat might, as the capitalists say, "make something of herself." As for Elena, opportunity was abandoning her. She had almost reached the point when the first and last thing that could be said of her was: *She is poor.*

(As for Marina, she could hardly bear even for me to look at her, so how could I say whom she reminded me of?)

If only Elena could have held a job, or better yet a lover! (For all I know, she did.) Why was she, like her grandmother, prohibited from entering the Cathedral of the Spilled Blood? Why couldn't she buy books and see movies?

In the end, I took Nina and Elena to a Chagall exhibit at the Russian Museum. I invited the entire family, of course, but only Nina and Elena chose to come. Perhaps Nina's only motive was to watch out for her daughter. In any event, Oksana conveyed them to the entrance, which was not many steps away from her begging-place. I had hoped that the old lady would join us, but she felt compelled to work, and maybe I should have told her that I would make up for her hour or two of lost earnings, but I could see no way to make this proposition in a way which would not have either insulted her or else somehow demeaned *me:* Why should I pay her to have fun? How much of her life would she lose in the museum, after all? Finally, how could I possibly know her true motives for refusing? Had she quarreled with Nina? Did she want to accomplish some secret business at the cathedral? I smiled and let her go. I never saw her again.

Nina and Elena thought Chagall mostly too abstract. They liked the happy paintings, especially the ones in which he and Bella were dancing in the sky. They loved his flowers on a table. A streetsweeper whom I thought merely boldly colored was too close to home for them; they thought him exceedingly depressing. Pretty soon they were shrugging suspiciously. Elena and her mother, who dressed like the fossilized Soviet-era women they were in their grey-drab and their dark (specifically, Nina wore a dark skirt and grey-tan jacket, while Elena had on a greenish-tan jacket and her slender legs were in dark trousers), made a sad contrast with Chagall's colors: green and red and white.

Nina kept drawing the interpreter aside to worry about her passport.

In a room of nudes Elena found paintings that seemed to speak to her. We left her alone to look. I bought her a catalogue, with best wishes of spreading the numbness to Marina. Nina, continuing numb to Chagall, whispered anxiously on and on into the interpreter's ear. Why not? After all, there was always a chance of rescue from this young woman whose unknownness had scarcely been exhausted. When I think back upon that bifurcated moment now, the two numbnesses of José González come to mind: first the stuporous vacancy of him and then the interval when he roofed himself in a golden house of music. And then I wonder: Why didn't he keep playing the accordion? Was I deceived by his dreamy face and beautiful music into believing that for him as for me it was an escape? Perhaps it was mere work. And yet I still believe that he played longer than he needed to. Meanwhile Elena, who did love to draw, momentarily distracted herself (at least so I want to believe) with the art of Chagall, and Nina entertained herself with transparent fantasies of "practical" hopes.

THIRTEEN

ESTRANGEMENT

*(USA, 1998; Ireland, 1848; Russia, 2005; Philippines, 1949;
Bosnia, 1992; Syria, 1968; Kenya, 1972; Mexico; 2005;
Colombia, 1999–2000; Thailand, 2001)*

I

Me, I'm kind of a loner, said homeless Mary, and when I asked why, she replied: Who knows what your friend's done? Maybe she'll start shooting somebody. Maybe she'll draw gunfire. You never, never, know.

Sometimes she slept down at the deconsecrated church at Tenth and Howard where *everybody has his own space*, but one night when she was returning to her hole in the fence, she got raped. The man grabbed her neck from behind, choked her, and announced that he'd strangle her if she didn't submit. In the end he agreed to use a condom. These were the things Mary told me. She said nothing about the worst part, and I thought it kindest not to ask. That Cambodian girl with the deformed nose, I had not felt protective of her because she needed no protection, being so richly local to this place as to be invisible; whereas Mary, whom I only met twice, nearly brought tears to my eyes. I made a photograph of her, but she feared to let you see her. She had flaccid, smelly flesh and wide brown eyes; she fell asleep in my lap and there were lice in her beautiful brown hair. After the rapist fled, she took his forgotten baseball cap to her social worker and the social worker gave it to the police to be tested for fingerprints;

then nothing happened. So tonight Mary was playing it safe. She couldn't come downstairs to see me because if she did, she'd lose the bed she had won in the shelter lottery, so I said I understood, and I chatted with her for a few more instants on the house phone just as two grim young cops came in. I asked her how well she would sleep tonight and what she would do until bedtime; she faintly replied: I'm thinking of you. Be good . . .

I never saw her again. After all, she was *kind of a loner.*

During the Irish Famine in the middle of the nineteenth century, her namesake, a certain Mary O'Brien, aged about thirty-five, with one illegitimate child, fell sick and *(as is customary here) was immediately turned out of her wretched lodging.* She lay under a graveyard wall all night. *When found by the relieving officer, she was supplied with food, and taken to the workhouse—but too late, as she expired in fifteen minutes after being taken in. There is no blame attributable to any officer of the Union.*

Continues the Parliamentary Report: *The inhuman conduct of the poor towards each other, when stricken by fever or dysentery, is incredible;* they abandoned their sick to die in the streets, being terrified of contagion.

2

Among the poor themselves, estrangement gets expressed either through fear of contagion (*who knows what your friend's done?*), or through fear's twin, hatred of the other. Sometimes it is associated with a more impersonal phenomenon: competition for scarce resources. I think that Oksana and Natalia disliked each other not least because rich passersby would generally give, when they gave at all, to one, not to both. And so they struggled for preeminence even in the misery department. —Are the police nicer to Oksana than you? I once asked Natalia. —They do pick on all of us, she said, but lately I have been more picked on than she. —Oksana said the opposite. —They tattled jealously about each other's earnings; they were each *kind of a loner.* (Turgenev, 1859: *One poor beggar is quick to espy another from a distance, but in old age they seldom become friends—and that is hardly surprising: they have nothing to share in common, not even hopes.*) While the rivalry of the two babushkas had inevitably become personal, an impersonal cause suggested itself whenever I escorted one or another away from their arena of conflict, the Cathedral of the Spilled Blood; for the wariness with which they regarded one another was never evinced toward any other beggar. After all, the success of these strangers could not hurt them.

Likewise, and here we return to Mary's tale, robbery and rape are two acts which, however personally they may be experienced by the victim, need not be personal at all for the perpetrator: he wants something, so he gets it.*

Between the poor and others, estrangement becomes class hatred. *The lot of the poor can easily be imagined,* runs a textbook on Filipino economics. *They are forced to eat unwholesome and inadequate food, wear*

---

* In wartime, estrangement evidently operates between citizens of antagonistic nations, no matter what their social class might be. In Beograd in 1998 I went to eat dinner, and the father with his two young sons at the adjoining table began staring at me. The youngest boy could not stop looking. When I had finished my meal, I greeted them in their language, but they would not answer. Passing the window as I descended to the sidewalk, I saw them still staring. And whenever I would walk down the street and gaze into a cafe or restaurant window, I'd instantaneously be met with what I call *war eyes.* Let me explain. It's said that civilians take much, much longer to react to sudden danger than soldiers. In my own country, which is largely comprised of well-fed, overstimulated individuals, I gaze upon my fellowman, and get a countergaze almost never. In an elevator or a subway, people actively look away from one another. When I look at a woman, it's true, she, all too accustomed to being perceived as prey, often shoots me an anxious or suspicious counterglance. But in Beograd I never needed to glance at anyone in particular; it sufficed for me to merely peer into an establishment in hopes of determining whether it was full or attractive, and before my eyes could move on, some crop-headed ex-soldier type would look away from his blonde or brunette, study me for much less than a second, then, deciding that I was no threat, turn back. I'd been caught out, perused, and analyzed. Not everybody did this, not even most people, but more did here than anywhere else I'd ever been.

ragged clothes, and live in unhealthful surroundings. When they get sick, they cannot afford medical care. The textbook continues: *They are responsive to the subversive preachings of wild-eyed agitators who make extravagant promises of social amelioration.*

3

What is poverty? Who are the rich? One night in Sarajevo in 1992 when the deep sullen thumpings and almost happy firecracker-poppings of small-arms fire had fallen away, a woman named Anesa said: Thanks be to the God! but Samir the militiaman, who was very proud of his wound, said: Who the fuck cares? and we saw a fat man and Samir said in great disgust: That guy's an asshole. Anybody in Sarajevo who's fat is an asshole.

This statement expressed class hatred at its clearest. Sarajevo's people were now divided into the (relatively) safe and the accident-prone, the well-fed and the hunger-pained—in short, the rich and the poor. (Don't ask me how pallid Anesa was, how gaunt Samir was, how they licked their lips over coffee grounds.)

4

How might that universal divide be perceived from the other side? I refer you to the Syrian criminal code. In 1968, not quite seven percent of that country's convictions were for *crimes of insolence* (5,994) and *crimes against wealth* (12,425).

5

Naked numbers sometimes reveal estrangement as shockingly as Samir's aphorism.

Can you recall the distinction between absolute and relative poverty?* The following data, furnished by Kenya's Central Bureau of Statistics for the year 1972, bring relative poverty to malignant life:

	CITIZENS	NONCITIZENS
Total employed	594,217	26,119
Unskilled labor	**246,834 (41.5%)**	1,395 (5.3%)
Skilled workers	100,704 (16.9%)	1,248 (4.8%)
General clerks, cashiers and		
bookkeeping clerks	6,839 (1.2%)	<u>268 (1.0%)</u>
Professionals	4,656 (0.8%)	**4,213 (16.1%)**
Top level administrators and		
general managers	<u>826 (0.1%)</u>	2,951 (11.0%)

Boldface indicates the greatest number in a given category of wage employment, <u>underline</u> indicates the smallest number. Totals do not add up to 100 percent since I deleted several line items.

While the inverted symmetry remains imperfect, it cannot be denied that nativeborn Kenyan residents were most likely to be employed in the most menial jobs, and least likely to win the highest paid, most lucrative positions, while noncitizens would most frequently be found working in the rather high-level occupations called "professional."

Even were unskilled labor to have been decently remunerated at that time—a suspect proposition, since the consolidated minimum daily wage was 9.25 shillings for men eighteen and over, 8.30 shillings for women eighteen and over, 4.50 shillings for the rest ($1.32, $1.19 and 64 cents, respectively, in 1974 dollars—the U.S. *hourly* minimum wage was then more than any of those)—the shocking differential between the opportunities open to citizens and to noncitizens must have escaped few workers. I imagine that a substantial number of Kenyans must have felt something akin to: *Any foreigner who works in this country is an asshole.*

---

* See p. 38.

6

I once met a young man in Mexico named Javier Armando Gomez Reyes [photograph 83]. Since he solicited my funds, I asked him: Why in general are some people rich and some poor?

Rich people have enough money to get a good education whereas poor people like me, we don't get ahead. For example, my family worked the land, so they had no money for my education, and after sixth grade I was out on the street. I can read a little. I couldn't go to junior high school or high school, because I didn't have the money for the books. In elementary school I didn't even have shoes.

Do the rich have any obligation to the poor?

No. It's not an obligation. It's what people feel in their hearts. For example, the people shopping here, with more money than anyone else, they say they have no money, but the poor will always give me something.

What he had just said began by excusing the rich from any responsibility for his welfare, but then moved to assert his resentment against them. I wanted to learn how far that resentment extended.

So are the rich selfish? I asked.

Yes. They guard what they have, because they know what it cost them to get it. They never think about other people. It could happen that they will lose their money and be poor in the street and it will be a poor person who helps them out.

Would you take part in a violent revolution against the rich?

Yes, because then you'll be helping the needy and not just yourself.

If they resisted and you had to kill them, would you do it?

Depends. If the rich man was defending himself and he might kill me, then I might defend myself. It's not because I have a bad heart!

7

The worst places are those where both inter- and intra-class estrangement exist. Accordingly, Colombia haunts me.

A teenager in Ciudad Bolívar's *barrio* Compartir reported that *we don't like the police. Police don't do good to the young man. Police see a young man, see a bad man.* And here I ask you to remember who the police were: scared, untrained, ill-equipped, underpaid representatives of the rich (by which I mean the beleaguered middle class, for the truly rich hired private security corporations); they hunkered down behind their riot shields, hoping that the militant poor, the guerrillas, and their antithesis, the paramilitaries, would not harm them. Every day in Bogotá, on the plaza or across the street from a quiet strike at a hospital, a line of police waited anxiously behind their riot shields, because poor people can turn ugly and infect the rich with their accident-prone-ness. I once saw this point made in a more jocular way by a homeless woman in Portland who sat grinning on grubby steps with a cigarette burning between her fingers, plucked flowers beside her, and then her all-in-fun sign (adorned with the face of a smiling woman just to keep up the mood): *DONATE HERE and help keep ME out of your neighborhood* [photograph 90]. The police in Bogotá could not do that, so I pitied them for being so few and so weak against the stinking carnivorous snarls of angry poor men all over Colombia [photographs 84–89], who waited everywhere wide-eyed and ready to attack rich people like you and me; sometimes they slung burlap bags over their shoulders; sometimes their teeth were broken; their breath was always foul and their hands always quick. Sometimes they leered longnecked with their heads forward like biting horses.

Dr. Gloria Suarez, the Bogotá morgue pathologist who has been quoted several times in this book, told me that in 1998, thirty-seven thousand people had died by violence. Much of this must be blamed on the civil war, which was essentially a class war: left-wing guerrillas against right-wing paramilitaries. The primary cause of homicide in Colombia was robbery, although in rural areas politics was a more important motive for murder than money.

Are you afraid in this street outside? I asked her.

Yes, she replied quietly. I've seen people attacked so many times. It's no use calling the police. No human power can help us.

Every day, Gloria paid up to one thousand pesos to protect her car from poor people. She made a point of not arriving too early in the morning. —At night it's also much more aggressive, she said. Sometimes they don't feel happy with only a thousand pesos . . .

Being rich like Gloria, I felt frequent fear on the street or even in a car in stopped traffic when tall men came rushing toward us.

They just take your mirror, one man said.

But on one of my visits to Colombia they burned cars with people in them.

A woman in a traffic jam in Cali was met by a man with a gun; she wisely gave him everything; later a policeman appeared and the gunman chatted relaxedly with him. Was the gunman poor or not? Who knew? Who could even ask him? For my part, I imagined him as brother to the crazed giant in Bogotá who stood in traffic holding out his hand; all the drivers he touched were intimidated into tithing. He was filthy; he must have been poor.

But in Compartir, the night before my first visit someone approached someone, who knew why, and got killed for his pains. Next they killed a small boy because he had seen the first murder. Then they killed someone else.

I was frequently assured, and I believe, that Colombia suffered very little from violent racism; it was not estranged in that way. (Mary's rapist had prowled that hole in the fence by night; so he must almost certainly have been a poor man, in which case their poverty would have united them; she brought her accident-prone-ness to the altar, and so her accident occurred. What did he bring, aside from the selfishness or desperation that every rapist carries? All Mary remembered of him was that he was Latino, she was white; and so there lay one more estrangement between them: race hatred.) But in almost every other way, strangers in Colombia distrusted one another—their watchword was: *you never know who is who*—and a journalist in Bogotá said to me: There are many armies inside, many different ideologies. There are people who are always angry, and other people who just think about kidnapping,* about revolution . . . He was silent, then said: It began as an ideology, and now it became—well, nobody knows what could happen if they win, not even them.

8

Just when I begin to feel certain that class estrangement is fundamental to the experience of poverty, I remember Sunee, and question myself. Moreover:

It is indeed cause for envy when a single private residence is honored by repeated imperial visits, and when it sees its daughters depart for the palace, one after another, to become Empresses, opines that famous eleventh-century Japanese chronicle, *A Tale of Flowering Fortunes,* and so far we would all agree; but the tale goes on to assure us: *Human beings,* in which are explicitly included *the humblest of the humble, derive pleasure from the good fortune of others, just as they feel involuntary compassion in the face of suffering.*

Did Sunee derive pleasure from the good fortune of her boss, the one who in her words had *a very bad heart?* More generally, did it

---

* If one got kidnapped and agreed to pay ransom, sometimes they kidnapped the ransom-payer. There was no social contract. And Colombia became emblematized for me by the boy I met who couldn't help running through scenarios of being kidnapped; what he dreaded above all was confirmation of what he called his weakness; he knew that he would strategize to ingratiate himself with the kidnappers . . .

please her to contemplate the class of people who were exempt from her routine of *eight in the morning until five-fifteen at night*? I cannot believe it. No matter how impossible it might be to change her destiny, no matter how much she believed that she deserved it *(I never thought anyone would come to visit; I'm not an important person)*, I refuse to suppose that she could vicariously enjoy my good fortune . . .

CHOICES

FOURTEEN

AMORTIZATION

(USA, 1993, 2005; Japan, 2000; Philippines, 1995)

I

The Marxist theoretician Amin argues with self-evident justness that the fair price for a commodity must include, in addition to appropriate remuneration for sellers and producers, reimbursement for the amortized cost of regenerating it. Thus, if a certain crop exhausts the soil, the producers should be paid a proportionate fraction of what they will need to rejuvenate their cropland. I remember how once upon a time in the solid black night I saw a fence of planks shored up here and there with corrugated siding, and behind it the scaffold of an unfinished building, and before it a platform of detritus on which a boy lay sleeping on a mattress with his knees up and his head on folded cloth on a pillow on a phone book on a box on a sawhorse, while at his feet a girl whose ankle-length skirt was hemmed with three patterned and possibly even embroidered stripes sat with her wrists together in her lap, gazing drearily out past the garbage into the darkness **[photograph 30]**. How refreshing was their rest going to be? What so-called nourishment would they swallow tomorrow? How long could they exist that way before succumbing to accident, malice, or disease? Meanwhile, for the goods they were expending, life and health themselves, nobody was paying them anything. —One commodity which poor people vend is themselves; and once the amortized cost of regenerating *that* obtrudes itself upon our consideration, we must admit that what they get for it may not achieve fairness's minimum. Prostitution is rich in examples. I know a forty-year-old in my home state who in between her other occupations of wife, mother, and student rents her body for two hundred dollars per hour in the escort trade—eight hundred or a thousand for all night. Even though the going rate has now reached three to five hundred an hour, L., like the Hanoi government worker who earned just enough for *cinemas, coffee, vegetables* but was happy playing cards with her colleagues,* makes fair price and better, since she receives not only money but also the sexual enjoyment and male attentiveness in which her marriage was lacking. Now consider amortization: She's learned how many sowings exhaust her soil. Three to five dates a week are enough for her. When she's gotten tired, she declines her calls. Every now and then she shuts off her cell phone for a week or more. This very sweet and sincere Caucasian lady, who occasionally calls herself Lotus, is not poor. She has saved her house from foreclosure and her children from the humiliation of shabby clothes. She controls her labor in all liberty. I wish her many years of contented moderate prostitution, and I hope that she escapes arrest.

In a slightly worse case, at least temporarily, was the Chinese bar girl who called herself Erica. She worked in the Kabukicho red light district of Tokyo's Shinjuku ward, where Sunee probably once worked also. Her cohort came to Japan to *get time*, as she put it, in two-week or three-week visas, and on arrival they found *an associate to introduce them to Japanese men*, in other words a pimp. Erica described what the

---

* See p. 35.

girls did: *They* all stand on the street and they use the technique. They all speak good Japanese for catch man. Most of the men is Chinese. They is really good for to talk to the news on the street. Shinjuku has a brothel image. So every Japanese know a lot of Chinese girls come to have sex, also to get a lot of customers catch. The owner wanna keep girl busy; they wanna have a lot of men from the customer.* The luckier girls such as Erica graduated from the streets to the clubs. Erica's bar got a thousand yen (ten dollars) straight up from each of her customers as a cover charge. Next, Erica flirted and poured high-priced drinks as artfully as possible, earning more money for the bar, with an undisclosed percentage for herself; then, when the sex act was consummated, the bar received nineteen thousand yen while Erica got eleven thousand. Erica's services appeared as a discreet item on the bill; a known, guaranteed amount whose reliability bore advantages for all. If the customer liked her enough, then *the second time he come by himself,* and Erica got to keep all thirty thousand.

It cost six to eight thousand yen per year for each one-year visa—a trivial amount, conveniently paid, for *after first year visa the Express Immigration call and Japanese man knows how to handle it.* A more significant price had been exacted for the preliminary permission to *get time,* for, as the interpreter put in (Erica was tired, and her English had begun to flag): *The girl tell me they had to pay a lot of money in China, like over one million to get one-month visa. Since they arriving in Tokyo, they have to pay it back.*

One million yen! Ten thousand dollars! At her maximum of five two-hundred-dollar escort calls per week, Lotus would have needed to work for ten weeks, completing fifty one-hour acts of intercourse, to reimburse that expense. At a hundred and ten dollars per

---

* At this early point in the interview Erica said "they" instead of "we" because she was still wary of me.

sex act, Erica would have been obligated to make the beast with two backs a mere ninety-one times. As usual, precision here is spurious; let's simply say that Erica needed to work twice as hard as did Lotus to achieve the same financial end—moreover, in a city whose cost of living was higher than where Lotus lived—and here's another moreover: *Lotus did not rely on her prostitution income.* Yes, she had mortgage emergencies and childrearing expenses, but subsistence food and shelter took care of themselves almost regardless. So it would be more consonant with reality to state that Erica had to work three times as hard as Lotus; she was, if you like, three times poorer.*

I asked: What happens if the girls don't pay back the one million?

Erica laughed. — Oh, the family got in trouble. The people try to help . . .

Then there was the actual cost of travel from China to Japan; and from time to time it transpired that the visa quota for pretty Chinese girls with no visible means of support had already been fulfilled that season, and even overfulfilled. Well, such difficulties were soluble, but costly: several of Erica's colleagues had paid three million for the opportunity to work on their backs. Let's employ the easy equation of a hundred sex acts per million yen. So a girl with a three-million-yen debt would need to do it three hundred times, plus as many other times as it cost to feed and shelter herself in the interval.

Erica said that a young girl could pay back the three million in two months. This computes to five sex acts a day, or as many as Lotus per-

---

* For one more reminder that simple arithmetic will not suffice to make such comparisons, consider the Filipina prostitute Juvy, who made 3,500 pesos (US $140) for an all-night date. Lotus made six times more for the same length of service. But Lotus had a mortgage to pay, and the cost of living in the United States was much greater than in the Philippines. Juvy was definitely better off than Erica, whose mortage (on herself) was horrendous. It is possible that from a standpoint of relative *normality*, Juvy was the best off of all.

forms in a week. Of course, since young girls find themselves more in demand, their unemployed nights are fewer, and their total living expenses during the debt period correspondingly reduced; moreover, if they are *really* young they can be rented for a higher price still. But the amortized cost of regenerating the commodity of youth is surpassingly high.

And Chinese girl, remarked Erica, they all get trouble! Can't eat the food in Japan, cannot find something for enjoy. They live make money a lot, so can't never relaxation.

Considerably poorer than Erica was the black street prostitute Tiffany, who wept to me: I'm so tired of being mean. I just don't want to be mean no more. Sometimes I act nice and soft and then they want a hard girl. Oh, I can be hard! It's like I got this jewel that everybody wants and they think it's between my legs but really it's in my heart an' so I built a wall around it and then a barbed wire fence and then an electric fence and then guards with machine guns. Like the way those hunters go out and shoot dogs, they shoot once to make 'em jump in the air and then they shoot again to make 'em and they've already picked out the poor little doggie they're gonna kill and they throw 'em a bone—here she burst into sobs—and he's *eatin'* it! Then they shoot 'im . . .

How much did she make per trick? It depended. What were her living expenses and conditions? Variable. I cannot quantify her poverty in relation to Erica's and Lotus's. But it does seem that her commodity was not regenerating and her cropland was not rejuvenating, at least not on that San Francisco night of breaking bottles when somebody yelled *I'm bleeding!* and whores' voices rose on updrafts of crack cocaine until they were shrilling like horses, and beside the mirrored bed of the window-boarded hotel room, Tiffany had written on the wall: IT HURTS ME and inside the chest of drawers, on the bottom of one bare drawer, she had written: **EVER SEE HOW A LOBSTER IS KILLED A LOBSTER MUST BE BOILED ALIVE BOILED**

ALIVE . . . IMAGINE THE PAIN IT MUST HAVE FELT. THAT IS THE SAME PAIN YOU WILL FEEL IN THE FIRES OF HELL.

2

Many people impoverish their bodies through dangerous labor such as prostitution. Others get impoverished by environmental degradation, as was the case for Oksana's family; and we will shortly see equivalent causes at work amidst the residents of Sarykamys, Kazakhstan. It may well "objectively" be that a poor person will get boiled alive no matter what, and his choice consists of being tortured by Satan or Beelzebub. Where education and even basic nourishment are lacking, as in the Congo (not to mention the case of Wan, who thought she was rich), choice could narrow to a literally lethal degree. And yet Big Mountain and Little Mountain remained in place a year after I first met them; Sunee's peripatetic drunkenness had not killed her; Oksana and Natalia were successfully getting old. They did possess some ability to choose. Because I wish to respect poor people's perceptions and experiences, I refuse to say that I know their good better than they; accordingly, I further refuse to condescend to them with the pity that either pretends they have no choices at all, or else, worse yet, gilds their every choice with my benevolent approval. Once again I submit the obvious: Poor people are no more and no less human than I; accordingly, they deserve to be judged and understood precisely as do I myself.

Lotus, Erica, and Tiffany could each have done something else. They chose prostitution; I respect their right to choose; on each of them falls my solicitude; each wears her own responsibility. To the extent that each one achieves what she set out to, she wins my pride in her; to the extent that each fails, she gains my sympathy. That is all.

I said that I cannot quantify Tiffany's poverty in relation to Erica's and Lotus's. But *qualitatively*, she was much poorer than they, somewhat richer than Wan.

Like most prostitutes, these three women were to varying degrees ruthlessly self-preoccupied. So were the people I met in Atyrau, which you will now visit. Lotus and Erica amortized themselves relatively well; Tiffany less than well. In my opinion, the citizens of Atyrau belonged to Tiffany's club. They were all "neutral" about the rapid environmental degradation of the Caspian Sea.

FIFTEEN

CRIME WITHOUT CRIMINALS

(Kazakhstan, 2000)

I

I'm going to tell you an ugly little story now, a story which sickens and shames me in my heart; but fortunately it takes place in a country most of us have never heard of, and, moreover, the saddest parts are all secondhand, without "hard evidence," so we might as well pretend that they're untrue.

In the year 2000, gasoline prices in my hometown rose temporarily, and the neighbors blamed it on the fire in the Chevron refinery at Point Richmond. After awhile it became clear that temporary meant permanent, and not just in my hometown. With one of his grand gestures, the President of the United States offered to open the national strategic oil reserve. There just wasn't enough oil, somehow! Of course Iraq had plenty to sell, but we were marking our tenth year of "sanctioning" them, to destruction we hoped, and we'd certainly succeeded in sending Iraq's children to hell—a hundred thousand of them went one perhaps inflated estimate, a million went another, were already dead from diarrhea thanks to the embargo. It would have been a shame to put a halt to *that*; so Iraqi oil remained beyond the pale.* Well, said our next President, we could always drill in Alaska's Arctic Wildlife Refuge. Who cared about a few caribou in urgent times like these? Actually, the times might not have been quite as urgent as the prices at the gas pumps pretended, because when the Soviet Union shattered into new nations, one of these became Kazakhstan, ninth largest country in the world, running from the Chinese border all the way to the Caspian Sea—a long, wide, irregular inkblot of a sovereignty none of whose topographic rivulets project much more or less than any other—and in western Kazakhstan, in a place called Tengiz, a joint venture between Chevron, Kazakhoil, ExxonMobil Kazakhstan and Lukarco B.V., was now gainfully employed in exploiting what the consortium's press releases labeled *the world's deepest supergiant oil field.* How deep was that, exactly, and how super and how giant? Well, their best guess was that Tengiz Field contained about *twenty-five billion barrels* of oil.

In deference to the principal partner, which retained a fifty percent share, the consortium called itself Tengizchevroil (TCO). I have in front of me a glossy booklet published by TCO. From it I learn that *Tengizchevroil's goal is to be a model of industry, ingenuity and accomplishment, as well as a major contributor to the economic development of the region and Kazakhstan.* Awfully nice of them, I must say. I'm also informed that *Tengizchevroil and all those working for TCO are very proud in operating its facilities in a safe and environmentally responsible manner, consistent with national environmental regulations.* What a wonderful world.

---

* We might note that the price for gasoline in Sacramento when I wrote this was about $2.00 a gallon. In Almaty, Kazakhstan, where gasoline comes from Kazakh oil refined in China, gasoline prices ranged from 38 to 53 tenge per liter, depending on quality. Let's call it 50 tenge per liter, or about 50¢ a quart, or also $2.00 a gallon. In Iraq, during my visit there two years earlier, it had been five dinars per liter, which works out to one cent per gallon.

2

Where oil companies set up shop, there's always an Oil City not far away. Kazakhstan's Oil City lies about two hundred miles north of Tengiz, almost in sight of the Caspian Sea. The name of it is Atyrau. My guidebook advises: *If you're not in the oil or gas business, there's little reason to drag yourself here.* Much of Atyrau's horizon-line is comprised of Soviet apartment-blocks all nearly the same height and all either grey or pinkish-beige like the mud-pocked, dirt-stained ice below them, the monotony of the sky itself merely a paler whitish-grey disturbed by nothing except one or two limp wires. At the base of these apartments, smoke creeps like an afterthought from still lower, grimier structures which interrupt the snowy courtyards more effectively than the rare dark-shrouded figures of human beings: a man in a sheepskin cap, or a woman who hides her hands inside her coat-sleeves. Sometimes after a new snow, Atyrau can appear almost beautiful, especially on a softly white and grey morning, with bundled people fishing on the ice of the Ural River (which happens to be the official dividing line between Europe and Asia), and beyond the fishermen lie small houses of brick, stone or concrete, with roofs of varying steepnesses, everything low, and huge crows flap rapidly across the field of vision, flying horizontally like the steam and smoke of Atyrau, which drifts and hovers rather than rises in the freezing air, attaching itself to each chimney or smokestack like a pennant. When I remember Atyrau, mainly I envision dirty snow, dirty slush, slippery dirty ice, mud frozen or unfrozen, litter frozen into ice, and those long boulevards of dirty, pale apartment-blocks through whose portals very occasionally pass one or two of the dark-clad figures, capped or hooded, who shuffle and skate along the glass-smooth sidewalks.

I also remember construction sites sealed off by barbed wire, construction workers on roofs and scaffolds; for, as I said, Atyrau is Oil

City. —Every time I fly in, it's different, said a Scottish oilman with a complacent smile. —I hardly recognize the place! —Next spring there were going to be two hotels, probably five-star ones, because many, many foreigners were going to be coming to Atyrau, on account of TCO. Soon there'd even be a direct flight from Moscow. Other wonders were just down the pipeline, so to speak. TCO meant to have an office building, naturally, a *real* office building, and the streets were going to get smoother and the brand new streetlights might be augmented. The receptionist at my hotel believed there'd be a new and better Russian Orthodox church. When I walked by the old church, workmen from Volgograd (which used to be Stalingrad) were already replacing the first of the tarnished brass cupolas with a fresh one made of plastic, steel and gilded foil. Ancient neighbor women watched happily. No doubt during the Soviet period this church had been a museum of atheism, or a storage depot, or some other such emblem of progress. The dome workers told me that they were going all over the former Soviet Union, fixing churches, mosques and synagogues as the market required. That sounded praiseworthy enough. They cut the cross off the old dome, which was going to get scrapped; they said they'd give that cross to the priest, whom I would have expected to be standing in the forefront with a shining face; yet for some reason he wasn't there. His residence, which lay next door to the church, was a sky blue little house with a cross on top. I meant to photograph it, but the light was already going. When I strolled by the next day, they'd torn it down and a bulldozer was smoothing out the earth. Atyrau was getting better and better by the minute; that was for sure! They were razing most of the one-storey houses of Old Town as part of their beautification project, all paid for fair and square with oil money.

I went to Old Town every day, trying to learn what the inhabitants thought about these improvements. (The house next to the priest's residence was already gone.) A grandmother who'd been born in her house, as her mother had been, said that next spring, when her time came, she was going to leave early; she couldn't bear to watch them bulldoze the place whose walls, by the way, had been carved in crudely beautiful patterns of hearts and flowers. I happened to be visiting her on a cold, sunny day just after it had snowed, so that all those little houses in Old Town seemed cleaner for lack of contrast with any muck, whose stinking refuse had been frozen into secrecy; everything was white on white and the houses looked especially homey with the pretty little curls of smoke from their chimneys. The neighbors across the street had been paid for their houses, but less than the destroyers had promised. I asked the grandmother what she thought about it all, where and for what she stood, and she raised her hands and shouted in cracked and desperate fervor: *Lenin-Stalin!*

My interpreter that day was a pretty young woman who translated negotiations for foreign businessmen. Perhaps because her parents were less than rich (by the standards of this book, they were rich enough), she regarded the poor with distaste. To her they literally all smelled, and maybe they did. When I made her come with me to Old Town, she hated it. She quit at the end of the day.

Do you feel sorry for these people? I asked her.

Not really. I'm neutral.

That was exactly what she was.

The pensioner who'd toiled all his life for the Soviet state and thanks to capitalism found himself penniless, the street drunk lost in muddy mirrors of slush (who knows what *he'd* been before?), the former school cook who now had to support her children by shoveling snow, the weary old market woman who sought to sell a handful of apples in the snowy niches between two not-yet-razed houses, and most of the other people I met in Old Town shared the grandmother's views. (I'll likewise not forget the twenty-year-old university student whose uncle still insisted on Stalin's goodness and whose teacher told her that the USSR had been the most perfect country on earth.) *Tengizchevroil's goal is to be . . . a major contributor to the economic development of the region and Kazakhstan.* How strange, that not everybody wanted to get economically developed!

Some of them thought that TCO's new office tower would be erected where their houses had stood, but others swore that the Turkish hotel would go there, or maybe just more apartment blocks; economic development is so deliciously unpredictable! That they'd get compensated for their homes they were all sure, but of course the valuations had been set so low that they feared they wouldn't have enough money to buy another place of their own. They could afford to live in the new apartments, but some were too old to climb stairs. Well, but *tak zhisn,* such is life. Lenin was their hero, "of course." Stalin was strict, but basically good. Gorbachev was the evil one; he'd destroyed everything. He who can understand will understand, they darkly said.

I would have liked to find out more about what was going to be done in Atyrau, but the officials in the *akimat,* the government office, refused to talk with me. They said that it was not their policy to release such information. Well, that was normal. Call the railroad and ask them at which town in Tengiz the train stopped, and they'd reply: We don't give such information. —Anyhow, the city fathers might have been occupied. Come to think of it, not many people had time for me in Atyrau. They were all busy getting rich. They loved TCO. Various interpreters took my money with incurious haste, then left me, their eyes on more lucrative jobs. Trying to understand this coldly dynamic place which was half raw, half stale, I wandered back and forth across the wide bridge with its two pairs of kiosks, the western ones reading in Cyrillic ЕВРОПА and then EUROPE, the eastern ones АЗИЯ and ASIA. My interpreters often preferred the Asian side with its raised pipes like white roots bursting briefly from the mud to remind me of the Canadian Arctic towns. They said that it was cleaner and newer; and indeed I remember one restaurant there whose napkins and tablecloths were made of gilded cloth as soapy-smooth as the sheets of a high-class whorehouse. The food was good, too. I myself preferred the European side with its billboard of the president of Kazakhstan and his family, all of them resolutely underlined by his famous promise that circumstances would be perfect in the year 2030. Old Town was on the European side. People rushed by, muffling their faces against the nasty wind.

According to an environmental activist whom I met there, the ethos of Atyrau could be best defined as *oil egotism*. He said that seals were dying off in the Caspian Sea by the thousands, possibly from fertilizer runoff, or maybe from underwater oil exploration. He thought that pretty soon, since 90 percent of the world's caviar comes from the Caspian, that particular delicacy might disappear.* He opposed offshore oil drilling, but even he supported TCO's activities in the Tengiz. —I understand that the economy of Kazakhstan should be developed, he said. Of course, before we had a 50 percent share and Chevron had 50 percent. Now, we get only 20 percent. Our government is selling off our share by parts . . .

I myself did not have anything against TCO. In fact, my plan was to compare the life of a worker at Tengiz with that of a municipal worker in Old Town—say, a member of the "Moskva Brigade" of snow shovelers; every day, there went that slow column of yellow-uniformed shufflers creeping along the slush-edge toward the new church [**photographs 91–93**]. I suspected that for one of TCO's hirelings life was better than ever before, while for the municipal laborers existence had been more tolerable under Communism. But I didn't know. Once upon a time there'd been a Soviet vision of perfect white living-blocks and towers, of futurity's pale blue windows, grey windows within, of a white sky resembling the "white nights" of Leningrad, since at this

---

* Five years later, as I finished this book, the importation of beluga caviar into the U.S.A. was banned in hopes of saving the species.

point it all remained on paper. In the taller-than-thou blueprints there are trees everywhere. Much of it, I haven't seen enough of the former USSR to say how much, never happened. However many millions the Soviets deliberately impoverished, let alone exterminated, whatever evil they did, the fact of that vision, hypocritical or not, remains.* What now was the vision of Atyrau's city fathers who were too busy to meet with me? Maybe if I'd learned it, this story wouldn't be as ugly.

The snow-shovelers all liked me. I photographed them day after day. Burly, laughing, heroically shooting that dirty snow into space, they told me to bring vodka some evening when their "general" had dismissed them from work, and we could have a party and I could ask all the questions I wanted. But TCO refused to grant me permission to visit the oil operation, which made my intended comparison rather difficult. So I decided to go to Tengiz without permission, and see what I could learn outside TCO's gates. I still didn't have anything against the company. I was just curious.

The closest village to the refinery is called Sarykamys, the environmental activist said. If you visit Sarykamys, you will find some things which are not right.

What things?

You will see. Tengiz oil has a large content of hydrogen sulfide—about 25 percent. That's why TCO has to remove the sulfur. Then the sulfur blows around. I think you will find some problems.

---

* You may remember that I did succeed in inquiring of Oksana and her dependents, and Natalia, also, whether the Soviet Union had actually done anything for poor people or whether its complacent announcements of progress had been as absurd as some painted nineteenth-century wood carvings of dancing peasants. Oksana was the most approving, saying among other things: "Under Communism some things were easier since we had assigned housing. Now we rent a place. An agency specializing in Chernobyl victims is trying to get us janitorial work." The other Russians expressed more sour opinions. In Atyrau's Old Town, on the other hand, everyone I interviewed missed the USSR. My richer interpreters certainly did not. I wish that I had been able to ask people in Sarykamys their thoughts on this question. As you will see, I was lucky to be able to ask them anything at all.

I told my interpreter that I wanted to go to Sarykamys, and after making a couple of telephone calls her face grew wooden and she looked down at the floor: They all say to me that I don't need to go there.

What does that mean?

They advise me not to go. I don't think that I could help you.

Oh, and why would that be?

Well, these are all Kazakh villages, and since I am ethnic Russian I might not be able to communicate with them . . .

But you communicated very well with those Kazakhs in Old Town today.

But in the village, well, relations are not always the same.

Suppose we were to bring a Kazakh interpreter, also?

Frankly, I am afraid of problems now. You see, they try to control this story you want to know about . . .

So I found an ethnic Kazakh interpreter, and she said: I will work with you here in Atyrau. But I'm afraid to go to the Tengiz.

Why?

I'm just afraid.

Finally I found another Kazakh who agreed to go. She had only lived in Atyrau for a few months. Maybe she liked the financial inducements, and maybe she didn't know that there was something strange about Sarykamys. I refrained from telling her what the other interpreters had said.

3

It was a long way to Tengiz. I asked the driver what he thought about the oil companies and he said: They are robbing us. And when there is a wind from the sea, there's a bad smell. But whether Kazakhstan or America does it, there will be pollution.

I asked him whether he might be against oil extraction, and he looked me up and down, laughed and asked: Which oil company fired you?

Nobody. I'm a journalist.

Anyway, no one will tell you anything. The doctors are afraid to tell the truth in case they lose their jobs.

Who can fire them?

TCO.

Do you know that or do you just believe that?

Oh, I don't know, I don't know . . . But I have an idea. Why don't you pay them? You can easily get a story then.

Pay whom?

Everybody. For fifty dollars people will tell you anything. They'll tell you there are mutants in Sarykamys!

4

On the snowy horizon, a train of cylindrical oil cars crawled beneath the moon. Then ash-grey twilight froze away into darkness.

I remember the bluish-whiteness of the steppes long past winter midnight, when from a distance the headlights of a rare oncoming car form an onion-bulb of glare from which a slender stalk of the same substance rises into the sky; and it is only possible to tell that the car is approaching because the stalk gradually sinks back into the tuber it originated from; and then when there is nothing but that one brightness withdrawn entirely into itself, a moment passes, and then another of sufficient duration to freeze my oilskin jacket into iron stiffness, after which the glow intensifies, splits into two, and by degrees becomes a painful assault long before any sound can be heard. An illuminated fox waits, appalled. And then the car is here and gone. It was never here. That was how the night was, and night came before five in the evening and stayed until after seven in the morning. The driver continued a steady thirty miles an hour along the icy road, too vigilant to spare more than a glance for the wrecked and turtle-turned cars we passed far too often; he was one of the best drivers I ever had. Thirty miles an hour; thirty miles an hour; hour after hour we crept through the darkness.

And then suddenly the road became as nakedly safe as any good American highway, and the driver sighed and sped up to fifty. We were coming into the Tengiz now, and this was TCO's highway. The many, many sullen lights of a "watch village" gleamed ahead like a prison Christmas. And *then* . . .

Well, even though it was already dark I now began to make out a sunset ahead **[photograph 94]**. But ahead was to the south, not the west. And this sunset, orange and purple, was more like a bruise in the darkness than that customary celestial luminosity which tinges the sky all around itself; if anything, the darkness seemed heavier and puffier around this purple glow which now began to resolve itself into multiple fires. The night paled into a cloudy sky whose clouds glowed like ruddy sores. There was no night there anymore, even though the fires still remained far away in the darkness over the snow. How many were there? Four or five of them, I thought, glowing high in the sky upon their smokestacks. What a beautiful peach color those flames had! Many, many lights attended them below. We came into a smell of sulfur. The interpreter held her nose. Plumes of smoke, plumes of fire! It was spectacular. But that smoke, how it crept and crawled and wriggled across the entire sky! TCO was doing its mite for global warming. That smoke would give the next generation another reason to curse us—two reasons, actually, for not only did it pollute the air and ground, it also burned off much of the fuel that was ostensibly being refined. Of course, a few members of the present generation would get rich.

And now we were past the great refinery, and the road became again an un-American road, a Kazakh road all lumpy and bumpy with dangerous ice. We crawled through the darkness all the way to Sarykamys.

The hospital bulked darkly in the darkness. Door after door proved to be locked. I found it hard to believe that such a place had received subsidies from TCO, or, for that matter, from anybody at all since Soviet times. We finally discovered at the top of some ice-slicked stairs, which gave a little underfoot, a door whose latch was actually less than immovable; and entering a cold and silent corridor we received our choice of three more doors, two of which were locked. The third allowed us up a flight of dark and even steps to another door outlined with light. We pushed it open. Here at last was a warm and illuminated zone, although the hallways exuded that eerie quality which I've felt most strongly when alone in a laboratory at midnight. Knocking at doors, we discovered a small ward of wrinkled, wide-eyed, bedridden patients, some attended by friends or relatives who sat around them wearing heavy jackets. We knocked at more doors. At last, at long last, we found two nurses whose own sallow listlessness left them at not much of a remove from their patients. When they understood that I was a journalist, their despondent apathy gave way to fear.

I told them that I had no plans to use their names; and I might even consider withholding the name of this village should they request it. All I really wanted to learn was whether the oil operation was injuring anybody here.

The nurses replied that they didn't know.

I asked what the most common health problems in Sarykamys might be, and they said that they didn't know. I asked what sicknesses the patients in the ward across the hall were suffering from, and they didn't know that, either. Folding their arms in miserable anxiety in that wretched little office whose only adornment was a poster for the American movie *Titanic*, they said, *Ne znayu, ne znayu*, over and over in their pitifully soft voices.

Finally I got out of the head nurse the information that, *yes, they are going to move, but they don't know when. They are just collecting their documents.*

Who will move?

Everyone.

Who told them to move?

Akimat told them.

As I said, the *akimat* is the administrative or government office of a place; and the *akim* is appointed, not elected. As one educated Kazakh explained to me, each *akim* is in effect the personal representative of the president. What the head nurse's disclosure meant was that the inhabitants of Sarykamys had received their instructions from the top, so to speak. The situation must be fairly serious.

The head nurse said: I'm so afraid even telling you this, that *some nurse in Sarykamys* might be mentioned in the newspaper . . .

I tried to get more out of them, but they both kept swallowing in fear. Finally, because I insisted and because they so desperately wanted to get rid of me, the head nurse telephoned the chief doctor, or perhaps only pretended to since she never could get through—well, but everything there was so decrepit that the telephone lines might truly have been out of order; after all, even in Atyrau a caller was as liable as not to get a busy signal in place of a dial tone, or even to hear somebody else's conversation. So why blame the head nurse?

At last the assistant nurse got delegated to direct us to the chief doctor's house. Down the dark, broken hospital stairs we groped, and then outside to the snowy dirt where the driver sat in the car idling the motor for warmth.

The doctor's house was not very far. Swinging around a browsing camel, we traversed the frozen dirt at the skinny little nurse's almost inaudible signals, until we arrived at a high metal gate on which I first tapped, then knocked, then boomed with my fist until the watchdogs came thudding and snarling against the other side. I gathered that the chief doctor's patients did not often visit her for consultations. There came footsteps and light at last. A boy, presumably the doctor's son, leashed the dogs, unbarred the gate and guided us across the frozen mud into the vestibule where the nurse, the interpreter and I stood crowded together amidst the household's boots and shoes, while the boy withdrew to the inner rooms.

There came slow footsteps. The doctor-in-chief appeared. She said that she had a temperature. She too was trembling now, just as both nurses had trembled, which is why I feel bad about telling you the name of the village, which really *is* Sarykamys, but even if that doctor and those nurses lose their jobs as a result of this story (which I sincerely hope that they won't), I must believe that what's most important is to tell the truth, for the sake of the four or five thousand inhabitants of Sarykamys whose health that doctor and those nurses ought to be protecting. And so our hostess fled behind the door, and we all stood there foolishly.

Please ask her just one question, I said to her boy. Is there a high rate of sickness here, and, if so, would TCO be responsible?

She will scream at me, he replied, ashamed.

The nurse had already rushed outside. There did not seem to be much to do except follow her.

Well, I told the interpreter, at least *your* job is pretty easy.

Ne znayu, ne znayu, she laughed, shaking her head.

So we went back to the hospital, and I tormented the pair of nurses a little longer, asking them what they thought about TCO (they didn't know), and whether they had ever heard of TCO (they didn't know, although from the hospital window you could almost see two devilish eyes of flame in the sky, and the purple and white smoke from them creeping across the horizon), and finally I asked them where the *akim's* house might be. They didn't know that, either.

After all, you said that he told the people to move, I remarked. So maybe you know where his house is.

Just ask anybody. Everybody knows. Only not us, the translator interpreted, and she could not help laughing again.

Leaving those two women to their fears, we descended the hospital steps for the last time. I stood in the cold, perplexed.

What now? said the translator.

Ne znayu.

She shook her head sadly.

Well, tell the driver to get us to the *akim*'s house, I guess.

The driver now began to convey us very purposefully along the dipping, icy, dead-earth swirls which in this village had to be called streets, and I was not paying much attention, relaxing actually after the strain of that visit to the doctor-in-chief, when it suddenly became apparent that he was undertaking the eight-hour journey back to Atyrau. It was like the doctor-in-chief's metal gate all over again: I had to question, reason, and finally loudly demand, gripping him by the shoulder before he would turn around. Then, whining sullenly all the way, he took us back to Sarykamys. He knew the mentality of those people, he said. I would never get anything out of them. I requested that he kindly stop and ask the first person we saw how to find the *akim*'s house. For a long time we saw nobody, and then finally the headlights froze and bleached the tan figure of an ancient woman creeping down the dirt street. I tapped the driver's shoulder, and he kept right on going. Seeing two men in a doorway, I shouted, and he kept going, so I opened the door of that slowly moving car preparatory to leaping out, until the interpreter laid her hand on my arm and said that they were drunks. Then, feeling foolish, I waited until we saw a family emerging from the doorway of a small shop. Reopening the door, I stepped out onto the ice, my jacket instantly puckering and freezing against my shoulders, and behind me the car rolled to a stop. These people readily pointed out the *akim*'s house, and offered to take me there on foot, but I could do nothing without my interpreter, and it seemed imprudent under the circumstances to leave the driver to his own devices, although he probably wouldn't drive off and leave me until he'd been paid. He refused to listen to the villagers' directions. All he did was argue and argue with me in a plaintive way which excited my pity; he too was getting afraid now.

What was it they were all afraid of? Much later, when I was back in the metropolis of Almaty, I went to visit a venerable newspaper's editor-in-chief, a rangy, pallid cigarette smoker whose desk lamp was upheld by a cast pewter figure of Lenin. On the wall hung a red Russian banner from the good old days: **WORKERS OF THE WORLD, UNITE.** The editor-in-chief said that in his opinion nothing bad would happen to any of these scared people. The doctor and the nurses would not lose their jobs, the driver wouldn't get summoned to KNB headquarters, et cetera. But in small towns the old *atmosphere* of repression might well remain. —Here we are in the center, you know, he said. And the center has become more liberal. But the provinces remain the provinces.

So in Kazakhstan is there freedom of the press? I asked.

The editor-in-chief replied: If you criticize the president or the parliament, you don't go to prison, but they close your publication immediately, and—well, you lose your luck.

The way I supposed it, the government of Kazakhstan did not want to stop getting oil money. For this reason, they protected TCO from exposure wherever they could. Do you remember the sentence I quoted from TCO's charming little booklet? *Tengizchevroil and all those working for TCO are very proud in operating its facilities in a safe and environmentally responsible manner, consistent with national environmental regulations.* —I didn't know what the national environmental regulations of Kazakhstan might be. But might they not be more lenient than the environmental regulations of, say, California? A journalist in Atyrau told me that he and his colleagues met with certain "obstacles" whenever they tried to write about conditions in the Tengiz. He preferred not to say what those obstacles were. He boasted that at least a small notice had once appeared in the Atyrau newspapers, referring to the Tengiz problem . . .

The driver was now warning that the interpreter and I might get badly beaten by the villagers. He said that these people were *wild.* Ignoring him, I persuaded the interpreter out of the car, and asked the family to repeat their directions in order for her to relay them to the driver, which she miserably did. She herself was not so much afraid as disheartened and cold. As for me, I was not afraid at all. I never felt, as the driver seemed to, that Sarykamys was a "bad" place, and indeed when we arrived at the apartment block in which the *akim* lived, all went well—for the *akim* himself happened to be out of town. His two sons, one a teenager, the other a little younger, were not sufficiently grown up to repel my intrusion as the doctor-in-chief had done. The interpreter and I found ourselves standing once again just inside the door of a residence to which we were unwelcome, standing side by side upon the tiny square of vinyl where an invited visitor would have stood to remove his shoes; we of course received no mandate to do that.

At first the elder boy said that he too knew nothing about anything; but when I inquired whether his father had in fact advised or instructed the people to move, he hesitated, and then the younger boy, who'd been lurking shyly in the kitchen, peering at us from the doorjamb, could no longer restrain himself from showing off his knowledge, and so then they both talked, the elder boy more and more wearily, as if he expected to get punished later for what he was saying. I could not worry about that then.

Two months ago, the elder boy said, a pair of Kazakh women had come to sample doorknobs and other metal objects. After that, his father told the people to move.

All of them?

Yes.

Well, and why should the people move? Is anything wrong in Sarykamys?

The elder boy shrugged his shoulders, and the younger one said: Some worker just now, he passed away from the sulfur.

How do you know it was from the sulfur and not from something else?

Everybody says it. Everybody knows it. After work, he wanted to have a dinner. Then he was dead when he was sitting at the table.

Was he old, then?

About forty years.

Are you two afraid for your own health? I asked the boys.

No, we never think about it.

Well, now that you're thinking about it, what's your opinion?

We'll see, the boys replied, gazing at each other almost slyly.

They told me that often in the early morning and often at twelve or one at night there would be a horrid chemical smell. They didn't know exactly what it was, or what the two women scientists had found. They thought that those women might be connected with Kazakhoil, but they weren't sure.

Well, well, I said. So everybody's going to move. Then what will happen to the houses here?

They're going to destroy all the one-storey houses. Houses like this one will stay here and become hostels for the workers. They're going to take from this very place oil. From under these houses . . .

And how do you feel about all that?

On the one hand, we think about our health. On the other hand, we think about money from oil.

And that was the point. It would be too easy to blame Chevron and the government of Kazakhstan for everything. But a man who smokes cigarettes surely suspects that his habit might be bad for him. A man who exchanges his health for oil money is similarly making a choice. All over the world I have heard the cry: *But what else can we do?* from opium growers, street prostitutes, terrorists and others whose actions might be considered controversial. If you believe, as I do, that everybody, even a condemned prisoner in his death cell, retains some degree of moral freedom, then the people of Sarykamys who express loyalty to that oil money (and I never heard a single soul in Kazakhstan explicitly reject it) become complicit in their own destruction. Of course, you and I are more guilty than they. We create the demand for TCO's product, we pollute the atmosphere with it, and about Sarykamys we don't give a rat's ass. And if you disagree with me about your own responsibility, read this story to the end and then decide whether you would be willing to forgo your petroleum addiction for a single day.

And will you be sad to leave Sarykamys?

Well, it's our native place, but we don't know . . .

They stood there then, the elder boy in the bright-lit doorway of a room just in front of us, the younger now off to the right in the dark living room or den, and because they were only boys and had already helped me more than anybody else in that town, I didn't have the heart to take advantage of them any further. So I thanked them, and the interpreter closed the last button of her coat. Trying to rid myself of the creepy and creepier feeling which had crept up my sleeves like the cold itself, I smiled at them, asking whether they had anything further to tell me; and had they been adults they would have replied in some manner hospitably or irritably innocuous, but they were not, and so the younger boy said: They had a meeting. Everybody here has anemia.

5

We knocked at the door of another apartment and a woman let us in [photographs 95, 96]. People were just sitting down to dinner over a long low table. Some of the women wore headscarves around their faces. They insisted on offering us bread. They said: There are sick women, sick children. Out of four thousand people here, 80 percent are sick.

What are their symptoms?

One lady replied: I've been here only two years, but I feel the influence of sulfur. When I wake up at three in the morning I smell the smell of sulfur and I have an allergy. I have a problem with my nose and my eyes. Those two ladies are my relatives. They're not from here, but they visit. When they are here, they have an ache in their legs. When they go out, the ache goes away.

An olive-faced woman in glasses said, talking faster and faster: After a rain, I notice on the gate a yellow dust. That's their sulfur, from their factory.

And you smell the sulfur every day?

Not every day, but almost. It depends on the wind.

Are you afraid?

Of course. I have children and grandchildren, and I worry about them. And TCO doesn't want to reveal the problem . . .

She was talking still more rapidly, almost gabbling now in anger and in terror.

Will you move?

If they help us. If not, we have no money to move.

An old pensioner with a white beard said: Because of sulfur gas, when we wake up we can't even breathe. That's at six or seven o'clock in the morning. Anyway, we should move. Why should our children die here?

Please send this story into America, a man pleaded. I know the Americans will do something.

(They wouldn't, of course.*)

A younger woman said: Sometimes our kids' hair turns white, we don't know why . . .

Now experiencing the feeling which they call "cold horror," I

---

* His belief in America, and my reaction to it, occurred during the term of President Clinton. Thanks to his successor, any such belief has been rendered ludicrous.

knocked on another door, and a woman held up her child and said: You see, he's one year and three months old, and he cannot walk. His brother might have something wrong with his heart but we're not sure. My husband has a heart problem. As for me, I have a headache every day, and there's a bad smell. In the summertime we can feel it all day, even the yard. We want to open the windows when it gets hot, but we can't, because of the smell. In the afternoon there is a little fire from the refinery, but in the evening there is a big fire, and more of a bad smell. Some doctors from Atyrau told us we have anemia . . .

Since this oil operation is making you sick, are you for or against the oil extraction?

If they close the factory, many people will lose their jobs, the woman replied, almost shrugging. It will be difficult to live.

<h1 style="text-align:center">6</h1>

No doubt in my ignorance of the "necessary" "realities" of oil extraction, about the virtues of America's God-given right to drive to the shopping mall, about the altruistic statesmanship and incidental greed of Kazakhstan's politicians, I am misconstruing all this. No doubt it is perfectly reasonable to poison the human beings who happen to live in Sarykamys, not to mention the uncensused seals and fishes of the Caspian Sea. After all, if the human beings say that *it will be difficult to live* if they're not poisoned, then their poisoning must be permissible, right? Their poverty seems as filthy as Atyrau's mud, which freezes, thaws, and freezes again, smearing itself by means of boots onto carpets and floors. They want to get out of it, and TCO stands so kindly ready to help. Besides, it was just a glimpse that I got of Sarykamys, no hard evidence, neither dead people nor dead seals dusted yellow with sulfur. I remember the taxi driver in Atyrau who'd quit working at Tengiz after a year because something had gone wrong with his liver; he'd seen his colleagues' hair fall out; he'd seen young men go to bed and never wake up. I asked him how he could be sure that this was from the sulfur, and he just laughed. How can I myself be sure?* All I know is that as soon as I returned from Sarykamys, here is what happened again and again: Very friendly people who'd talked politics with me before agreed to appointments for interviews and then at the set hour hung their heads and mumbled a refusal. —It's not that I'm afraid, said another of my ethnic Russian interpreters. It's only that I don't want any kind of problem.

What kind of problem? Would you be expelled from school, or lose your job, or go to prison?

Of course not.

Well then, what?

Eighty percent, nothing would happen, she said with a rigid, stubborn guardedness. But I don't want any problem.

What problem?

Biting her lips, she stared into space.

As for the friendly brigade of snow-shovelers, at the time we'd set for our interview they weren't there, and next time I saw them they were sullen and scared. —It's very strange, my interpreter said. It's as if somebody has talked to them . . . †

---

* The toxicological studies available to me bore out some, but not all, of what the people in Atyrau told me. The discrepancies do not necessarily invalidate the things I was told, since the studies were conducted under subacute conditions. References to acute cases of sulfur poisoning, such as the infamous London fog of 1952 which killed four thousand, specify bronchitis as a common cause of death. I did not encounter anybody in Atyrau who was coughing. But there was also no smell of sulfur during the brief interval of my visit. It would seem that if these self-reports of illness were true, and if sulfur and its oxides were the cause, then these people must have suffered from a cumulative chronic condition that sometimes became acute. For more detailed discussion, see the penultimate note to this chapter in the "Sources" section, pp. 309–10.
† I did pay a call on one of the brigade's three women, who during the open, welcoming time had given me her address and invited me to interview her anytime.

The foreigners don't care about us at all, said one woman with whom I got to be friendly. —They want to suck us dry. But of course our own government is just the same. —She had spoken like this several times, without fear. When I asked to meet her one more time, she said she'd be happy to help. But when the time came, I found a note inside my locked hotel room saying that *for some reasons I cannot talk to you,* and that she might not be able to see me before I left Atyrau. I understood, and left her in peace.

7

Without TCO, Atyrau might well retain its low houses, painted and unpainted boxes behind their gates of scrapmetal, all overhung by the smell of exhaust and guarded by mounds of snow topped with filthy slush (the obverse of snow-capped mountains). Between those houses, there's nothing but oozing slush and dark mud carelessly hidden under snow like congealed saliva-froth. Instead, thanks to TCO, Atyrau is becoming an international administrative center, with nice hotels, and all the latest poisons out of sight.

One of the men from Volgograd who was replacing the church dome, a thoughtful old worker, said to me: Communism was worse in a way, I suppose, but at least it guaranteed our future. We didn't have to hunt for a job all the time, gamble all the time. Communism and capitalism have both failed. Maybe there is some middle way, like the socialism in Sweden . . .

I wished so. But I scarcely thought so.

She and her little boy rented a room in one of those rosette-carved, soon-to-be-demolished little wooden houses in Old Town. When I came, she was angry and terrified. All she would say about her life was that she had been a schoolteacher in the Communist days. Now she had to shovel snow just to survive. She was not built for such work, and she was always tired and in pain.

SIXTEEN

SNAKEHEAD FEAR

(Japan, 2001)

I

The late-night taxi driver confirmed the street, saying that it was here that Chinese girls who could barely speak Japanese stood on the sidewalk after ten o'clock, inviting men into the bars they served. Whenever they hired this driver, usually around dawn, four of five of them at a time would crowd into the taxi and direct him to an apartment which they all shared. I asked him why he thought they had anything to do with snakeheads, and he replied that their uneasiness and their language difficulties, in combination with the fact that they invariably hailed him from that street of prostitutes, branded them with illegality; and since the business of snakeheads was smuggling human beings from China, and since in addition everybody knew that snakeheads collected money from Chinese prostitutes, bar owners, street vendors and the like, well, it all added up. I admired his reasoning, especially since while strolling up that selfsame street on that cold cold night I'd met a hooded and shivering young Chinese who stood presenting pink fliers which were adorned both with snapshots of smiling girls in bathing suits and with snapshots of the same or other naked girls on beds hiding their faces from the camera, some of them offering upturned buttocks, the others uplifting breasts or touching pubic or should I say public hair; and the shivering man explained that snakeheads came here at midnight, sometimes to his establishment and other times to others like it* —oh, there were places and more other places, all right there on that street on the edge of Kabukicho. The shivering man said that one could recognize a snakehead by his belligerent bear-shambling gait, which he imitated for me. I never ever saw anybody walk like that. I strolled that street night after night, and all the men looked the same, not only to me but also to whatever guide or interpreter I happened to bring with me. I asked the shivering man to introduce me to a snakehead, and he said that he would try but that he was very afraid. He tried. After that he always avoided me, saying in an anxious voice that he was busy. An old Korean laughed at me and said: Don't you see that he's afraid?

Since the shivering man had become unpromising, I pursued other conduits, such as the detective agency which proposed to arrange a meeting for half a million yen (more than four thousand dollars), this fee to be split between the agency and their Yakuza[†] go-between. The snakeheads themselves would also want a present, the detective said. He didn't know how much. And if the snakeheads refused to meet me, I'd still have to pay the four thousand. I didn't much care for that method.

Then there was the smallish Yakuza family with some of whose members I'd made friends on a prior occasion; they would have been willing to introduce me to snakeheads, they said, except for the fact that if my article offended somebody they would lose face or worse. They were very very sorry, they said. Perhaps they were afraid, too.

-----

* Not to the one down the street whose sign proclaimed SUBWAY MOLESTERS (offering a golden chance to enter a crowded room full of girls for a specified period of time and grope them in an explicit simulation of the fondlings and molestings which occur on a rush hour subway car)—no, that was for Japanese only, said the sign.
† Japanese Mafia.

There was the well-connected, notorious, longhaired man of part Chinese descent who fixed boxing matches; he said that what I wanted was very, very, very difficult, probably impossible, *because right now snakeheads very, very nervous, Mr. Vollmann! Very complicated! Because international police cooperation right now, so snakeheads very, very nervous!* He was right about that.

Then there was the shady journalist I knew who knew another journalist who knew a man who told me that what I wanted was more than impractical but that if I wanted to take the train up to Chiba then we could at least talk about it.

He met my interpreter and me in a Denny's restaurant in sight of the station, and this proved to be an inspired choice for discretion because in the course of those three hours the waitress never came unless we summoned her, and only a little girl in the next booth paid us any heed, peeping over the partition to gaze at my white skin in amazement. I paid him three hundred dollars for three hours of his time, and given what he risked, that was a bargain. Both he and the notorious longhaired man (who encountered him through other channels when he was trying to help me) separately warned that if these words allowed the snakeheads to deduce his identity, he'd be murdered. So you're not going to be told who he was. Are you beginning to get a sense of how nice the snakeheads were?

Why were they called snakeheads? I never found out. What did they look like? Not like shambling bears at all; more like ordinary people. The Yakuza had their proud and brilliant full-body tattoos of dragons and demons, but snakeheads, I was told, owned at most a small black dragon hidden in the armpit; I never got to see that. In fact, for all the risks I took and all the expense money I spent, I never to my certain knowledge met a single snakehead in the flesh. This essay on snakeheads and their relationship to poor people can thus proceed only by indirection, sketching the shadows which snakeheads cast as they flickered through other Chinese and Japanese lives. Disciplined, secretive, and utterly expedient—they had no permanent organization, meeting only to finance specific ventures in alien smuggling—they wriggled through the bowels of Japanese society, sheltered by that society's xenophobia which drove even law-abiding Chinese underground. Example: When I mentioned the name of somebody I'd met on the plane, my Japanese friends wondered aloud whether she might be Chinese. —Oh, no, she insisted. My father just gave me a weird name. —Later, in confidence, she confessed that her father was in fact Chinese, but she couldn't bear for anybody to find out, for fear that she might then be regarded as "less Japanese." Relatively cosmopolitan, possessor of a Caucasian boyfriend in California, with a Mexican vacation fresh under her belt, she still craved to normalize herself in that sad fashion. And she was only half Chinese, remember. In Japan, full Chinese, like Koreans and Burakumin "untouchables," tried to pass for ordinary when they could. The snakeheads were good at that. Whereas the Yakuza gave out business cards (and these cards were nearly as flamboyant as their tattoos), whatever telephone numbers or addresses the snakeheads offered were sure to be out of date within three months at most.

The man in the Denny's restaurant said that while police agencies generally agreed that the yearly income of the Yakuza was approximately thirteen billion yen* (which would have comprised a respectable gross domestic product for a small country), nobody knew how much the snakeheads might gross. He called them *the darkest organization in Japan.* —Even the police cannot see the underside of this, he said.

When did they first appear?

About ten years ago.

And when did the general public begin to be affected?

---

* In January 2001, this would have been about U.S. $112,069,000.

Maybe two years ago.

From a shopping bag he began to extract a pile of confidential blue binders borrowed from the police. He got right to the point. He told me: In Japan we used to say: water, air, and safety are free. Now safety is no longer free.

He gave me newspaper clippings about the latest crimes: an attack by four Chinese upon a bank van, another robbery ten days later with forty-six million yen stolen and one person killed, et cetera. As an American, hence violence-jaded, I could scarcely feel impressed. But, as the cliché goes, everything is relative. Not long after the Columbine high school shootings, I happened to be in Colombia, where my acquaintances expressed amused surprise that we Americans could get so worked up over thirteen deaths. In Colombia, thirty people at a time got killed in villages all over the country every week! So I could get the Colombians' drift, and I could likewise see the point of this well-groomed, greyhaired, youngish-faced Japanese in his business suit. Life was getting less safe in Japan. And that was in considerable measure the snakeheads' fault.

He said that thanks to the collapse of the "bubble economy," even Japanese-born university graduates sometimes failed to get jobs now, and so I should be able to imagine how it must be for everybody else. How could the crime rate *not* be going up? Turning the pages of those confidential blue binders filled with gangster organizational charts whose circles and squares were all dizzyingly interconnected, he began to lay out the details. The snakeheads charged three million yen* for passage to Japan, usually in a dangerous, overcrowded boat.† No doubt this generalization omits details and discounts; you may

---

* U.S. $25,650.
† Frequently the boats, which held on the average a hundred and fifty illegal passengers, were chartered from the infamous "Fourteen Karat Families," who had once comprised an anti-Communist Chinese nationalist organization funded by Taiwan, but who now were simply an international criminal syndicate.

recall that the Chinese prostitute Erica, whom I had interviewed one year before,* had quoted me the price of one million for a one-month visa (here she was almost certainly speaking of her own case) and three million yen for vaguely specified other circumstances and other colleagues. Her travel broker might or might not have been a snakehead; she began to squirm when that issue arose. The man in Chiba remarked that of course one could find high-class snakeheads and high-class clients who got to fly into Japan with forged documents in their pockets and phony-baloney Japanese spouses right beside them, but these were usually urbanites who paid up front, no matter if the price were five or six million. Most illegals found the three million difficult enough. For a Chinese farmer, this fee amounted to *thirty or forty years' earnings.* Of course in Tokyo it was possible to make fifty thousand yen in a day if a worker were skilled and lucky, but most clients of the snakeheads lacked one or both of those qualities. After all, weren't they poor people? The three million yen needed to be quickly repaid,† the snakeheads not being known especially for their patience, and one way to pay it back was crime.

Before you judge these criminals too harshly, imagine, if you will, their arrival in Japan, the snakeheads detaining them in a warehouse rented from the Yakuza, then allowing them their phone call home to China to plead for the money, in many cases with a snakehead literally holding a knife to the caller's ear, and if the money didn't come, off went the ear, and if the money still didn't come it was murder time. (After they paid off the snakeheads, then it was time to get to the point of the enterprise and build themselves nice houses back in China. Judge them for this, if you wish. I am spared judgment thanks to the limits of my own richness, which ultimately forbade

---

* See p. 166.
† The snakeheads used to require all the money up front. Now a down payment of 500,000 yen was often enough; and in some cases they required no down payment at all.

me from peeking into the otherwise unimaginable lives they came from in China's Fujian Province; this chapter, which cost me between five and eight thousand dollars to write, fails worse than most of the others to achieve the minimal object of basic description; the chapter on Kazakhstan at least suggests certain horrors; but the sights and smells of those Fujian lives ought to be set against their illegal equivalents in Tokyo, and I cannot do that; perhaps I never could, in which case the chapter on Big Mountain and Little Mountain achieves the most success, being the bluntest confession of inadequacy; but unlike James Agee, I fear to give undue prominence to the joys of self-laceration. Agee writes that we "cannot even face the fact of nature without either stone blindness or sentimentality," so I will leave you and me stone-blind to that unknown but surely ghastly life in Fujian which they must if they failed return to, assuming that they could return at all.)

How often did illegal immigrants get murdered for non-payment? Unknown. My personal belief is that this happened rarely, murders being rare in Japan. Were I a snakehead, I'd rather keep my host organism alive, anemic blood being more nutritious to me than none.

Why did anyone seek out the snakeheads to help them with their do-it-yourself immigration projects? In fact, until recently, when Japan began to watch and restrict them, Chinese had entered the country legally in tour groups, then simply overstayed. In September 2000, three men vanished in this fashion. When I wrote this chapter, the Japanese police were still looking for them. It cost the vanishers only one million yen to take this gamble at self-enrichment—a third of the snakeheads' price. (Again, recall that this was the first figure quoted by Erica.) But now that loophole was closed.

So they fell back on the secret nightmare trip in the overcrowded boat, followed by the phone call with the knife against the ear. If they were willing to further indebt themselves or their families, the snakeheads could do other things for them. Recently a snakehead from the Shanghai Mafia was arrested in possession of a Japanese passport. It was straightforward to get that item for anyone who could pay. An already legal Japanese citizen presented his residence registration and his family register to a private agency, together with his photograph, except that after pocketing a fee provided by some generous snakehead, he inserted not his own photograph but the likeness of a Chinese client. A week or two later, the agency sent him a postcard when his passport was ready. He gave the postcard to the snakehead, who passed it on to the client, who went to the agency to pick up the passport. The officials asked him only his supposed name and birthdate. That was all the Japanese he needed to know. That cost him about half a million yen, of which the Japanese pawn received a smallish portion.

Then there were the marriage tricks.* In West Shinjuku, ten minutes' walking from Kabukicho, there is a steel-girdered, concrete-walled underpass along whose grimy sidewalk-lips hasten salarymen, office women in high heels, cyclists and everybody; but along the graffiti'd walls, behind a platoon of bicycles whose handlebar baskets are hoarded high with newspapers and cans, run two files of card-boxes inhabited by those who do not hasten, the homeless men, one of whom, a stinking drunk, told me with his own lips how six months ago a snakehead whose name was something like Big Fish Dragon had come and paid him eighty thousand yen† to enter a taxi which conveyed him to a windowless apartment in the Okubo district near

---

* It was not only the snakeheads who arranged such marriages. One cropheaded man inside a tent in a park, everything shipshape because he used to be a construction boss, sat cross-legged on blankets, smoked cigarettes, the rainy afternoon light shining through the roof, and he said that he knew for a fact that Filipinas often paid Japanese men money to marry them, and so did Korean women. Each nationality generally went through her own group's Mafia. "Some time ago," he told me, "a Korean Mafia guy visited me and asked if I could sell my family register for a marriage. There were five or six of them around my tent, quite threatening. They had guns."
† Approximately U.S. $685.

Kabukicho, where he was instructed to shower, then loaned an approximately fitting suit and necktie which he wore to another apartment filled with shy downcast Chinese women one of whom was also all dolled up; a snakehead took a formal portrait of the happy couple—how sweet to see two poor people benefiting each other!—and then they got married. They would never see each other again. The homeless man guessed that his wife had paid Big Fish Dragon about half a million yen* to arrange her nuptials, but he'd felt too awkward to ask her. She was beautiful, he said, a real princess. Perhaps she'd gotten a good "dating club" job after that . . .

Were you ever tempted to go see your wife? I asked him.

Oh, no! Because this was snakehead business, you understand. So I was afraid—

He still had the wedding picture, which he showed me; they'd contemptuously allowed him to keep that . . .

Sometimes the marriage knots got tied more elaborately. There were several cases known to the police in which a Yakuza married his girlfriend or mistress to a snakehead, and then in return married the snakehead's girlfriend. Now the Chinese couple could legally reside in Japan, and the Yakuza got paid for both marriages.

All of these unions, registered at the appropriate municipal office, were absolutely legal. Sometimes after a year the immigration police telephoned the bride and groom to make sure that they were still married, but that phone call probably wouldn't come in my homeless friend's case, since the groom had no address† and the bride was most likely a rolling stone herself, working (depending on her looks) as a

---

* About U.S. $2,825. According to that well-informed man in Chiba, the homeless man usually received a fee of anywhere from thirty thousand to half a million yen, while his bride paid between eight hundred thousand and a million yen.

† I'm informed that when the man wasn't homeless, the woman had to pay more, and that if the police called after that first year of marriage and he agreeably promised that his wife was right there, the woman had to pay extra, which again enriched both him and the snakeheads.

"lady bar" hostess, a lookout in a sweatshop for illegal laborers, or a low-paid domestic; accordingly, even though a special unit of plain-clothesmen had posted such suspect marriages into the police record with its neat chart of names and addresses, four of which the man in Chiba permitted me to copy down, the addresses quickly went out of date, as I discovered when I set out to visit them, thinking them to be surefire because some of them were used by five or even ten women at a time. The discrimination against foreigners for which Japan is so famous, reified here in their outright racist and accord-ingly mutual impoverishing fear of these Chinese immigrants legal and illegal, a fear perhaps all the worse for the atrocious things that their army had done to them during the Second World War, which were themselves doubtless the worse for all of ancient China's influ-ence on ancient Japan—three particular strangenesses whose degree of conspicuousness in Chinese-Japanese encounters I'll never know—combined with the impossibility of coming up with security deposits, led our happy Chinese wives to accept the snakeheads' kind offer of a temporary home, no matter that it was crowded and that the snakeheads charged each occupant an amount equal to the total rent. I foolishly imagined that the snakeheads were sufficiently cost-conscious to use at least some apartments over and over. If I knocked on one of those police-recorded doors in, say, early afternoon, when bar hostesses were likely to be just waking up, and if when it opened I happened to see a crowd of scared-looking Chinese ladies within, why, then I probably would have discovered a snakepit. That was my reasoning. Most of the addresses were in Okubo, where the homeless man had discovered himself to be so instantaneously and profitably married; and each place was difficult for each white-gloved taxi driver to find because when he checked his city atlas the alleys all crowded together there in many, many lines of color. The last address lay close to where a Japanese dentist had recently been stabbed in a robbery committed by four Chinese men, and the driver remarked: Not all the Chinese are bad, but I think the police have to enforce the law. I feel afraid. It's a new situation. It's been like this in my neighborhood only since last year with the lockpicking and everything, and they say that the Chinese are doing it. —And wending our way through a maze of apartments where Chinese-style clothes sometimes hung from the laundry lines, the interpreter and I discovered that that address was now a vacant lot. Had it always been? How could I say?

The next address lay in an alley by the train station in Okubo where there were many Chinese prostitutes, and, passing spilled garbage in the entranceway, I met a wary old Chinese and his innocent-eyed teenaged son who said that they had lived there for a year and that the Japanese treated them very, *very* well but he really had to go. Not wishing to become one of his insulting and frightening discomforts, I declined to keep him, having found out from him that the addresses given me by the man in Chiba were at least a year old.

Third was the old Taiwanese apartment manager whose window was taped over; fourth was the domicile of a Korean woman who seemed terrified of us and slammed the door as soon as she decently could, audibly locking it from the inside. In each case I'd had the interpreter at the last moment whisper into our unwilling interviewee's ear: *snakeheads*, —and in each case the answer was a claim of utter ignorance concerning any snakehead doings. What did that prove? If poverty is commonly associated with any given mood, that would be sadness; whereas in the case of these poor people connected however indirectly with the snakeheads, the ambient mood was *tension*. Therefore, to an even greater degree than with the other heroes and heroines of this book I failed to establish even a temporary sense of "who they were." What Sunee truly thought of me I can't imagine; probably having any guest at all, let alone a foreigner, made her feel vaguely important, and there was always the certainty that I would give her something, and the possibility, unfortunately not to be realized, that I would make her rich. Vimonrat was shy before me, but I hope that by the end she considered me kind. Natalia disliked me, I imagine; Elena liked me; the rest of the family hoped like Sunee that I could do something significant for them. Perhaps they liked me as well. Big Mountain and Little Mountain were grateful for the money I gave them, and then they forgot me. The people in Nan Ning might have worried that the visit of that foreign journalist could get them in trouble; mainly they grieved and raged over their destroyed houses. And all that they or I could do was our meaningless best; and they were as visible to me as the gloamings in a dark room; now what I can see of them are snapshots of those gloamings, pored over most likely beyond stringency into fantasy. At least I was able to peer far enough into each apartment to discern that the floor was not occluded by many mattresses, that each apartment seemed to house a decently small number of tenants. —The snakeheads are very smart, agreed the man in Chiba without surprise. They move, move, move. If you need to telephone them, you know what they do? They go to a coffee shop and rent some stranger's cellular phone for three or four hours, just like that. Very difficult to meet them . . .

So much for the services provided by the snakeheads. When it came to repayment, pretty girls had it easy. As an American street-walker once remarked to me: I'm literally sitting on a gold mine. — One night, an interpreter and I went to the hostess bar whose Chinese barker had found us on the street right there in Kabukicho; and, bargaining the cover price down from a hundred dollars apiece to a hundred dollars for two, we sat at a table while bored dull Thai women refilled after practically every sip our glasses of water flavored with some kind of cheap whiskey or cognac or brandy whose main purpose seemed to be to color that water; finally we lured a big tall raw-faced Chinese prostitute next to us, but this new never-to-be-paid acquaintance replied with such serene ignorance to our every whispered query about snakeheads that I was in despair. She said that she had been sent by her parents to study Japanese (which as it happened

she barely spoke), and she didn't know whom or how much they had
paid. Summoning the Chinese Mama-san, whose vivacious smiling
ruthlessness had impelled me to pay in advance and get a receipt,
too, just in case there might be any sudden additional charges or fees,
I asked about snakeheads, to which she expressed her regrets that she
had no contacts with such people; indeed, she went on, in such sacred
regard did she hold her obligation to protect her girls that she never
allowed Chinese men to enter, especially since mainland Chinese
and Taiwanese were at loggerheads nowadays. And on the subject of
the girls, she wanted me to know that every one was perfectly legal,
as I was at liberty to verify for myself; and so, thanking her for perfect courtesy, I sat gloomily back on the cushions, while the Thai
farmgirl across the table (thanks to several visits to her country, I
could at least conjecture the obscene mysteries of her own sort of
poverty) tonged new ice cubes in my glass. The next afternoon I got
my interpreter for that time, a nice anti-nuclear activist named Mari,
to telephone that same bar, I having coached Mari until in her head
and heart the character of a fictitious friend of hers named Miss Lee,
unfortunate Chinese farmgirl and virgin, who was willing to do *anything* to repay three million yen to the snakeheads who were now
threatening her family for repayment, had come most plausibly to
life. When Mari relayed Miss Lee's difficulties to the Chinese bargirl who answered the phone, a lady of experience who fifteen minutes later when we called back with new lies would be *busy for an hour
with a customer*, she replied that Miss Lee's problems were quite routine and could all be taken care of. Illegality was no problem; Miss
Lee simply should visit the bar to work things out . . .

What if the snakeheads' debtors happened not to be attractive females? In that case, they could work in construction and other trades
that required only the physical labor at which these Chinese peasants
were already so capable; others became burglars, for eighty percent
of all Japanese locks are still of the easy old cylinder type. That was

why that white-gloved taxi driver in Okubo was so afraid. One of the hallmarks of these new criminals was the gag comprised of gummed tape, which offered rapid convenience to the gagger, no matter that a year before, one Japanese homeowner got kicked in the stomach by a Chinese burglar until he began to vomit blood which the gummed tape prevented him from expelling from his mouth, so that he aspirated and died. Other illegals carved out fine new careers for themselves in kidnapping and armed robbery. Persons of a more analytical bent went into fraud. Some made fake cards to win money at the *pachinko* gambling machines. Bought-off convenience store clerks furnished the snakeheads with customers' credit card numbers, and with this information those immigrants with the knowhow and the proper machine could forge credit cards which they could use themselves, sell back to the snakeheads or peddle at the Thieves' Market in Kabukicho. On the east side of Shinjuku I met a victim of one of these credit card affairs; the police couldn't tell him how or where the crime had been committed, but the perpetrator was undocumented and Chinese. In jail he refused to say how he'd entered Japan.

That knowledgeable man in Chiba with the shopping bag full of confidential police binders, of secret tables of snakehead organization which I was not allowed to copy or even to view except upside down (and I couldn't read Japanese anyway), had written down for me the address of a Chinese restaurant in Kabukicho. Smiling, he drew the edge of his hand across his throat. —There was a decapitation, repeated my interpreter in English, a head cut off by snakeheads. No, three people, killed with a big Chinese knife. We can visit. Snakeheads meet in the deep end, in the far room.

And indeed I went to that tiny room filled with Chinese men in black suits, beyond which lay another even smaller room, windowless, where faded prints of traditional Chinese beauties adorned the walls, and at red tables Chinese and Japanese were drinking beer from big bottles and eating sliced eel and tofu noodles and greens from wet, slightly unclean little plates. Were any of them snakeheads? Without an introduction I could think of no way to find out. Baffled, I paid my unreceipted seventy dollars for an undistinguished dinner and went out to wander amidst Kabukicho's vertical, brilliant signs of mis-spelled English phrases and illuminated photographs of Asian wom-en's faces, buttocks and naked bodies; while alert and wiry young boys pawed at me, following me for half a block each with their excel-lent and various lists of reasons why their hookers in their "dating club" were better than the hookers next door.* These individuals surely cherished their own likely chances of improving their material lives beyond desperation. I wandered the alleys searching for snake-heads, while girls in white thigh-length synthetic bunny-fur jackets tried to persuade me why I should get massaged or sucked; one was a Chinese girl with a fresh new Japanese name who spoke a little En-glish, and when I said that I actually hoped to meet some snakeheads she darted back into the doorway, whipped out a tiny pink cellphone and glared at me with eyes of terrified rage. After that, every time I strolled down that street at night, the wiry boys would point and whisper: *Journalist!* It seemed a problem almost impossible of solu-tion, this so far perfect secrecy of the snakeheads; and if in despera-tion I began to get more direct, more insistent, asking every pretty, plaintive Chinese whore on the street whether she could help me, her eyes would widen, then, once she was sure she wasn't hearing things, the lovely lips would snarl back as she too snatched out her cellphone.

---

* In one club I paid to discover that it worked like this: The customer paid thirty thousand yen (about U.S. $256). The lady got nineteen thousand of this, the wiry boy with his laminated and pictorial list of reasons got ten thousand, and the poor Mama-san got only a thousand. The Mama-san was counting on next time, when if the prostitute had properly done her job the man would come back to her, now cut-ting out the wiry boy entirely so that the Mama-san got his share; moreover, the Mama-san didn't pay her girls any part of the revenues of the watery, overpriced drinks. —These prices and subdivisions differed from the ones in Erica's club (p. 167).

I knew that I was being stupid, that if this door I pounded on were in fact to open, out would come a monster.

And, speaking of monsters, that man in Chiba had opened one last police binder and copied down for me the address of the snakehead boss who was suspected to be the ringleader in those decapitations in the Chinese restaurant where I had eaten. —Go there, said the man, if you're brave enough.

He showed me a photograph of the snakehead, a mild-looking young man in spectacles. He said that very likely the snakehead wore no spectacles now, or a different hairstyle. Late one afternoon I took a taxi to that subdistrict, and after a quarter-hour of searching building numbers and twisting alleys found at last the shuttered two-storey house with its long walkway. To me it seemed a sinister place, but only on account of my errand. It was one of those dangerous, reckless things that I was doing, knocking on the door, wondering what would happen. Several times in my career I've done this, each time wondering if the door would open upon my death. To my relief and disappointment, the door did not open. I heard footfalls within, soft and quiet—maybe a bodyguard, a servant perhaps, and maybe just another perfectly harmless old person who was afraid of strangers. So I'd achieved exactly nothing; and the same thing happened with another snakehead address which the man in Chiba had given me.

So I fell back on the notorious man whom I have already mentioned. He was a special friend of mine, although I was enough in awe of him to wonder (and this I still don't know) why this cult-notorious associate of artists and criminals, this connoisseur of women from squat dark Ainu fertility goddesses to smallbreasted, full-tattooed Japanese sadomasochists, would take the trouble to help me. Perhaps it was because I myself was an artist. Whenever I came to Japan, I brought him my latest book or woodblock print. Did he respect me or was I merely amusing to him? In any event, it was the notorious one who'd arranged my interview with a Yakuza boss two years before. He knew the whereabouts of almost everything. And now he emerged from the shining elevator of the five-hundred-dollar-a-night hotel in which I was staying so as to prove that my status was high enough to warrant a gang boss's time. He liked that hotel. He approved. Tall and monkish in his long dark robe of a jacket, his white hair flowing down his shoulders, he told me that we had to leave at once. He took me by taxi to an office on the edge of Kabukicho, a dingy office high up in a business tower, and in this office men were sitting around a table drinking the Korean rice-wine called *soju.* I wish I could tell you the business in which these men were engaged, a perfectly legal trade which is emblematic of our time because it manufactures unreality, and maybe I could do without making any trouble for them, but since these men, one chubby, bearded and dreamy, the other two hard-faced, had connections to the snakeheads, I would have been betraying the trust with which my notorious friend was honoring me had I even asked whether it was all right to describe them more fully, just for the sake of a little local color. Bowing, they laid out their business cards on the table before me, and one of the cards was emblazoned with a blood-red rising sun and on the obverse with a golden flower similar to the devices which I had seen on the cards of Yakuza bosses. They were all right-wingers—*very patriotic,* explained my friend with a smile. For an hour I sat at the table nodding and smiling awkwardly while they talked amongst themselves in Japanese. Every now and then one man would make a phone call. My friend explained: Because snakehead very *nervous,* you see. Control is too tight, you know. I do my best. I do my best.

So we went out for dinner in Kabukicho, where they served me the best of everything and kept filling up my glass with hot sake, refusing to let me pay, and then they took me to another hostess bar where sad-eyed Czech and Russian girls kept refilling our glasses with watered-down brandy, clapping like automatons when somebody danced. Most of them could hardly speak Japanese. They were in debt to the Yakuza, and one of them told me (and the notorious man agreed) that she would be killed if she ran off. But she didn't care. In two months she'd be done. Then she was going to have some strong words with her "promoter," she said. My notorious friend called my name, and we all went out into the midnight chill. He'd paid for everything. The other men said goodbye and went away. My friend bought himself and me a bowl of ramen at an all-night automat and then brought me back to my hotel, where we sat drinking my Scotch until two or three in the morning, talking about love and reincarnation. In the morning he telephoned my voicemail while I was out breakfasting on potato chips and coffee at a convenience store to save the money I might need for information or a surprise obligatory dinner which could easily cost five hundred dollars, and the message said: Listen. I'm trying my best still but they're all refusing to contact with you. I can get the small type any time, but this means nothing for you. I know you need the big one. So. I meet them this afternoon after four o'clock directly. I do my last trial. —He did his last trial, without success. The snakeheads were afraid.

So they'd refused to meet me. They refused to meet everyone right now, because Interpol was hunting them. And why *should* they meet me? Unlike the Yakuza or even the secret terrorists of Malaysia, they had no "image" to project; they were not "about" anything but money. Publicity was bad for their business. That being the case, what can I say about them?

First of all, they were no longer just Chinese syndicate gangsters moving Chinese illegals into Japan. Some of the Russian dancers in Kabukicho told me that they'd entered Japan via the snakehead route. One man who'd been researching the snakeheads for some time (like all the others, he begged me not to print his name, saying that he needed to protect himself; he was afraid) told me that they now operated in Cambodia, working in conjunction with travel agents where many kinds of passports could be forged. Every so often I'll open the newspaper out here in California and learn that such and such a number illegal Chinese have been intercepted in a container ship off Los Angeles or San Francisco. As long as there are geographical boundary lines between the haves and the have-nots, snakeheads and their ilk will prosper.*

Second of all, by compelling a large proportion of their clients to repay them rapidly and by any means necessary, the snakeheads, as we saw, inevitably increased the incidence of property crimes. By so doing, they also escalated local xenophobia against both legal and illegal immigrants (just think about that white-gloved taxi driver saying in his veiled way: Not all the Chinese are bad, but I think the police have to enforce the law . . . —thereby driving those immigrants even further into concealing their origins.

My prediction is that if the snakeheads get more successful (and who can stop them?), and if their clients accordingly ravage the host society ever more noticeably like rapidly reproducing parasites of violence, that society will in self-defense begin to transform itself into a police state. In the U.S. we see this happening already, beginning at the ever-lengthening Mexican border wall with its auxiliary police and sensors and freeway checkpoints. In Japan we find ever stricter scrutiny of Chinese tour groups and increased surveillance of Japanese marriages with foreigners, not to mention of Chinese immigrants generally. As crime increases, police measures will become more extreme.

As a result of all these factors, everybody is going to become more afraid of everybody else. Japanese will fear Chinese, Chinese legals

---

* For instance, consider this dispatch from England: "Five millionaire gangsters have been identified as key figures in the illegal cockling industry . . . The gangsters, all British and from the Liverpool area, are said to make tens of thousands of pounds a week profit by hiring hundreds of illegal Chinese immigrants on slave wages and making them work in unsafe conditions . . . Most . . . are 'bought' from so-called Snakehead gangs, an offshoot from the Chinese Triad criminal groups . . ."

and illegals will fear each other, and everybody will fear the snake-heads. The snakeheads will fear exposure, no doubt, and they'll take whatever ruthless measures they need to for the sake of business as usual. When I think back on what everybody said to me when I was asking questions about the snakeheads, one word tolls in my memory: *Afraid, afraid, afraid . . .*

2

From this book's point of view, the snakeheads despite their unpleasant fascination are, like TCO, not protagonists but *circumstances*—which is certainly convenient for me, given that both of those parties declined to be interviewed. In the foreground stand the poor Kazakhs and Chinese who choose to amortize themselves.

In the case of a resident of Sarykamys, the question is this: *How can I most profitably amortize my health?* Or, if you like: *Should I live in poverty, or should I take the most feasible escape, which may kill me and will almost certainly poison me to some extent, and my family, too?* We know the preferred choice.

In the case of a Chinese peasant from Fujian Province, the question is: *How can I most profitably amortize my labor?* In other words: *Should I live in poverty, or should I take the most feasible escape, which will probably require me to do things I would otherwise refrain from doing (prostitution, theft, et cetera) and which will definitely indenture me to brutal masters in an alien land?*

In Colombia, many of the urban street criminals are refugees displaced by violence from their rural homes. It may well be that for these people, the only alternative to begging in Bogotá or Medellín is getting murdered in the fields they came from; it may also be that begging fails to sustain life, and that in the atmosphere of class estrangement they've breathed all their lives as Colombians, begging naturally supplements itself with extortion and worse.

Similarly, an illegal Chinese in Tokyo may feel that having already imperiled himself and his family at home to commence this adventure, and having broken any number of laws in any event, then having been frightened, humiliated and angered by Japanese xenophobia, he experiences no crisis of conscience when it comes to breaking other laws.

And in Sarykamys or even Atyrau, who am I to even try to imagine what it must be like to be poor?

It is certainly safe to say that the poor people in these places take calculated chances, actively, spending themselves and others as they think best. Poverty, like richness, most frequently expresses itself in selfishness. And the selfishness of the desperate can partake of an urgent ruthlessness. And here once again I remember Sunee clawing at the air, as if she could not breathe.

HOPES

SEVENTEEN

"MORE AID, BETTER DIRECTED"

(1997)

I

It must surely be time in this book to pay lip service to specific policy recommendations for improving poor people's lives.

One organization proposes political, education and social empowerment, equality for women, *pro-poor growth*, meaning prioritizing full employment, equality and economic growth, small-scale agriculture, technological development, environmental protection and education, all the while reducing family size; *managed globalization*, the maintenance of *democratic space*, forgiveness of poor countries' international debts, conflict prevention and resolution, the creation of new global markets, and of course *strengthening the United Nations' role and leadership*, for it is to the United Nations that we are indebted for all these proposals. Most emblematic of all is the following request: *More aid, better directed*.

More aid, better directed! Couldn't we all use that? And what if the universe enacts less aid, more poorly directed?

The Mongols are coming. They'll slaughter us all. Shall we recommend that they not come?

I support every one of the United Nations' suggestions. Had small-scale agriculture been more successful in the village where Sunee was born, she might never have toiled and drunk her life away in Bangkok. Had she been taught to read and write, had she come into a culture of full employment, perhaps she could have escaped poverty.* It is my hope that all such proposals will be implemented, and that poverty will someday, as the United Nations puts it, go the way of slavery.

Alas, slavery remains with us.

I assume that some people will always be poor, as some people eternally have been. I see before me Big Mountain's hand, more hard and wrinkled than mine; his sadly shining eyes as he looks out at me from the darkness of the box house, breathing inconspicuously through the clean white germ mark. I fear that he will die poor and soon. Should I be wrong, so much the better. Meanwhile, absent *more aid, better directed*, there is little that you and I can do for people like him, and not much they can do for themselves.

What *can* they do? *Hope, accept, escape.* Acceptance and escape are kindred forms of making one's peace with existence. Hope is an eternally unknown quantity. Its goal is either realistic or unrealistic; therefore it leads either to acceptance or escape. More aid, better directed, may be obtainable, given the accomplishment of certain stratagems. Then again, it may be a fantasy. How can poor people know and how can I know? Well, for them it's straightforward enough: They can ruin their health or pay a snakehead; then they'll find out. As for me, all I need do is turn into an accountant of their amortizations.

In a multilevel, air-conditioned Chinese bookstore, I watch the

---

* One volume of the 1961 census of India concerns itself with "Special Tables for Scheduled Castes." In Table SC-I, the unemployed are pigeonholed by their educational level, and the results are shockingly consistent. Consider Manipur: 6,718 "persons not at work," of whom 5,106 are illiterate, 1,329 are "illiterate (without educational level)", 270 are at the primary or junior basic level, 13 have won through to "matriculation or higher secondary," and in the highest category, "above matriculation or higher secondary," we find nobody at all. Consider Tripura's 77,434 jobless people, whose membership in those respective categories falls the same law: 71,305, then 3,827, followed by 2,234, then 42, and finally 26.

young people sitting from morning until night, reading the books they cannot afford to buy. Will they learn the magic engineering or negotiating formula to save them? Or will they open a romance to page one, win the Kingdom of the Jade Princess for the afternoon, then go home smiling to their hovels? Either way, aren't people better off hoping and not knowing, waiting for the numbers rider to bring them lucky happiness? —*Money!* prayed Sunee. *About ten thousand baht for the youngest's education* . . . —If I'd given her that (as I could have done), wouldn't her life have turned perfect? *Please send this story into America,* begged the sick man in Sarykamys. *I know the Americans will do something.* —Oh, yes; oh, *yes.* —*Hope dies last,* sneered Oksana's granddaughter Elena.

2

Two homeless men were cooking beside their crate-houses on Sumidagawa Terrace.

Why are some rich and others poor? I asked.

I don't know why, said the young one. Probably the rich people know how to use the money . . .

Are you rich or poor?

I am poor, replied the old man, very poor.

Why are you poor?

Because I don't have a job.

And why is that?

Due to my health problems.

Do you see any hope for your situation?

I'm just waiting for my death, said the old man, and the young man laughed in brassy sadness.

What will you do if they move you out?

Without weariness or self-pity, certainly without hope or even defiance he pointed to his box-house and said: I'll make another one.

3

Since hope dies last, why not place it first?

The terminal cancer patient who believes in cures, isn't he better off? The "healthy" soul who looks forward to tomorrow, which is a day nearer the grave, the man who knows that the Americans will do something, the homeless men who marry prostitutes for money, the strivers and the opium addicts alike, the devotees of placebos and the strategists who can solve all difficulties provided only that it is given to them to dispense more aid, better directed, why not cheer them on instead of pity them?

I propose that false hopes are as good as true, provided that they cause no harm; and that anyhow between true and false we can but infrequently tell the difference. —Oksana had said: I was the kind of person who always had hope and never begged. —Now she *always* begged. —Shall we demean her former hope by calling it wrongheaded?—Until he's dead, who I am to say that the cancer patient was truly terminal?

EIGHTEEN

THE RIDER

(Philippines, 1995)

Gary truly was a family man, I'd have to say. He'd told his Filipina wife not to ask too much about what he did—not that what he did was bad, only illegal. She didn't want to know; nor did he himself reflect upon his livelihood as much as grapple with it—another reason for silence. You see, he played the numbers just like everybody else, always hoping for the big score. (He asked me to choose three digits; maybe as an outsider I'd bring him luck. I didn't.) On the other side of the scale, he hated to see poor people throw their money away—possibly because he himself so frequently lost. Over and over he'd say to me: If I knew what was going to win, I'd hop on my bike and ride all over the island, buy up that number everywhere, just *go go go* all night! I could make four million pesos . . . !* —But that precognition had never come and never would. On balance, his affirmation of the product lay as pale as a road in the night: It was wrong, but then he got his wages. Frankly, I think that he was too hard on himself. Gambling, drug-taking and love can all be classed as rituals

---

* About U.S. $160,000. In 1995, the Filipino peso was approximately equal to the Thai baht, wavering at around 25 to U.S. $1. One peso was 100 centavos.

of hope. That these three varieties not seldom prove illusory in their effects is one reason that our heaven-sent Inquisitors like to make them illegal. But other kinds of hope also suffer from unlikeliness, almost by definition; for when the getting is easy we find small cause to wish for anything. I don't bother to *hope* to get over this cold; I *expect* it. But I sure hope that the aching in my testicles isn't V.D. Shall we then alter the Marxist line? *Hope is the dope of the masses.* Hail to hope-pushers! Better to let their clients lose ninety-nine percent of the time (maybe even a hundred percent) than to take away hope.

As I said, Gary did what he did without wallowing in notions about the rightness of it. He was a rider, just a rider! He made two hundred and fifty pesos a night,* which was good money for that island. He did what he did, the motorcycle headlamp shining before him like a miner's helmet, leading him speedily down jungle passageways to the rich veins and mother lodes of coordinators whose tally sheets he must harvest for the manager on the other side of the mountain.

The game of jai alai, so they say (and by "they" I mean above all Gary), is rigged in Manila. That is, the archangels, great figures, supposedly join together to decide which players will win, as was done in our country during those televised quiz shows of old. But I do not know this allegation to be a fact, and its veracity seems of little importance. Suffice it to say that the game, like so many other enterprises in the Philippines, gives off the sour odor of corruption, and that with the exception of a few piously misinformed souls and prepaid mouthpieces, nobody minds. Jai alai in and of itself is perfectly legal. Tip sheets, sold on the street for 25 centavos (the list price of mine was 1 p, 25), are also legal; and right across the top they even quote the law which says so. The "street ushers," who are often children, flowergirls, or the like, come and go like prostitutes—not flagrantly, in other

* About U.S. $12.50.

words, but it is still pretty easy to pick them out: Look, here comes a small boy, selling hope! Three old ladies giggle and twitter like virgins as they buy three portions. When I bought mine, I didn't have to worry about being arrested, although whenever somebody caught sight of it he'd grinningly shake a finger. Why? I possessed the road map, but I did not yet own hope, which is to say the *use* of the tip sheets; yes, technically that's problematic, because betting on jai alai is as illegal as it is widespread.

When somebody gambles on the outcome of a game, he plunks down a minimum of one hundred pesos in mildewed bills, which buys him one number. The street usher gives him a betting stub, pockets a twenty-five percent commission for his pains, and records hope's number onto a handwritten tally sheet. The usher then remits these, along with the remaining seventy-five percent of the sales money, to a coordinator, so called (yes, numbers runners can be bureaucrats, too!). The coordinator is but the householder or innkeeper who collects what the usher brings, and stores it secretly until nightfall when Gary the dispatcher comes riding his motorcycle up the jungle paths.

And now I have a little more to relate about Gary himself. He had established himself in this island's society, I don't know how many years back. Whites of long-term residency in one Asian country or another are not exactly lacking, whites who get local friends and colleagues, even sweethearts, even wives. But the majority wear psychic spacesuits which they take off only upon entering their little moon-bases, in which they can breathe the oxygen of their own upbringings. Gary, however, wore psychic shorts. He blended in, speaking Visayan even at home with his family, none of whom seemed comfortable in English—such was his success. With the tourists of the resort he spoke a strange English from nowhere, so that at first I took him to be Australian, then Canadian or maybe South African. It was as though he'd installed in his larynx one of those electronic voice-disguisers which continuously encoded him in new accents like a spook's hand twiddling a radio dial to make this station or that station fade out, adding *good one*, *mate*, and *aye* and *OK* like mutually exclusive call signals to confound the enemy. (Wiry and small with a pock-marked face, he would have made an inconspicuous operative.) I could hardly believe it when I learned that he was American. He'd visited our failing country not long since to see about a job, but within a couple of days he drew his pay for good. — Over there I'm nothing, he said. I'm lower class, and I get no respect. I'd be so poor I'd have to live in a bad neighborhood and send my kids to dangerous schools. It's just not safe over there. Over here, people know me and maybe look up to me a bit because I'm a family man and I've made a home. By lo-cal standards I'm getting old but that's OK. My kids will take care of me when they grow up. I'm respected. —But to me the most remark-able badge of his assimilation was that he'd become a rider. His white face stood out in the jungle night, but he'd managed to do it. He said that the benefits were great—meaning I think the drugs.

By the way, he was one of the best teachers I ever had. Let's say he taught me skydiving, although it wasn't that. When it came to techni-cal matters I'd call him incredibly clear. He was patient, too. If it took me ten times to get something right when another student could fig-ure it out the first time, he'd go through it ten times with me, and then an eleventh. He never showed impatience, even when I made the most egregious mistakes. Because skydiving had certain bad associa-tions for me, I sometimes found myself afraid, but he made it easy, like a potbellied old cop I once met in Sacramento who'd been deadly accurate shooting his forty-five one-handed; and at the shooting range he'd showed me how to hold my own pistol better, with my in-dex finger not touching the grip but parallel to it, and the three lower fingers squeezing like a vise—an unnatural, punishing way to keep that tool in hand; that day my hand was sore, but I got much better groups. I've shot in that style to this day. What I remembered and respected most was the relaxed way that the old cop stood and moved

and carried himself. He had mastered his skill and felt correspondingly easy and joyful about hitting the bull's-eye time after time. So I
felt relaxed, too, and became a better shooter. This was how Gary
likewise taught. It was as if he'd been, say, my scuba instructor and
had brought me deep underwater, then sat smiling and winking at me
on the sandy bottom, let the mouthpiece of his regulator float away,
exhaled calm bubbles, and then slowly pivoted his right arm, brought
his fingertips down to his shoulder, found the regulator hose by feel,
traced his hand down it to the mouthpiece, inserted it back into his
mouth, finished exhaling to clear it, and then took the first breath.
Now it was my turn. This was for me a kind of gambling. I knew that
if I let my mouthpiece go and then couldn't find it again, I would be in
big trouble. Maybe I'd even drown. But he had just showed me that it
could be done without looking. He'd smiled at me. If something went
wrong, he would help me. I trusted him. I was afraid, but I let go the
mouthpiece, reached up to my shoulder, found the hose, found the
mouthpiece, inserted it, took a deep breath—and choked on the sea-
water I'd forgotten to clear with an exhalation. For a second I almost
panicked, but there Gary was, his eyes huge and calm behind his
mask (underwater, everything looks twenty-five percent larger), and so
I coughed the water out, hit the purge valve with the mouthpiece just
at my lips, and took the next breath, which was effortless and silky
and nourishing. Now I understood. Now I could do it. I signaled for
permission to try again, but first Gary made the wait signal and repeated the drill for me. No motion of his was problematic or hurried.
He blew laughing signal-bubbles to show me how easy it was. I took
my mouthpiece out and let it go, found it and put it in, breathed out
and in. There was nothing to it. This was the kind of teacher he was,
gentle, proficient, and good. He knew everything. With him I always
believed that sooner or later I'd get it right.

He expected me on time for lessons, or better yet, five minutes
early. Being, like Trotsky, a dutiful schoolboy, I did arrive on time

every day except one, when I was three minutes late. For a moment
he pretended not to see me. With him everything had to be just so.
Once he lay staring at a wall of his house which had been plastered in
an improper fashion, and although his wife told him not to torture
himself, the lacuna swelled before his hyperfocused eyes until he
couldn't withstand the imperfection of it anymore. Leaping up, he
smashed it and replastered it himself. This is, in a sense, a hellish way
to be, but please remember that he didn't rely on gambler's hope to
make the wall better; he took charge. I respect that.

One afternoon at the end of a class (it was, let's say, a jungle orien-
teering course), we'd stripped off our boots and soaked them in the
bleach tank, we'd washed out our canteens and placed the black an-
odized compasses back on the shelf, and now it was just Gary and I
in the classroom. Somebody had left a map unfolded on the table;
someone else had placed two sheets of paper askew, and an orphaned
pencil lay out of kilter—intolerable these phenomena to him, just as
wet cloud-stains in an otherwise featureless midnight sky might have
enraged some astronomer. Swearing, he straightened everything. I
wanted to help him but he refused, I'm not sure whether because he
didn't want to put me to any trouble or because only he could arrange the classroom in the way that God demanded. He was a funny
one. No, let's say he was perfect for his job, which was perfect for
him. When you teach, let's say, a demolitions course, everything had
better be just so.

He frequently spoke to me about his wife (who the one time I met
her seemed old, sad and silent, perhaps because they were having
money troubles). He told me how much he loved her and respected
her. He said that he wanted to be a good father to his children.

When he went on the job at night, the jungle seemed not unlike
the tropical sea fifty feet down, where cliffs studded with vein-
branches, brown aortas and immense fungoid organs loom out of the
blue murk; the jungle was as densely strange as that, the full moon

(richly yellow) as remote and alien as the surface of the ocean seen from below, which is a lashing, writhing mirror of transcendence. As dreamlike to go deeper into the jungle as it would have been to go to the moon! Gary stepped on the gas. Every mechanical thing that he did, he did perfectly. He was going very fast down the bumpy path but he knew it by heart and at night it was almost empty—oh, every half hour or so he might see a couple of young girls out for a prome-nade (and, speaking of young girls, Gary remained scrupulously faithful to his wife), or an old lady coming home late with a sack on her back, but these pale figures so suddenly trapped in his headlights never shocked his unswerving alertness. He left the town behind, and past the bus station parked the bike in a tongue of mud between immense trees. The night was wet like the sea, neither hot or cold.

Gary walked down a hill, down a field, down a steep wet slope, and across an irrigation ditch in the pitch-blackness. A light was on. He took off his shoes. This was Freddy's place.

Freddy was the manager he worked for. Freddy was the one he had to bring the tally sheets back to. Freddy was the one who gave him great benefits, firstly the reefers (Freddy's cabinet never ran out of excellent grass dried brown), and secondly the ice, which is a liquid white concentrate of methamphetamine said to be dangerously ad-dictive, like gambling; our Inquisitors declared the same thing about heroin, crack cocaine, marijuana, alcohol, caffeine and sugar, and they were always right, which is beside the point, because Inquisitors take away hope. The spermy drop vaporized upon the sheet of foil folded lengthwise; smoke rose, its bitterness more milky, less defined than crack smoke, into the glass tube, then descended throats, reached lungs, and at once it was as though a gentle hand had elevated the brain from behind, making it more buoyant within its meningeal sac, more happy and steady and watchful. This was why Gary so fre-quently came to Freddy's at night as he started work, just to be blessed with those aforesaid benefits.

The house was quiet at that time because they were still out selling numbers. Only Freddy, Freddy's boy and another Filipino were
there, the boy a little feverish that night. Ripe smoke descended,
hazing a lightbulb around which moths flitted like white sparks. On
the wall hung two lacquered puffer-fishes, faded to the color of
wood, not silver anymore as in the fabulous sea. The men lit up, and
the evening became bigheaded and pleasant.

Freddy had some greenish Ming porcelain that he'd dug up out of
cemeteries, and a Spanish silver coin from 1820 which he'd found in
a bulldozer's wake. He showed them to me and then we sat listening
to the crickets. A spider crawled upon the ceiling. Gary was worry-
ing over the tipsheets, trying to pick the lucky number that would
make him rich. It surprised me at first that he would fall for this, but,
after all, why should it matter one bit to the rank and file whether the
game is rigged? If none of the bettors can predict the outcome, then
the bets are fair.

Now for the palm trees and empty dark road. Now for the dark
puddles and bogs, the thick black mud. To Freddy and the other man
and the boy Gary said goodbye in his quiet way, put his shoes on, and
ascended the jungle to his motorcycle. He was the hope artist, the
one who might conduct anybody on this island to heaven if the passenger had only bought the right ticket.

He was flying down the road now at the maximum speed commensurate with safety and skill, lit by the red glow of his cigarette.
He told me later that when he was doing this job he didn't think of
anything but the motion and the velocity. Sometimes the trail was so
narrow that I, riding behind and against him, with one hand on his
shoulder, could touch foliage on either side. He was as kind to me as
always, but I knew that I was interrupting him. He usually wore
headphones to fill him full of music just as he filled himself with
happy smoke.

He rarely had problems with the police. Once there had been a crackdown on gambling, and glimpsing with his rapid eyes the checkpoint ahead, he'd made a tight U-turn and taken another way which required him to carry the motorcycle up a steep flight of a hundred steps near the church. They hadn't caught him then. Another time they had, and Freddy got him out. It was nothing personal on the cops' part. They wanted some squeeze, so Freddy's riders got the shakedown. That was business, not the Inquisition. Speaking of business, Freddy and his people got forty percent of the take, which after the ushers' twenty-five percent left thirty-five percent in the pot to pay riders, coordinators, and naturally any winners; that night the cops had been the winners. That was years ago. Since then, the protection that Freddy bought had stayed fresh and good.

Following dark fence-skeletons, Gary pulled up in front of the first coordinator's place, which was a rickety jungle cafe infested with drunken smiles. They greeted him cordially. From their air of detachment I guessed that they themselves didn't bet, merely collected and deducted. For them, the rider exemplified not so much hope as *steadiness*.

He came quickly back to the motorcycle with the tally sheets under his jacket and bulleted away. The next place was a shack halfway up the mountain. A man came out. I heard a baby whimpering inside. The man had also discovered a Spanish silver coin, this one with a date of seventeen something. He was very proud of it, and gladly brought it out to show me. In the moonlight the coin, which had been well polished, seemed astoundingly bright. Gary took the tally sheets. And the man, who was already rich in hope thanks to his piece of silver, which might bring him millions, stood gazing after us with excited gratitude. Gary offered him still another possibility, just in case the silver coin didn't pan out, and if Gary didn't pan out tonight, then maybe he would tomorrow night. Isn't anticipation the purest pleasure of our lives? Now we sped down a very bumpy road which almost dislodged me, but the ice I'd smoked gave me strength.

Gary's daughter was at Girl Scout camp. Last night he'd stopped to visit her, but tonight as we went by we heard group singing and saw upraised torches, so Gary figured that she was probably too busy to be embarrassed just then. I don't think I have ever met anybody who more calmly and certainly loved his kids.

There was a night carnival park in the next place and Gary disappeared behind a tiny glowing grocery stand. The place after that was a skinny alley at the back of a house. Then it was time to go up the mountain. Brilliant light bulbs in thatch houses trembled past like numbered chances, and then the humidity of transpiring banana trees swallowed the rider. Again it was like rising to the surface of the sea as we neared that coolly swimming moon. There was a certain bend near the last coordinator's house where Gary always stopped to light up a reefer. The jungle was gently alive all around. This was life—Gary's life, at least, although, like all of us, he occasionally disparaged it, felt trapped, felt oldness creeping on him, was tired of this job and the other job, wanted to accomplish great things, wanted to be rich, wanted to make his wife happier. Call him incomparably wealthy in dreams and schemes. Although I'd disappointed him by refusing to smuggle his excellent heroin into the USA, that notion wasn't over and never would be until Gary died. What he had won, I thought, was his destiny, his quiet life of secrets which hurt no other gambler who did not pay to get hurt, his chance to mount his gas-powered horse, don the earphones, turn the key and make every night his own, controlling the details, flying here and there, always trusted, always vivifying people with beneficent illusions. Yes, he'd won; his hopes befriended him with eternal druggy dreams.

He came back into Freddy's, took off his shoes in the low back kitchen where the boy was lighting a mosquito coil, and handed over the tally sheets. He flicked on the lighter (actually that required several flicks). Guested by cats and dogs, he put a cigarette in his mouth.

He leaned forward with his elbows on the table and spoke quietly in Visayan with a gentle-looking man who kept breaking off bits of some dirty rock in his long fingers. Each rock was the size of two fists. I wondered what it was, but they wouldn't tell me.

Gary patted the cat. His knee jigged. The other cat basked upon the concrete partition between sink and sooty pots, her fur rose-colored by the light.

In the front room where the real business was going on, hope peddlers were working with a calculator and a stack of tally sheets. A lean man stretched his arm across his knee, gazing and watching. There were three at the table: the boy with the calculator, and the two men with pens wiggling. All the sheets were crammed with tiny numbers under the columns of those magic ten digits. So that made four, including the watcher, and a fifth man sat facing the wall, slowly summing by hand upon a yellow pad. The radio sang softly, it not being time yet for the game results; hope's accountants murmured together, moving forefingers down the columns, the boy clicking calculator keys while glittering black beetles crawled between their toes.

Gary didn't usually stay around for all that; it wasn't his job. Besides, his wife would worry if he were late. He would go back to the house that he had built with his own hands and reread an old paperback or maybe even *Reader's Digest* because he had read everything he could get his hands on; books were hard to come by in his kingdom. Three times now he'd read some story by David Foster Wallace, torn out of the pages of *The New Yorker*; he gave it to me to read, too, but the cabin I was renting offered only one twenty-five-watt bulb and I didn't feel like standing close to the light straining my eyes while the mosquitoes bit me. Freddy had just finished reading *Papillon*. He offered that to me. I had never read it and would have liked to, but the same mosquito-logic applied, and anyhow I hated to deprive him of it. Freddy was a kind man, and so was Gary. They wouldn't take any money for the drugs they gave me.

Gary put on his shoes and said goodbye. In the morning he'd learn that the two numbers he'd bet on had lost again. The motorcycle buzzed down the road, its headlamp making a progressively smaller slice of luminescence, until it vanished abruptly in the jungle.

NINETEEN

UNDER THE ROAD

(Everywhere)

I

Between Phnom Penh and Choeung Ek the road got busier each year, and in the ravine beneath the bridge, which was closer to the former killing fields than to the town, the shantytown kept growing, as might be expected in one of the seven countries in which the United Nations' Human Poverty Index (HPI) happens to exceed fifty percent of the population as I write. How is the Human Poverty Index measured? Never mind. It won't make poor people any richer.

In that shantytown, whose name I never learned, the laughing faces and stroking hands of children formed a wave of which the puppy dogs' straining ears and noses were the crest, a wave of fun **[photograph 97]**. And when I saw those young lives rushing across the wall of thatch, I was reminded once again that, to an extent, life really is what we make of it. The freedom of slum children to play with puppies instead of getting schooled will, in *the market's* threatening terms, *cost them later.* I do not envy their lives. And yet it would be false to say that these people who by the United Nations' definition were poor were at that moment unhappy.

I remember all the Canadian Inuit towns I have visited. Alcoholics and gasoline-sniffers, suicides, incests, and assaults define those places to social workers. But I also remember the happiness of children there, the freedom they had to wander together under the midnight sun, their parents trusting, and with good reason, that they would take care of each other; they roamed wildly as my child never can, and as I in my childhood rarely did.

On the Filipino island of Cebu, against a corrugated wall, a ragged, bright-eyed child sits on a plastic stool on a blanket on the sidewalk, looking at me from beneath long and shiny bangs, while two other children lie sleeping with splayed legs on that blanket, and it is night and I see neither mother nor father and the child sits patiently scratching at the bites and scabs on its legs, and it is looking at me, *looking at me*; and if you turn your attention to that image **[photograph 127]**, those eyes will also be looking at you. But since this book privileges the consciousness of rich and poor, and wants nothing better than that consciousness can make its own choices, shouldn't I consider some ways that poverty can enrich itself with happiness? My God, who am I to disapprove of Sunee's daily drunk?

2

In an earlier chapter of this book I quoted the critic I. A. Richards on stock thinking. What makes poetry mediocre? *Every item and every strand of meaning, every cadence and every least movement of the form is fatally and irrevocably familiar to anyone with any acquaintance with English poetry . . . the mental movements out of which they were composed have long been parts of our intellectual and emotional repertory and . . . these movements are few and simple and arranged in an obvious order.*

Why are you poor? I'd asked the old man at Sumidagawa Terrace.*

---

* See p. 223.

Because I don't have a job.

Call this answer *fatally and irrevocably familiar,* fatal being an especially appropriate descriptor because when conceived in such limited, monotonous terms (appropriately so, because poverty is limited and monotonous), his situation feels tautologically hopeless.

It may be (why not hope, since that chemobiological entity dies last?) that if one avoids this conceptualization of existence, rearranging the movements of one's consciousness into something more multitudinous and complex, or arranged in a less obvious order, one might be able, however provisionally, to feel less impoverished.

A few steps north of the Mexican border, I was once panhandled by the worn-looking, impressively intoxicated Julio [photograph 102]. We satisfied his requirements and mine by means of a paid interview in the nearest vacant lot (he would have preferred my hotel room, but the best thing about paid interviews in dirt lots is the feasibility of their endings). He had labored as a campesino,* not only in Mexico but also in California, where the work was harder but more lucrative. He generally worked in tomatoes.

Are you poor? I asked.

I am *not* poor, because poor are only stealers. Look at my T-shirt! Look at my tennis shoes!

Why are some people rich and others poor?

The rich are rich because they work hard. I am not poor because I am a drunk, he said with pride. I have enough money to get drunk!

Perhaps he was merely expressing the bitterness of class estrangement; perhaps he was in the throes of numbness adaptive or maladaptive; either way, I applaud his answer for its unexpectedness.

---

* Field worker. Sometimes this word refers exclusively to work on the Mexican side.

3

The Japanese poet Okura (ca. 660–ca. 733) composed a graphic "Dialogue on Poverty." We first meet a poor man, whose soliloquy conveys a melancholy enough impression of an existence wasted in shivering in sleet, wrapped in every rag he possesses as he gnaws on blackened salt. Once he swills down his poor man's elixir of sake residue, alcoholic numbness warms him into a temporary self-satisfaction. *I am not poor because I am a drunk. I have enough money to get drunk!* Even so, he's still cold. *So what of you, whose wretchedness surpasses mine?* This question is addressed to his neighbor, the rock-bottom destitute man, who owns but one rag to shiver in, and whose soliloquy drags us down from bad to worse. In his broken cell of straw and dirt, his parents freeze together, *while down below my wife and children lie and press upon me, groaning in their misery,* and in the cooking pot there is nothing but a spiderweb. Meanwhile, the tax man menaces them in the doorway.

Someone is always better off than I, and someone else is worse off.

In the chapter on dependence I quoted Montaigne on those people who are *continually tossed about by the tempest of the diverse passions that drive them to and fro; depending entirely on others.* His opposite need not be a rich man, but a composed and contented one. Okura's poor man is absolutely and relatively richer than the destitute man. But what if the destitute man also possessed the power to get drunk?

4

Elena's drawings, and Vimonrat's **[photographs 110–111]** took both of those impoverished girls to another place. The common gloss on *imaginary,* name *nonexistent,* does the concept an injustice. *I am not poor because I am a drunk,* and Elena was not poor when she was drawing. I believe this with all my heart. I know the love of pen and paper and line; I have seen that love in Elena's face when she showed me her drawings.

I assert that that place was as happy as long afternoons in some Cambodian beauty shop far in the ricefields; the family men lie in their hammocks slowly sucking on long cigarettes while the mother shampoos a lady's hair and her five-year-old son fills the rinse bucket, singing. —Child labor! rich people might say. —And they would be right. What does the boy lose, thereby, and what does he gain? Does the fact of his singing signify anything? Negro slaves used to sing in the fields of my own country; does whatever happiness their singing gave them mitigate slavery? What is poverty? What are riches? *A chicken in every pot* was once the slogan of the moment. Does that mean that on rainy days we should also aspire to have an umbrella apiece? After all, isn't being rained on one of the penalties of poverty? But full joyously I remember a Burmese afternoon when it was still raining a little but it was sunny with pure white clouds and people walked with or without their umbrellas down the water-sizzling streets, and a woman in sandals sat on the sidewalk before her plastic-covered stand, her cheeks painted in big yellow circles of pigment; and past her came two ladies walking hand in hand under a single umbrella.

5

What about Okura's destitute man? Could rain have caused him joy? —Well, I suppose so, if the merely poor man gave him means to get drunk enough . . .

6

Many times I have witnessed and enjoyed the happy music and cigarette smoke of the Cinnabar in San Francisco, all the whores singing along at the top of their voices to a jukebox tune which one of them

called *those boom-booms comin' in.* —I'm winning! stuttered the prostitute who after months of speech therapy was not much improved, because a man had hit her over the head harder than necessary. Her name
was Linda, and she was half Chinese. A lean old white whore got up
from the bar and whacked the cue ball, *haw!* and Linda giggled, put her
hair up, strode over to the table and took her turn, the pool cue gently
wavering between thumb and forefinger, then slamming hard against
the white sphere and thereby racking another solid into the pocket;
and it made me so happy to see Linda marching round the table with
her head proudly back, stalking the perfect angle; now she leaned in
like a warrior with a spear . . . *Make me nervous!* she confided to herself.
No, no, no! And as the men on the bar stools grinned, she wiped her
sweaty palm, walked around the table once more time, using the cue as
her walking stick, then stopped, squinted fiercely beneath her baseball
cap, spread her wide legs wider, chalked her cue and then . . .

7

A man walking on rubble, a skeletal man in an open shirt gesturing
around at the rubble, men on shifting, clinking bricks . . . —we are
back in the "Africa" of Nan Ning. Sandaled men stand on shifting,
clinking bricks. Why must they bear this?

How can it be anything but an insult to tell them that they should
have hope?

Well, what would you propose instead? Should they wait for *more
aid, better directed?*

8

A tea-seller all in flowing grey squats high on his concrete throne,
before him an array of ancient teapots of various colors. His small
hand flicks milk from an immense cauldron into each, then flicks

sugar. A tap of water runs continually into the dirty cups beside him. Beside him there is also a dish of clotted cream, not to mention two immense porcelain goblets, each taller than he, and each filled with boiling water awaiting his hand-flick on the tap.

Seated on charpoys, blanket-wrapped men, his customers, greet each other with a *salaam alaykum*. Their milk and tea is served with *nan* bread. They smile; they caress the heads of their sons. By my financial standards, they almost surely dwell beneath the road, which is certainly better than resting underground.

I admire these long moments they seem to possess. In my country there used to be few cafes; most of those which now exist are franchises; and even in the local coffee shop where I like to greet my neighbors in the morning, time itself has been franchised. —I've got to go! my rich neighbors are always saying to one another. And off they run. It admit that there is an afternoon crowd whose members linger awhile—students, mainly. I have always liked the sleepy atmosphere of college towns; my coffee shop partakes slightly of that in the afternoons. But poor countries are often richer than ours in time. People work longer, to be sure, but their work can be slow and filled with conversation—at least when they are working for themselves. The customers in this Pakistani teashop are not working, obviously. They sit hour on hour, speaking softly and with grave smiles. Of course some men sit sullenly alone. But the most silent man of all, their Emperor on his concrete pedestal, how can I not respect his imperturbable reign? His apparatus obeys his will, his boy-servitors distribute his beneficence in the half-washed cups. As busy as an octopus, he seems to dream all the while. Once he sends me a sweet smile.

Montaigne asserts: *Poverty has nothing to be feared but this, that it delivers us into the hands of pain, by the thirst, hunger, cold, heat, and sleepless nights that it makes us endure.* It may well be that if one descends beneath the road with sufficient care, one can find teashops to sit in, puppy-dogs to play with, cheap spirits to drink, oceans of time to swim in at the price of a bearable increase in discomfort.

Suppose that the case is worse than this? Montaigne again: *He who has learned how to die has unlearned how to be a slave.*

9

Montaigne, it seems, was terrified of death, and sought in his writings to comfort himself.

I have seen a man die in screaming fear and bewilderment. As far as I could tell, he died without learning how to die.

The tale of Natalia's children, whatever its nasty truth might have been, and the brief autobiographies of Oksana's dependents, are sadly ordinary accounts of living death. But why should poor people, so often impoverished in thinking and learning as in everything else, be expected to learn how to live or how to die?

Seneca observes: *Greatness of soul is a virtue that is seemly for every human being, even for him who is the lowliest of the lowly. For what is greater or braver than to beat down misfortune?* But here as usual, although poverty's misfortunes are likely to be more formidable than richness's, the deck gets stacked against the poor; for Seneca continues: *Yet this greatness of soul has freer play under circumstances of good fortune, and is shown to better advantage on the judge's bench than on the floor.* Set aside the context: Our essayist was vainly attempting to bring out *greatness of soul* in the richest man in his known universe, Nero. Rhetorical strategy therefore required him to elevate richness over poverty. All the same, we can reject the value judgment while profiting from the situational analysis, whose accuracy is undeniable: It is not merely that the poor man, being invisible, cannot hope to have his bravery *shown to better advantage.* The consciousness which must engage with misfortune is more likely than a rich man's to be numbed and tattered. Moreover, the misfortune at issue, being closer to *normality* for a poor man, offers less "drama" to him; the ordeal may be more drawn out than for a rich man, who presumably spends less of his life under clouds of bad luck, but its ending, however it goes, will be less impressive to all parties: A man already half dead gains less credit for dying well; and should chance go the other way, he will be restored not to life but merely to half-deadness.

A friend of mine for whom I have very fond feelings managed with considerable heroism to resist smoking crack cocaine for the entire last month of her pregnancy. The baby, her seventh, was born crack-addicted like the others and surrendered forever to the California foster care system. The mother returned to her own addiction immediately upon her discharge from the hospital. Why deny Sherri her victory? But why also pretend that it might not have been *shown to better advantage* had she enjoyed *circumstances of good fortune?*

This having been said, I confess that in the half-dozen years I knew her, I never heard her mourn for her children, nor even for herself. She was in fact a cheery, energetic person whose adaptive and maladaptive numbnesses insured that her existence would be, at least in her eyes, *shown to better advantage.* She had eternal hope that something good would come along.

(Caressing Vimonrat almost shyly, Sunee said to me: I hope she can be a teacher. I hope her life will be easier than mine.)

For a grander case of soul-greatness than any of the foregoing, consider the Sacramento panhandler Reverend Steele,* who believed that we were in heaven *right now* and that after we died we fell into oblivion. Hell was prison, hell was paradoxically death and hell was contradictorily here, at least being out on the street (a rich man would say, under the road). Demons hounded him to commit violent crimes, and in his dark sunglasses and with his stench this man, who said he survived on five dollars a day, seemed indeed diabolical; but his derangements divided the world into the camp of *the enemy* and the good side. The tensions

---

* See footnote, pp. 59–60.

of his existence with their immense stakes might well have informed his life with more meaning than my own. Would I choose to be him? Never. But he reminds me, as did drunken Julio, that people who live under the road have developed their own *normality*. Seneca takes a stroll down there where slender green trees burst from Madagascar's red hillside and tall slender treeheads roof the mountains with myriad moisture-caves; here he finds half-dead wretches. But they are actually quite alive, thank you. A woman in a yellow sunhat and a yellow dress, holding her baby, stands in the shade at the side of the road, her head high. A man in a red loincloth and a girl in a bathing suit, both very brown, sit on a mat in the sun behind a bamboo fence where the Hotel des Amis restaurant is, and they do not look at the passing train. In Brickaville a dark little girl bounces a ball on the sandy street while her brother watches, he seeming darker than she thanks to his shining white T-shirt. In grass-roofed houses on stick-legs, hidden beneath immense fruit trees, live people who are technically to be considered poor. Their poverty contains a barestriped hillside of stumps; no doubt its erosion will cause them difficulties later. A brown woman hugs the doorway of her hillside hut, peering shyly out. I greet her, and she smiles. Around her live clusters of green bananas on the trees like grenades. There comes a hot tobacco breeze. I swelter, and so does she; I wonder how much of her life is passed drowning in a hot sea of air; but soon enough there's rain in the street, bright white sky, weird pale green trees spreading in the square, dirty kids laughing, showing white teeth . . .

Normality may well school its subjects adequately enough in how to live and how to die.

10

What is your *normality?* I will never know. You are a Congolese beggar-girl staring down at her blanket-wrapped knees [**photograph 29**]. Is your secret numbness, or estrangement, or simple pain? Do you tend toward acceptance, hope, escape, or none of the above? Whatever road I take, you exist unknowably beneath or above it; I cannot ever *see* you.)

II

Every man is rich or poor, says Adam Smith, *to the degree in which he can afford to enjoy the necessaries, conveniencies, and amusements of human life. But after the division of labour has once thoroughly taken place, it is but a small part of these with which a man's own labour can supply him.*

Well, then, what if, as did Thoreau, one rejects division of labor?

Children, the unemployed, artistically inclined imaginations such as Elena's, all such people live in an undivided or at least less divided world.

People who by First World standards are underemployed, people with slow lives, divide their labor less than others.

Might there accordingly be some way for them to redefine their necessaries, conveniencies and amusements back within reach? From under the road I remember the laughing, tilted faces, the puppies straining to be free, trusting from the hilarity of the hands holding them that they almost instantaneously would be; they knew it was a game; and in fact the moment released itself as happily as an ejaculation, in running, laughter, and excited high-pitched barks.

Hope dies last, insisted Elena, but why not hope that if amusements can be so freely communalized, why not conveniencies, too, and even necessaries?

This book is not "practical." It cannot tell anyone what to do, much less how to do it. For all I know, the *normality* of our epoch may render resource-sharing substantially impossible. But *what is greater or braver than to beat down misfortune,* or at least to try? One does try when one indentures himself to snakeheads, or plays oil roulette with one's health. But whether *I think I am rich,* or *I know I am poor,* to the extent that one's degree of richness is indeed a matter of thinking, so must also be the case with one's degree of estrangement. Do you remember what Javier Armando Gomez Reyes said about the rich?* *They guard what they have, because they know what it cost them to get it. They never think about other people. It could happen that they will lose their money and be poor in the street and it will be a poor person who helps them out.* Doubtless he was romanticizing his own class here just as egregiously as Seneca had done. All the same, if you and I were both poor in the street and helped each other out, might we not each at least enjoy the prospect of being better off?

12

Every man is rich or poor to the degree in which he can afford to enjoy the necessaries, conveniencies, and amusements of human life. In this connection I remember the old houses of Atyrau, which their original owners might well have built themselves. (Here again I think of the houses in Nan Ning's "Africa.") Five years of the wrecking ball have gone by since I saw them. Perhaps there are a few left. Some survive in my photographs [112–116]. In my hope-drugged fantasies, at least, their ornamental carvings prove existence of those who build for themselves. (I always paint the walls of my studio as suits me.) Weren't they poor people? How could they have justified the expense of wooden heart, flower, or wheel? Or perhaps in old times they were *not* poor people, at least according to the *normality* of the time, and for them commissioning building was cheap, in which case the decorative elements likewise escaped the cash nexus. These reliefs were abundant in Old Town, yet ever unique. Seemingly neither over- nor undervalued (Adam Smith reminds us that every commodity has its "real" price), they enriched the snowy, muddy landscape under the road to a modest

---

* See p. 158.

degree. I suppose that some of the people who dwelled in those houses took pride in them, or at least were sustained by their familiarity.

I was born here, said the old Tartar lady in mittens. She had a downturned mouth. —I wish to have an apartment, she said. Maybe they'll give me an apartment, maybe not. When they tore down the old houses on the other side of the road, they didn't give them enough. They said they'd give twenty thousand dollars and gave only fourteen thousand. Some of the people bought horses and some of them bought apartments. So some of them are now in debt.

Peering from the tight drawn hood, she informed me that she had seen seventy-five years. The windows of her house were set in tallish shutter-wells appointed with elongated bas-relief diamonds whose centers had been cut out like eyeballs. Just out of curiosity, I asked an American contractor how much he would charge me to make something like that for my windows, and he said that he was not sure he could do it, but if he could it would cost a couple of thousand.

Of course the Communist time was better! the Tartar lady shouted. We used to get a good income from the government.

Who is your hero? I asked.

Brezhnev—Lenin—Stalin! she cried out exultantly. When Brezhnev was in power, we had enough and everyone lived in peace. Russian people are always live people, but Kazakhs are addicted: They take drugs and they don't behave in public . . .

That was her adaptive numbness: comforting fantasies of racial superiority, not to mention the superiority of the past, where her hopes and enjoyments mostly lived, like the deep-carven leaf- and tulip-shaped holes in the niches between an old house's windows. Unlike Oksana and her family, this woman chose to bless Comrade Stalin as the treasurer of her necessaries, conveniencies and amusements. If nothing else, she found more companions for her point of view than could Sherri or Reverend Steele.

In another old house, around the corner from the one with wooden flowers the size of wagon wheels on the fence, each petal grooved all the way through so that it might have been a separate piece of wood, the grandmother said that their turn was to come next spring.

Do you know what's going to happen to you here? I asked.

Yeah, we know, said the children.

Where will you go?

To a hostel, they said.

Will it be nice there?

We don't know.

They had lived in a hostel before with their mother, but their grandmother said that that had been *very different*.

Still another grandmother, who lived in the house her grandmother had been born in, said: I don't know where I'll go. I'll leave before they tear it down. I don't want to see it.

Deducting the uncertainty associated with any change and accordingly magnified in the perceptions of the old and powerless, subtracting the distinct likelihood that the authorities of Kazakhstan, like those elsewhere, did not govern with the interest of the governed uppermost in their minds and therefore would not give fair value for the doomed old houses—supposing, in short, the absurdity that the poor people of Atyrau were actually going to be transmogrified from under the road up to the level clean heaven where rich people play—I still submit that a certain crude handworked beauty associated with under-the-roadness was going to be lost, and that the grandmothers' laments in part reflected this. Under the road, where time is slower and cheaper, not only does the division of labor sometimes insist less on itself, but so does the division between labor and art. Well, goodbye, goodbye! Simple, crownlike flowers on short-plucked diagonal stems spread their angled wings and hovered darkly on a house's pale wall, under-the-road blossoms awaiting the happy day when oil's thoroughfare, preceded by its herald, the wrecking ball, would uplift everybody into a superior *normality*.

13

As for us, reader, why not wander back beneath the road, where among the many young shantytowns in the folds of Bogotá's wide Ciudad Bolívar slumscape lay an ordinary specimen: shacks in the gulley, steep-sloping mud and clay? The community *junta* president of a neighboring squatterville assured me that eighty to ninety percent of the homes in Ciudad Bolívar were illegal.* As in Colombia, so in our world: For every Nan Ning or Atyrau whose deeded properties are being bulldozed, a multitude of illegal settlements arise somewhere else. As for the place in the gulley, four years before nobody had squatted there. But the location was convenient: only two kilometers from the water pipeline (which was not much thicker than three fingers). The owners of this land were nice; they never complained about squatters (perhaps because doing so might have gotten them murdered); they'd expressed willingness to deed the land to the city, but they wanted twenty-four million pesos.† On a cool, wet afternoon flavored with gasoline fumes, some of the squatters gathered around the pool table and unrolled a drawing of the hoped-for legalization. The drawing itself cost ten million pesos, they said.‡ They needed thirteen dollars apiece over their six hundred and thirty-nine lots ($8,307.00§) to *make the legalization.*

---

* That other shantytown had begun only five or six years ago. (To explore it one climbed over rubbishy hills, for each house was above or below its neighbor.) Its inmates were mainly refugees displaced by the leftist guerrillas. The *junta* president said: "Too many problems with violence. The big, big problem is the water. From five years we bring water to houses by horse. Big trucks bring and sell it to them now. They start to construct a canal, but there is no water by proper tubes. Some people take it by hose." His name was Pedro Jose Arías. I asked him whether his class views were the customary ones. —"That's true," he allowed, "we hate the rich, because in Colombia the money talks."
† U.S. $13,559.
‡ U.S. $5,650. I find this difficult to believe.
§ 14.7 million pesos. As so often with poor people's numbers, these three figures do not appear to cross-check.

The place that dreamed of legalizing itself was fittingly named Nueva Esperanza (New Hope). It was here that that eight-year-old schoolgirl had gotten chased home by two boys with knives.* I met her grieving, angry, helpless mother on my very first visit, and every time I went back, there had just been another such ugly demonstration of accident-prone-ness. Their poverty was around and under them, like smoke and dirty water rippling under traffic.

Is it dangerous here? I asked the people gathered around their map.

No, no! they said indignantly.

A man in Taliban Afghanistan once said to me: *When there is no job opportunity, your only chance is to take arms.* And in Nueva Esperanza, the baker in his torn apron, gilding his egg-shaped breads with sugar, salt, flour and rich yellow butter, explained: *We can't work on account of the paramilitaries; and the guerrillas won't let anybody plant in the fields.* What symmetry! But the baker had in fact found a way to work. Leaning on the greased metal table while he rolled out the bread dough while his wife of forty-six years pulled forth the long trays of dark-blasted rolls from that oven whose transport here had made such a story (carried on a pole through the hills by four strong people), he said: We used to be just like any animal, just one meal a day. —But the oven had now squatted here for three years; and he and she went on rolling out dough with their hands; all the time we chatted there were soft slapping sounds as they altered the long snake into spheroids like hardboiled eggs beneath the corrugated roof which echoed with cool rain, accompanied by the voices of children and of a howling dog, and all the bread was going to get sold. Granted, in six years a sack of flour had increased in cost from nine thousand to forty-eight thousand pesos. He had accordingly raised his prices by eighty percent in the same period. But as long as the authorities, paramilitaries and guerrillas

---

* See p. 138.

paid him no mind, the old baker, whom I would not characterize as poor, possessed every prospect of a future solidified by the corn-rich smell of the dough. Moreover, his bread-work seemed both to content him and (if this is not too presumptuous) to become him; he reminded me of the Emperor of that teashop in Pakistan. His wife worked more wearily, but under the road as well as over it we had better take our happiness where we can.

The instant I left him, his neighbors drew me into their hovels and begged for *more aid, better directed*, glaring at me with desperate eyes. Just as the baker had been once, so were they: one meal a day, usually soup. Some of them did not even have that. I remember that their homes were chilly and clammy. I gave a little to the people I particularly pitied (always being careful not to let them see how much money I had); while others equally poor or poorer I put off with excuses, not daring to refuse them outright, because *when there is no job opportunity, your only chance is to take arms.* Two visits later, my interpreter advised that we not return to Nueva Esperanza anymore . . . *

Earlier in this book I wrote: *What can they do? Hope, accept, escape.* The people who stood around their map refused to accept and saw no escape, so they were determined to finish building a school soon; right now there was not enough money for third grade. — Oh, what hopes they all had! My friend Dr. Carlos, who ran a clinic for poor people in a more urban subdistrict of Ciudad Bolívar, was sure that

---

* The baker and his wife had a daughter named Gladys who lived with her children in another illegal settlement. I visited them several times. She said that she felt no fear in Ciudad Bolívar (and indeed, this beautiful, cheerful, friendly young woman **[photograph 120]** was also brave, strong and tough), but she had on occasion felt afraid in Centro (downtown Bogotá). Then she said: "I'm practical. I don't feel scared in general. I was robbed one time by an Ecuadorean. He just tried to be friendly the entire time. That was in Sur side . . ." — Another time when she got off work at four-thirty in the morning, a man followed her two and a half blocks from the bus stop, masturbating. She threw a stone at him. A few days later she passed close to the bus stop and saw him again. He later did the same thing to one of her friends. He was *loco*. After that he never saw her again.

conditions would be better in twenty years. —Twenty years? my driver laughed. Jesus tomatoes! When I was a kid, Ciudad Bolívar was all jungle, nothing! Twenty years ago it began. Twenty years from now, my *God!* — His derision approached actual despair.

Priority number one is to finish the clinic building, continued Dr. Carlos very calmly. Right now the priest comes for Mass.

His wife was the morgue pathologist in Bogotá who has already spoken to us in this book. Because she possessed a strong stomach for horrors, I call her a realist, and because she was a realist I decline to discount her worries about her husband's safety, particularly at night. Dr. Carlos was a brave, optimistic, practical man, a hero to me, and I hope that no one has harmed him.

The people in Nueva Esperanza rolled up their map, and afterward they played pool and drank beer, singing songs which the rain muffled as everything got muffled in that illegal squatters' town in a ravine above Bogotá, lost in the dreary sparkle of streetlit raindrops in Ciudad Bolívar . . .

TWENTY

DIRTY TOILETS

(Kenya and USA, 1992, 1996)

I

One night in New York City I met a black girl in the street. She came running up and threw her arms around me. She wanted me to buy her some cosmetics.

You wanna come see my room? she asked.

She led me to the elevator and we rode to the sixth floor. She said hi to all the teenagers and children who were living their lives in the corridor, said wait a minute, knocked on her door (649)—and no one was there. — I don't know where they went! she said in amazement.

The ladies' room was out of order, so she excused herself to the men's room. It was very dark in there and stank of urine. Someone had stolen the light bulbs. Someone kept stealing the toilet paper. She came out buttoning up her jeans. —I can't believe we have to live like this, she said.

I asked her how it was, and she said: Them toilets, let's just say they've got so bad I just piss on the floor.

Gotta go see my friend on the first floor, she said then. Her baby died.

What did it die of?

Natural causes.

They said she flushed it down the toilet, explained one of the kids. The cops came.

They *did?* Shhh. Don't talk about that in front of him. Shhh.

She took me down to the mezzanine and then she asked me: What do you feel like doing?

Just keeping you company.

She leaned against me and said: Now I really gotta be makin' my money. Do you want to do something with me? Get serious.

I don't have any money.

Name a price.

That bitch really gets on my nerves, said her friend who'd lost her baby. Always trying to get in my room to do her thing. I don't care, but when she's finished being with somebody I have to *live* in that room. Also, where I come from, you give a girl something if she lets you use her room.

Robin, do you have the key? my companion asked her.

Uh *uh*, said Robin. One of my kids got it.

You hang out with her for forty-five minutes, said my companion, whose name was Dinah. I gotta get some money. Then I'll be right back.

I left my husband in South Carolina, said Robin. Now I'm as free as a bird.

That's nice, said I.

I like to hang out with men, said Robin. I learn so much from men. Know what I mean?

No, said I.

We were standing outside now, and there were four of us now, drinking beer out of straws. The night was scarred with star-tracks. One of Robin's whore-daughters came up to her. —Mama, you have the key?

No, I don't have the key.

Mama, I'm cold.

Go sit in the mezzanine.

Mama, where's the key?

Can't you see I'm talking to this gentleman?

I'm your daughter. Isn't that more important?

No. This is more important.

Her son came up to her. —Do you have the key?

I don't have the key, motherfucker. Now you respect me.

As soon as they were out of sight she winked and showed me the key. —We can go up there anytime.

Now, aren't you just the devil, I said.

You gonna stick it in or not? I don't got all night, you motherfucker.

Just then, she got into an argument about money with another prostitute, and at that convenient moment appeared Elaine, who was missing alternating teeth.

You want to spend some time with me? she wanted to know. I'm not no street whore. I always use a rubber.

Don't have any money, I lied. I'll give you the rest of my beer, though.

Robin whirled on me. Hey, you giving away *my* beer!

Elaine was ashamed. —Oh, I didn't know you was with her.

It's all right, Robin told her finally. Keep it.

Thank you, said Elaine humbly.

I have my own apartment, Elaine remarked to me.

She's a man, whispered Robin.

2

I can't believe we have to live like this, Dinah had said, meaning in particular the filthy toilets; but in a slum in Nairobi I once spent days and nights with a prostitute named Rose who with all her neighbors shared one toilet, which was a concrete closet with a hole in the floor, and of course neither light bulbs nor toilet paper. From a standpoint of income, their *normality* was certainly inferior to that of the inmates of that transient hotel in Times Square; all the same, they took turns keeping their toilet clean.

They stole from one another, to be sure; they lived amidst jealousies sometimes criminally and even homicidally expressed; but they kept their toilet clean. I never saw them putting their children out of their own homes so that they could do business. They did not habitually menace each other, nor did they publicly grasp and snatch and struggle over each other's rights and possessions.

I would not want to live in either of these two places, but if I had to choose, I would rather spend the rest of my life in that Kenyan slum. And this gives me hope, because if one group of people whom *the market* defines as poorer than other can actually live a richer life, then poverty itself may be more malleable, hence less to be feared, than other nightmares.

3

Once again, and in full: *Every man is rich or poor to the degree in which he can afford to enjoy the necessaries, conveniencies, and amusements of human life. But after the division of labour has once thoroughly taken place, it is but a small part of these with which a man's own labour can supply him.*

We divide up the labor. It becomes someone else's concern to supply the light bulbs and toilet paper. Still another party cleans the bathrooms, and gets paid for doing it. What then is my interest in flushing the toilet, especially when none of my neighbors have that interest?

I can't believe we have to live like this.

4

Could it be that sharing resources and responsibilities works best when there is not much to share?

In that case, people with almost nothing and people with almost everything might be better off than the ones afflicted with relative poverty—who have enough to lose but not enough to be happy.

I prefer to hope and believe that a culture of communalism, however attenuated it may become as a result of material enrichment, can mitigate each and every one of the phenomena of poverty. Invisibility, deformity and unwantedness cannot defeat true neighborliness, at least not all the time. Dependence and accident-prone-ness are more powerful monsters: A band of refugees, or the dispossessed homeowners of Nan Ning, might start their journey to hell with all the mutual goodwill in the world, but should the impoverishment be poisonous enough, *any* resistance to it, single or collective, will be ineffective. But even if no other sustenance is available, unfortunate people can offer each other comfort, as they can when they have no medicine for pain. I remember the mothers and fathers who sat with their sanctioned children in Saddam Hussein Pediatric Hospital; my government would not let any medicines through, a freedom-loving policy which the doctors bitterly assured me had caused numbers of these children to die needlessly; but surely they were better off dying with than without their parents rocking them in their arms. As for numbness and estrangement, the same considerations apply.

5

What motivates someone to clean a communal toilet, and, moreover, to do so anonymously and without pay?

One immediate answer is that in that slum in Nairobi everyone lived so close together that there was no anonymity; the next person to use the toilet would have known, and announced, the identity of whoever had befouled it.

The word *responsibility* is easy to use and abuse in this context. I could patronizingly suggest that Dinah, Robin and Elaine "take responsibility" for the toilets, but in that case they would merely find themselves in the situation of the Pakistani immigrant I met in San Francisco who, valiantly upholding for an entire year the custom of paying for the lunch of the man behind him in the cafeteria line, never found any stranger willing to pay for *his* lunch. Sunee and the other cleaning ladies in Thailand taught me that assuming responsibility for one's poverty at least offers the comfort of finality; and if I were Dinah it might conceivably be "good for me" to clean up the bathroom once in awhile, but the most likely result would be scorn, abuse, intimidation, and eventually an assault or rape in some dark and filthy stall.

What is Dinah's degree of responsibility for the dirty toilets she uses? What is Natalia's for the loss of her children? Were I informed of every relevant division of rights and obligations, down to the last statutory or unspoken rule, would I be fit even then to judge the person?

6

So much for *responsibility*. What about *community?*

One mother who lived in Nueva Esperanza said that Ciudad Bolívar was getting worse. I asked why, and she shruggingly replied: If they let it go bad, then it goes bad. If they don't want it to go bad, then the good neighbor should help you.

And who are our neighbors, good and bad? Why, everybody. That is why a teenaged girl in a built-up section of Ciudad Bolívar expressed almost unbearable bitterness when she said: When the government gets a new president they come to the poor and make promise. But after that they don't keep the promise.

PLACEHOLDERS

TWENTY-ONE

I KNOW I AM RICH

(USA, 2005)

I

I am sometimes afraid of poor people. They are by no means the only people of whom I have been or can be afraid, nor am I *often* afraid of poor people; nonetheless, my fear of people whom I define as poor is part of what defines me as rich.

I am a petty-bourgeois property owner. My building is an old restaurant on a corner parking lot just under the railroad bridge from the homeless shelter. People sleep in my parking lot. Some of them stay for months; others I see only once. My visual memory has deteriorated since I suffered a series of minor strokes; and I put names to faces only when those names have been repeated to me several times, insistently. The people whom I do come to recognize tolerate me, joke with me, and, I fondly believe, like me. I believe this because I always tell them that they can camp here as long as they wish. Sometimes, when I know them and they ask me, and occasionally even when they do not, I will give them small things such as a bottle to get drunk on or a little money. I bring my little girl to greet them whenever she is with me, because I would not wish her to grow up disdainful of poor people or needlessly afraid of them. I am not afraid of the people whom I know. In addition to liking me, they probably make remarks behind my back. I would, if I were them. Their jokes often refer to the hilarious impossibility of my inviting them into my building so that they can drink my whiskey and copulate in my bed.* I always come out to them; I never let them in to me. In the words of a fortune cookie received by my best friend Ben, *love all, trust a few.* That is why my blinds are always drawn, and I have taped tinfoil over the insides of the windows which face the parking lot.

In the nighttime, when I come out from my building, I frequently see people whom I cannot remember seeing before, and they are sometimes less friendly than the people whom I know. Perhaps it is one of them who defecates on my outer wall. Sometime soon I will buy a hose to wash away this filth, but where will I keep it? If it stays outside I will have to lock it in a box bolted to the wall. If it comes inside, it will cause its surroundings to reek of the urine through which it has been dragged.

These nighttime people are most numerous in summer. Sometimes they build their campfires closer to my building than I would like. I say nothing, not because I am afraid, but because I consider it a tactical error to issue demands which probably will not be obeyed and whose compliance I cannot verify more than sporadically. My best weapon for preserving my building, therefore, is the good will I seek to gain. Of course I am kind by nature; or at least I sincerely believe that I am. I try to be kind for no gainful purpose, and certainly not to express ingratiation in the face of intimidation. In the night I approach the campfires and crack flames of tall men whom I cannot see, extend my hand, introduce myself as the property owner, and tell them that

---

* Frantz Fanon, 1961: "The native town is a crouching village . . . a town wallowing in the mire. It is a town of niggers and dirty Arabs. The look that the native turns on the settler's town is a look of lust, a look of envy; it expresses his dreams of possession—all manner of possession: to sit at the settler's table, to sleep in the settler's bed, with his wife if possible . . . And this the settler knows very well . . . he ascertains bitterly, always on the defensive, 'they want to take our place.'"

they are welcome. If they are sitting or lying more than two feet from my steel door, I refrain from telling them to move. In truth I do like sheltering people, and it makes me happy to feel that I am being a good soul. These night people accept my handshake unenthusiastically, but sometimes with goodnatured surprise at my boldness. They and I know that they could hurt me in the darkness and that I would have no recourse.

When I first took possession of the property I signed up with an alarm company. The parking lot came with motion detector lights. Night after night, the alarm company would awaken me at home with the news that power to the alarm had just been interrupted. For reasons having to do with the California fire code, a circuit breaker switch hung on the outer wall. I came to presume that my motion detector lights annoyed the people who slept in my parking lot, and therefore they flipped the switch. They assured me that they had seen the culprit and warned him away; he was Puerto Rican, they assured me, not black like them. I pretended to believe them and hired a contractor to enclose the switch in a padlocked metal box. The alarm interruptions ceased that night.

Someone pried a bar off one of my windows; someone else yanked at the bars until the stucco required patching; people left chairs on my roof. None of these halfhearted actions scared me. But I was well aware that the alarm would not save my property; it would only make a loud noise.

My building got graffiti'd every now and then, and I painted the graffiti out. I don't believe that my homeless friends did it. They said they'd seen the taggers, and described them to me; I pretended to pay attention.

Once in a great while there were thugs in my parking lot at night, men who were demanding, menacing and, from my petty-bourgeois perspective, insolent. I made a point of declining whatever they asked of me, but I spoke more politely to them than I wished, because I was afraid. Were they poor? They must have been poor in something, to entertain themselves in my parking lot . . .

On New Year's Eve I fell off a ladder and injured my knee. It was midafternoon. I was hobbling back from the convenience store and was two blocks from the parking lot when three black boys in their early teens insisted that I give them my food, half of which was intended for me and half for the two men who were then my most regular parking lot sleepers.* I refused, and the leader's insistence became a command. All the time I had continued to creep homeward toward my fortress, seeking to ignore what I could not help. The leader's command now took on gruesome overtones. Again I refused, and he furiously demanded that I tell him why. I said that I just didn't feel like giving them anything. I was past them now and so my back was turned to them. I was filled with hatred and anger that they had chosen to pick on me in my condition, but my primary emotion was fear.

All right, boys, said the leader. Let's get him. One, two, three!

I kept dragging myself along without looking over my shoulder. Nobody was in sight. Any moment I expected to feel them kicking me down. But I refused to acknowledge them. I remain proud of this.

Aw, just kidding, the leader finally said.

A few nights later he was at the streetcar stop where I was waiting, and suddenly lunged at me. I stared into his face, refusing to react because I knew all too well that any reaction I could invent would be not merely belated but insufficient, and a tall man grabbed him from

---

* This was considerate on my part, but no great sacrifice, because I was rich. Engels's First Law of Consumption runs: *As the income of the family increases, a smaller percentage is spent for food*. In 1938 and again in 1945, "wage earners' families" in the Philippines spent a bit more than half of their monthly disbursements on food. Therefore, an economist concluded, probably rightly, that the Filipino standard of living was low. As for my friends in the parking lot, how much of their miniscule incomes did they spend on food? The homeless shelter fed them most of the time. But liquor is a food of sorts; so perhaps is crack, not to mention methamphetamine; these necessary expenses the shelter sadly failed to cover.

behind at the last minute and shook him. I said nothing and opened a book.

But they were not poor people, were they? They were just punk kids going bad.

Call them poor people, the ones who kept defecating on my outer wall. I made inquiries about renting a portable toilet for them but was told that I could be cited by the city for creating an attractive nuisance.

Two days after I spent a Saturday scrubbing excrement off my wall and paid a hundred and twenty dollars for a contractor to pressure wash it, I went inside for an hour one midafternoon and there was more excrement in the parking lot; the next morning there was more on the wall, and just then the one man who had slept there and whom I therefore suspected of having done it came up to me whining for money. I wasn't short with him, but I gave him nothing. I was a rich man with a sad face; I felt exploited.

You're going to have to fence it off, my friends kept saying.

Sometimes I worry that they will come through the roof. I come back from out of town and find a chair or crate leaning against my wall; I wonder whether they have been trying to get onto the roof.

2

In Hanoi, on the shore of Lake Hoan Kiem, the pagoda sports a big door which only kings could enter. That was my steel door in Sacramento. Among my first year's crop of neighbors—my guests, if you will, or even my tenants—dwelled obsequious Carty, who insisted on calling me sir and whom I never trusted; in order to express my feelings without hurting him (last I saw of him, he was set to depart the state), I have changed his name here. His handshake was soft, brown-smeared and feculent. Let me expand on this, because it is by this that my rich man's memory so frequently defines him: Natalia had no odor, and neither did Oksana; Sunee kept herself clean; Big Mountain and Little Mountain smelled a little of smoke and damp wool but not much; the gleaners of their own destroyed houses, if they smelled of anything, could not be smelled through the dust; but Carty smelled always of excrement, and his handshake stank up my hand; whenever my little girl was with me, I'd have her shake hands with Daddy's friend, which she did willingly; then we'd go inside and I'd have her wash her hands and I would wash mine.

Less frequently than I believe I did, I gave him money or booze. He slept sometimes on the concrete slab which made my palace an island upon its parking lot, or on other occasions beside the garbage bin on my property line. He breached the king's door indeed: He came right through my doorway one rainy afternoon when the deliveryman and I were unloading my new mattress. The door was open for only forty-five seconds, and Carty was on the far side of my parking lot by the garbage bin, but that was enough of an interval for him to appear in my sanctum. He wondered if I needed help, he said. It was probably the case that Carty would have gladly held up a mattress end for me for a dollar or two, but why couldn't he have looked for me outside by the truck? It is a rule among all the transients I've ever met—all the stay-at-homes, too—that one does not enter someone else's camp uninvited. And so I swiftly, steadily declined his proposal, blocking his way so that he could not well investigate my layout or possessions, and although he stood there dripping I did not allow myself to pity him. A quarter-hour later, when the deilveryman had gone, I locked my steel door behind me and sauntered across the parking lot to chat with him, so that there would be no hard feelings. He received me pleasantly, standing beneath the overhang of the neighboring building with his shopping cart pulled in as far as it could go, so that there was no room for me, and I was soon wetter than he. I stood there ignoring the rain while he looked at me, and then after the neighborliness had been concluded I wandered slowly back amidst the puddles to my king's door. Then I went in, and shut Carty out. Why had I bothered to be courteous? One could say that I "liked" Carty while distrusting him, and this would be true. I believe that he also liked me. Whether or not he would have stolen from me if he could, whether he might have been one of my passing wall-defecators I cannot say; had I known for a fact that he was an active thief I would not have stopped liking him, whereas if I had seen him defiling my building, my opinion of him would have gone down, for the achievement of gain by any means need not be "personal," but the other thing is sheer meanness. At any rate, Carty went out of his way to call me sir and I went out of my way to drop in on him and ask him how he was doing. Rousseau opines that it is the rich who have most at stake in creating and preserving social forms, since *the rich having feelings, if I may so express myself, in every part of their possessions, it was much easier to harm them . . .* But can that really be so? Might not the continued existence of my domain behind that steel door have been a perpetual offense and harm to Carty? It is true that his poverty eternally threatened my richness. But I defeated him again and again; every day I shut him out into the rain.

3

I always tried to treat him as my equal, so whenever he called me sir I called him Mr. Carty. Sometimes something I asked with innocuous intention pricked something shocking and baleful within him; his red eyes would glow with hate. The first time I called him Mr. Carty I provoked this reaction in him; he must have thought I was making fun of him. He had already explained that since he came from the south he just naturally called men sir (although I never heard him say sir to anyone but me); so I explained back that I was simply trying to return the respect, and after that he accepted it; and to the end (he stayed in my parking lot for about a year) I felt an equality between the two of us. Did he feel likewise? I have not so hollow a soul that my perceptions of others must mirror those of me; I can respect those who hate me, and perhaps even like them; but it is an open question whether there can be such a thing as one-sided equality.

All the same, once upon a time in Belgrade, hearing a shuffling sound, I saw a legless man at my elbow, young, bearded, well-clad, with his bluejean legs sewn into pockets around his stumps. Most likely it had been a land mine or a shell. I gave him a five-dinar note and he thanked me in a deep and serious voice. How can I say that I know him as a person? Would I even recognize him again? There are so many legless beggars in this world! But the transfer of money was nothing more or less than a handshake between two citizens of Earth, either one of who could have been the giver or the receiver. It was a transaction without egotism on either side. He expressed through his noninsistence my right not to give him anything, and the little that I did give was simply my recognition of him as he was. The more I write about this moment, the more I degrade it; for making it significant cannot but seem a pretension to generosity or superiority on my part, or at least a magnification of his deformity. But the significance was precisely in the insignificance. We saw each other; I gave; he accepted; we forgot each other.

And once upon a time in Battambang, in the restaurant whose floor-tiles were imprinted with M. C. Escher cubes, whose immaculate girl in a Heineken sash stood ready and hopeful at the table, whose menu offered a hundred things from banana-fish-lemon-flower soup to deep-fried frogs, whose wall said **GOLDEN DREAMS COME TRUE FOR YOU** and whose Khmer-dubbed Chinese video shrieked at the world, mendicant soldiers came in, and amidst them was a legless man, crawling across the floor, smiling ingratiatingly, tapping my ankles, feeling the laces of my shoes. I had no small money to give him, and the previous night I'd shared my dinner with him and he had eaten little of it. Moreover, here came the soldier on the crutches, then the soldier without arms. What did I do? Whom did I give to? There was no possibility that I could act in any particular way and feel satisfied.

Must charity satisfy me, then? It was not charity to give to the legless Serb; that was like giving to myself, moving money from one pocket to another.

Would it be a fair vulgarization to say that I, a rich man, demand that the poor grovel respectfully to me when I give? I do not think so, because when Carty groveled, that did not please me, either. But in Russia I had felt flattered that both Natalia and Oksana crossed themselves and blessed me (what did they say when I wasn't around?)

Again, must charity please me? Is it incumbent on me to feel a specific way, or do I demand a certain standard from others? If it feels like charity, have I failed?

4

Lloyd, who was rude and sometimes obscene, I ended up "liking" better than Carty. Lloyd's girlfriend Linda I "liked." (Why do I continue to put "like" in quotation marks? Montaigne has his man of royal wealth complain that no one keeps him company for true friendship, *for no friendship can be knit where there is so little relation and correspondence . . . Their liberty being bridled on all sides by the great liberty I have over them, I see nothing around me except what is covered and masked*.) I tried to treat them all the same. If I brought a beer for one, I brought beers for others. If I gave whiskey, I handed it to the nearest one and said that it was for all. Was that right?

I was kind to them in ways that cost me little. Then I went across the parking lot and shut my steel door on them. Was that right?

5

When I was a decade younger, on a cold and windy day in Minneapolis I was stopped by a man who seized my hand in friendliness, and because he was tall and poor and black, I expected no good to come of it. This is a "racist" statement. At the time I made it, in a private notebook, a white couple was walking their dog four blocks from the house where I lived. A car pulled up. One of the men inside got out and shot the woman in the leg. When her husband bent over her in fear and love, the man shot him in the back. The newspaper in its delicacy did not mention the race of the men in the car. When a television report did say that they were black, several readers complained, I think with reason, that listing the race of those evil men would at least allow them to exclude carloads of men of other races from their fears. The newspaper's ombudsman replied with a lengthy and even-tempered defense of the policy. He said that the newspaper refrained from indicating the race of attackers anymore unless there was reason to suppose that the case was a "hate crime," or unless additional physical characteristics of the assailants were known. He said that the reason for this policy was to prevent racial stereotyping in America from getting any worse. I think that the policy is correct. How many blacks have been lynched simply for being black? I also think that the policy is wrong. It can never be right to obscure a fact.

Having asserted that credo, I cannot now back out of confessing that I am afraid of many tall, poor black men whom I do not know—not of all black men by any means: not of black businessmen in suits; not of poor black men who appear too weak to hurt me; not of tall, poor black men in black countries—neither tall black men on the buses and streets of Nairobi and even in the slums, nor of tall black men in Mogadishu during the war (unless they were shooting), nor of tall black men in Yemen even after September eleventh; the tall black men in Antananarivo who pursued me by twos and threes in daylight, in the midst of a crowd, I did fear, because they meant to rob me, but only for that reason. I am afraid of tall, poor black men who stop me in the streets of my own country. I am afraid of them because I know that they want something from me and because I believe that they believe that I am the enemy. I do not want to be anybody's enemy if I can help it. I do not believe that black men are inferior or superior to me. The question of whether "society" owes them something for slavery, Jim Crow and all the rest I answer in the affirmative. But I do not believe that *I* owe a black man more than I owe any other man, or any woman, for that matter. Does that mean that I owe him nothing? I would say: I owe him no more and no less than he owes me: respect, sympathy, neighborliness, help in an emergency. What if his life is an emergency? To this question I do not have a consistent answer.

The black man in Minneapolis who blocked my way, having snatched my hand and introduced himself, next confiscated my cap to adorn his head. He did this in a smiling, joking way; he admired my cap, and then he returned it; all the same, he did not ask me before he pulled it from my head. I had just returned from a country where it is worse than rude, in fact almost blasphemous, to touch another person's head. The idea is that the head is the highest part of an individual, hence the noblest, most spiritual part of his being. Of course this tall, poor black man in front of me could not be blamed for unawareness of my experiences and associations; but by the standards of my homeland and his, it is not polite to touch a stranger or his belongings without permission, and my blood boiled.

The man talked on and on. I waited for him to ask me for money so that I could give him something and leave him. My intention to give him a coin or two was not motivated by fear of him; although he was tall, poor and black, he did not intimidate me with any prospect of violence; he merely expressed a mild, perhaps unthinking disrespect of me as a person. (Tadano Makuzu, 1818: *Women of town origin who become concubines and attendants consider nobles to be their enemies. Similarly, although low types such as servants and porters support themselves with money they earn through their employment, they have nothing but scorn for their employers. Why is this the case?*) Several times in this book I have expressed my skepticism about the traditional divide between the "deserving" and the "undeserving" poor; I would rather think that any poor person is deserving, no matter whether I dislike him. Had he threatened me, then and only then would I have considered him undeserving of anything from me.

I wanted him to go because I was hungry. There was a restaurant across the street. I asked him if it was any good.

I can take you to a much better place right down the street, he said. Real home cooking. I eat there all the time. Come on; let's go.

I knew that there would be a fee imposed for his trouble, and this suited me; for, as you know, I have a positive fetish about equality, and I truly think that it must be better for the self-respect of someone who receives money from me to feel paid for value received, not given charity. Besides, the restaurant across the street did not look very good and the one he knew might be interesting. I was resisting my suspicion that since I was white and he was tall, black and poor, he would not play fair with me. He led me for two blocks, crossed the street, and brought me into an alley halfway back the way we had come. I'd agreed to give him a dollar, which was all I felt like giving; he'd wanted two, then one-fifty, but a dollar was truly all that I wanted to give. We stopped in front of a boarded-up storefront, where three tall, poor black men leaned. Call it a restaurant by all means; but it was not me who would be dining.

Pay up, my conductor ordered.

His friends stood around me grinning, and one of them began to lay hands on me. I no longer feel bitter about what happened next, although for several days afterward I was afflicted with the shockingly vivid shame and anger which remains so incommunicable between victims (poor people, for instance) and the world at large. As robberies go, this one was not brutal. They even allowed me to keep twenty dollars.

I sometimes fear tall, black poor men in America not for their blackness but because poor blacks are so often *really* poor; perceived as deformity, their poor blackness is also unwanted, dependent, accident-prone, painful, and most definitely estranged, estranged not numbly but angrily; and poor men who are taller than I and also angry are dangerous to me. *I sometimes fear tall, black poor men in America* thus equates to *I am sometimes afraid of poor people.*

Carty was black. Lloyd was black. Lloyd's girlfriend Linda was white. I "liked" them all. I shut my door on them all.

6

After all, didn't they shut their doors on me?

I have come to know the way that some of them are with each other, the couple sitting on the sidewalk laughing, hugging, then staggering off somewhere, returning an hour later, holding hands. Their arms fly around each other. Those two love each other, living in that faintly feculent smell like a barnyard, one of poverty's many aromas. Do they still dream the desperate dream of richness, whose fulfillment might require many a nightmare twist; or are they rich enough? I could have made friends with them, if not with the dogs in their street cages. I have on occasion blended into the backpacks, tarps, bungee cords and blanket-topped shopping carts that lean against the walls; once upon a time I was even close to the longhaired, scabby woman who sits on a bench twitching her ankles; she placed me in the hands of God; now she has forgotten me. — You're in my prayers, she murmurs to someone else, giving off a faint smell of sour milk. As for me, being a rich man, I came, went, and got excreted from these people's consciousness; now they gaze at me with bitter wariness, mimicked by their barking dogs.

7

That was in Sacramento; and in Mexicali on a hundred-and-fifteen-degree afternoon, almost in sight of the American border, Señor Hugo Ramirez [photograph 2], who looked to be in his forties and so was probably a decade younger, sat on a bench before the open door of a shop whose music blasted through my breastbone; Hugo Ramirez shook my hand with a hand whose once-white mitten was nicely on the way to filthifying; and when I asked him why some are rich and some are poor he drew in his shoulders, gazed at me with cautious slyness, and replied: *Robbers.* — Do the rich rob the poor? I inquired, wanting to understand him; but Hugo Ramirez merely replied: *Robbers.* I asked him what obligation the rich had toward the poor, and he said: None. We all have to work . . . —But then he grew cunning and cautious again. I wondered what unimaginable accidents he had suffered.

An hour later I saw him several blocks away. He refused to greet me; perhaps he'd forgotten me; let's say he'd shut his door on me.

8

I shut my door on them, just as when we who are in first-class train compartments pull our glass doors shut to drown out the poorer sort in the corridors, who will be standing or leaning all the way across Romania; of course my shut door gives them something to lean against; I'm doing them a favor.

9

The Sacramento real estate king Scarpia* once said to me: They defecate and they urinate all over the alley and the building. They crap all over the lot. Alan's made several citizen's arrests. These people are constantly along the alley. We're constantly having to clean up the alley and paint the building. This is their urine right here. I've spent forty thousand dollars for cleaning. We spend hours and thousands of dollars doing what the downtown partnership is supposed to be doing. I mean, the graffiti, the swastikas! Alan and I have spent more dollars repairing those fences . . . Emma's Tacos burned. The transients evidently lit that fire. If I don't laugh I get so pissed off—

Your car was broken into here, right? said he to his aide. Your wife's car, right? —He's found all kinds of belongings, he explained, turning back to me. He's found more unbelievable stuff! They wanna make money to support their drug habits, so if they can't do it they dig for bottles. Look! They dug the entire foundation out! We had to spend thousands to fix it! Can you believe this? The building was literally *suspended* here with no foundation . . .

One has to admit this has a lot to do with city policy, he continued, makin' 'em feel comfortable here. And I am tired of being a victim. We live in a society where the bad people are predators. Anyone who intrudes on our property should be a *victim* if I have anything to say about it. A law, say that again!

He took me under the sidewalk and showed me the charred beams and brick stalls, the rusty corrugated roof. I wasn't a property owner in those days, so his millionaire woes merely bemused me. He showed me a switchbox open, the wires cut, copper half pulled out; poor people could make money selling copper by the pound.

I think places that are feeding these people, they need to conduct

---

* His name I have also changed, to spare myself from a frivolous lawsuit.

drug tests and weapons tests, he said. And there should be programs of work. Just put people to work for four or five hours a day.

(Perhaps Scarpia was right. Right or wrong, he was my brother. Hadn't I wanted to make that tall poor black man in Minneapolis work for his dollar? This is what I remember of Scarpia: a receding hairline and shiny black shoes, sunglasses, a tie, a pager, a white shirt and folded arms. At the time I was appalled by him. I still disagree with him, but in my memory he's now mellowed into an entertainment, as have some of the poor people who menaced me; he's a story I tell.)

And I also think when the new jail comes along and there's room to arrest all these people with warrants outstanding, he said happily, I think the problem will start taking care of itself.

Listen! he cried out. *We're paying taxes, and what are we gettin' for our money?*

I remember the deep square tunnel under the brick wall. Nineteenth-century Sacramento had built itself down there. After too many floods, they dumped earth on top of their lives and started over. Subterranean rooms and passages remained. Some of them were still accessible from Scarpia's lot when I met him, although they have since been closed off. I remember an old meat slicer in the dark; and another basement, an adding machine, lamps without bulbs, a smell as of rodent droppings, candle wax, feces, a long tunnel, and suddenly a choking smell of shit. That was the smell of poverty, perhaps. Here came another long tunnel, and the flashlight slanted between beams.

We stood on the edge of it, and it was hot and stinking.

And right here they actually *broke holes* through the pawnshop to steal stuff . . . he said, the aide looking around wearily.

They steal it and take it into the alley, he said. The guy who owned that restaurant was arrested for fencing merchandise.

I'm sick and tired of doing it, sick of it! he shouted. They're coming under city sidewalks and breaking into the building. These people can do seemingly anything. They can cut through anything.

Yes, I was slightly sorry for him, but he was a rich man; he had deep pockets. I thought that I was on the side of poor people, who after all did need to defecate and whose theft of copper wire struck me as more remarkable than egregious. Now when I consider the possibility that the poor have supernatural powers, that *these people can do seemingly anything,* I wonder: What if they do something to me?

I keep my windows covered with tinfoil on the inside, or else the blinds are down. In my second year of ownership I finally slid one window a little open for ventilation. At once a poor man shouted out at me from across the street; parting two blind-strips very cautiously, I placed my eye to the opening and spied on his avid, gloating face. An hour later, I heard a noise. Someone had reached through the bars and folded back several strips of my blinds. I refolded them as straight as I could, taped it into place, closed the window and dropped my strip of wooden molding back into the groove. (My friend Kent, a commercial photographer, had his studio a few blocks away from me, and he once said: It makes you want to leave, and leave everything behind. — The auto store owner from whom people stole copper piping might have felt the same.) How safe was my window? *They can cut through anything.* Later that year I hired a contractor to weld steel mesh over the bars.

10

What do I owe the poor? For instance, what do I owe the men in Minneapolis who robbed me?

Oksana's son-in-law, the Chernobyl victim, had made the case that my interest entailed protecting them from poverty to at least some minuscule extent. Specifically, he'd said, as you may remember: *The rich always want to become richer, and squeeze the last bit from the poor. They don't understand the natural equilibrium: If they make everyone poorer, the economy gets poorer and they get poorer, no matter how many mansions they build, no matter how many guns they keep.* I disbelieve this. First of all, while I do want to get richer, so does everyone else, including the poor; therefore, whether it's good or bad, the impulse to enrich oneself appears ineradicable, as the Soviets found when they "dekulakized" rich peasants: All that happened when they impoverished people in the interest of equality was that other people, or even those selfsame people, became rich all over again. Accordingly, let's call the fact that *the rich always want to get richer* irrelevant. Now, it is certainly true that many rich people, although hopefully neither I who am writing nor you who are reading this book, *squeeze the last bit from the poor* when they can. But what precisely constitutes *the last bit?* Marx wrote of mill owners paying the workers the bare minimum that would allow the latter to reproduce their labor, namely to pay for food, shelter and new proletarian children. As a result, the mill workers could, in a fashion, survive. *The last bit* remained. One reason that the inmates of Jewish ghettoes in Nazi-occupied Eastern Europe did not rise up until almost the end, and frequently not then, was that the system of deportation quotas and work cards convinced people that prudence, hard work, payoffs and good connections would save them, whereas rebellion would be punished terribly; their murderers were cunning; *the last bit* got extracted in increments. Continue with the Nazi analogy. *If they make everyone poorer, the economy gets poorer.* While this might have been true in some respects—some Germans protested vainly against the extermination of skilled Jewish shoemakers, on the obvious grounds that shoe production would suffer—all the same, the nationalization of Jewish businesses, the reduction of Jews to slave laborers and the extraction of gold from Jewish corpses were profitable, at least to individual profiteers and at least in the short run. *If they make everyone poorer, the economy gets poorer,* but what if they only impoverish *some* people? A person who exploits others in order to lower his product's manufacturing cost still requires the existence of people who are rich enough to buy it. But I see no reason why it should be impractical (that is, unprofitable) to hire workers at a pittance to produce some necessity to be sold to poor people at a pittance plus ten percent.

In short, self-interest does not require me to enrich my neighbor. It merely requires me to leave him *the last bit*. If I do choose to help him, I am but pleasing myself.

11

Self-interest further advises me to bear in mind relative as well as absolute poverty. Somebody outside my window may own more than *the last bit*. All the same, if he owns less than I (or even more than I), he may still want what I have.* And so I keep my blinds down. And so I shut my door on them all.

12

I dislike it when people attach things to my building. I have to draw a line somewhere, don't I? On one rainy day, a man left his sleeping bag up on the concrete threshold of my steel door, and I felt disrespected although most likely I remained entirely out of his equation; he might have assumed that the place was abandoned, as did the teenagers who sometimes pedaled round and round my parking lot with increasing speed until they were ready to slam their bicycles into my wall. At the end of the day his sleeping bag was still there and in the way of some heavy boxes that I was moving. I didn't want to trip over it; my bones were aching as it was. So I picked up the poor man's sleeping bag, which gave off a stench, and I threw it crabbily out into my sodden parking lot. An hour later somebody had energetically vandalized my

---

* Against him please set Oksana, who, at least in retrospect, had been happy enough as a young woman at the Kolkhoz Jakob Petrov; no matter that by my standards she was *always* poor.

fortress; this might have been the sleeping bag's owner, enraged at the prospect of a wet night. What should I have done? Was I obliged to let that sleeping bag block my door indefinitely?

The previous summer people had been camping on my threshold, some in sleeping bags and some in tents. They smoked crack in lovely orange flame-flittings in the darkness; some of the women were prostitutes who did their business on the other side of the building. I welcomed them all and shook their hands. When my little girl was with me, I made her shake their hands, too. Wasn't that good enough?

Some of them kept pissing on my wall although there was a free toilet a block away. I had to repaint it eventually. How much was I supposed to put up with? *Listen! We're paying taxes, and what are we gettin' for our money?*

I never ran them off. I've never run anybody off. Eventually they move on, or the police devour them. Then new people come.

In another season I discovered a heavy blanket folded neatly behind the parking sign which had been nailed over my window-bars. The blanket was out of sight, and probably did me no harm, but I pulled it out and flung it into view in my corner weeds, so that it could be claimed. The next day it was still there, and I was feeling remorseful. Behind a garbage bin, someone had laid out cardboard to sleep on. I picked up the blanket, which was very greasy, and took it over there. Eventually it disappeared.

13

A big man pounded on my door. He needed help; he'd run out of gas. While I reached into my pocket to find some change for him, he tried to shove past me. I kicked him hard in the knee so that he fell back outside. Then I slammed my steel door on him. He pounded on it for a long time, shouting murderous threats.

Later someone knocked on my door, and I refrained from answering. Was it my task to save everybody on earth? *What are we gettin' for our money?*

14

Once when I stood in Jerusalem looking out at the Via Dolorosa from the Ecce Homo Arch, watching Muslims stride up that narrow cobbled way, a young Palestinian boy found me and tried to sell me his postcards: *Come on! All different!* I refused with thanks. *Five shekel! All different! Have a look!* — No, I don't want any. — In disgust and anger the child stabbed his elbow almost into my chest, cursing me obscenely. After that, when street vendors made my acquaintance along the Via Dolorosa, I continued to be as calm and courteous as ever, but I braced myself against possible assaults of sudden anger.

I also remember a snowy Sunday afternoon when a woman in that snow-shovelers' brigade in Kazakhstan* told me that under Communism, she had been a cook and janitor in a school. But now that job was no longer possible. She worked eight hours, and it was *very challenging,* she said. Just to ensure that I understood her, I asked, innocuously, I thought: Which is better, Communism or capitalism? — I don't know, she said bitterly through her teeth. Anyway, there are poor people in America, too. — And I could feel that at that instant she hated me.

15

And so my face has become the face of Bogotá: green or tan or white high walls overstrung with barbed wire, private security guards who shrink away from every stranger, even from me if I come on them suddenly; truckloads of police in the streets, broken glass atop brick

---

* See p. 194.

walls, caution and suspicion, masked by the appeasement of panhandlers who refuse to go away, getting angrier and angrier, striding up to my interpreters scowling and threatening; call them proud emblems of the tallest wrath; sometimes they kill drivers and set cars on fire. Seneca relates that the Roman Senate once debated a proposal to require slaves to wear a certain livery; *it then became apparent how great would be the impending danger if our slaves should begin to count our number.* By the same logic, I avoid wearing a rich man's livery and refrain wherever possible from pulling my wallet from my pocket. And at home, whenever it comes time to take the electric trolley, I approach the fare machine with exact change already clenched in my hand.

At home I strive to be moderately careful. I try to prepare myself for the eventuality of losing what I have. In Bogotá one must be more careful than that. All the admonitions I received on my first visit there made me so apprehensive that by the time I finally moved to a sleazy hotel in the Candelaria (on the way, a bearded man with blazing eyes stepped out onto the street and stopped our car; the driver later said that if he hadn't rendered up the hundred-peso toll, the extortionist would have snapped off the mirror), I felt uneasy. Marcos, my second interpreter, and one of the bravest men I ever knew, insisted that I wait in the car while he visited the lobby. Oh, how he wished that I would stay in his apartment instead! He'd charge me nothing; he pitied me; he worried about me. In retrospect I wonder whether he bribed the desk clerk with his own money to encourage her to protect me. We accompanied her up to the room, where he insisted on testing the lock, which of course was nearly useless; he checked every window to see who could come in; finally he left me, miserable and anxious. He turned on the TV, and there was a program about a man who broke into old ladies' apartments and murdered them.

16

Padlocking my luggage, I went out ten minutes later. Crossing the street to a fleamarket, I kept waiting for something to happen, so well had I been advised that something would. No one paid me any attention.

And in New York a month after September eleventh, business took me to a radio station near the attack site. I saw a few people in gas masks, their demeanor scared and sad; this was so shocking to me, for I'd gotten used to feeling fairly safe behind the border-blinds of my own country. But nothing happened to them, either.

It is not impossible even for rich people to visit the streets of this world.

17

I find a man's shirt on my parking lot, heavy with his excrement; he has left this gift for me, the rich man. I can pick it up with my gloved hands and dispose of it, or I can leave it alone so that it gets worse.

I leave it alone. After a couple of months it no longer stinks. I go inside and shut my steel door on it.

18

To Thoreau I am a member of *that seemingly wealthy, but most terribly impoverished class of all, who have accumulated dross, but know not how to use it, or get rid of it, and thus have forged their own golden or silver fetters*—and this he writes in spite of his frequent acquaintance with *the degraded poor,* whose forms *are permanently contracted by the long habit of shrinking from cold and misery, and the development of all their limbs and faculties is checked* (this is the category I've called "pain").

As for me, I consider myself to belong to the lucky class. Closing my steel door on others' problems, I withdraw within my own skull, where even my own problems sometimes fail to penetrate. I have lived in tents and happily kept rain and mosquitoes out. I have observed the sufferings of human beings, done a little to alleviate them, and left them behind. My sensations in doing so are sometimes as smelly as San Francisco's rainy uriney Tenderloin streets, where in a sunken subway plaza homeless ones are reading, snoring or snarling in sodden sleep bags; infected by misery, I look away, but my eyes meet a man's red-eyed glare on those rainy steps in the dark; I could remember him or I could remember the woman sitting on those steps, singing; her pants and her jacket are soaking wet in that night rain and water runs out of her hair into her eyes; her titanic thighs are blotched with eczema and she keeps scratching them; she reeks, but she is smiling as she sings; of course the only honest thing to do is remember them both—in my tent. I am a rich man. I'm one with the man in Bogotá who said: I'm scared about the poor people coming to take everything from me.

TWENTY-TWO

I THINK YOU ARE RICH

(??)

I

Reader, who are you? Some of the people who send me letters about my books are in prison, and some are prostitutes, and some are dying from AIDS—impoverished ones, in short, whom I am flattered and privileged to hear from, because I am rich and I want poor people to like me.

I write to please myself, not because I am selfish (although I may be that), but because the world owes me no living, and the idea of *capturing a market* repels me. If you like what I have written, thank you; if not, I bear no you grudge.

But who are you likely to be? I have been told that my books are difficult to read. If that is so, then my readers must be people who do not mind difficult books. — The beautiful, dirty young woman in dirty rags in the place they called the Burned Land **[photograph 1]**, gazes steadily into my face with what might have been the beginning of a smile, crooking her elbow around the Y-shaped branch which supports the roof-beam of her open shanty, a small child who must have been hers staring at me from her other elbow, his shoulder level with her fist, which she has wedged against her hip-sash, and all around her everything has been cut down and burned for the sake of a survival unable to amortize its own cost, which is why the rivers of this island, Madagascar, run orange-red with silt from deforestation; she gazes at me in patience and the gentle hope that I might do something for her. The man who brought me here was thrilled to get my cast-off sodapop bottle; he carried it all the way across the Burned Land. As for this young mother, whose life for no reason that I could see was so much harder than mine, she will take anything and give everything. The interpreter advises me not to give her any money to save her from getting murdered . . . None of them can read, although the interpreter paid a professional letter-writer and so concealed her own illiteracy from me for years. What can this book possibly do for any of them? — Under the road there may well be leisure for this and that; and in the homeless camp beneath the freeway in Miami where I once passed a night or two [photographs 3–9], I did meet readers, but because they were poor they had to content themselves with the cast-off books which fell their way. When this book is published I will give away several copies, as I always do, to whomever then happens to be living in my parking lot. Whatever its cover price will be, it will probably be too much for very many poor people to take a chance on. Whatever it thinks it knows about poverty, they will know more truly, and more deeply if less broadly. As for the style, although I have striven to write simply, why *shouldn't* people who cannot afford my Ivy League education be discouraged by long sentences?

So allow me to suppose that you, like me, are rich.

2

What is it that I need to tell you? That I look upon us both as Sunee's mother gazes upon her daughter's lifelong drunkenness? That I wonder what will kill Natalia, her drinking or her fits or something else, probably not her impoverishment itself? That for some reason Natalia's face is to me of all the people's in this book the most beautiful? These prattlings of my heart might be thrown away, like all the individuals, including you and me, that they concern. Poor people and rich people, we have in common our mortal insignificance.

3

You are rich, so tell me: Who does that make you? What would *they* have been had poverty not diminished them? Would they be any happier? My rich and intellectual friends are happy and sad; the sun also rises, and goes to its appointed place; and isn't it as I always say Natalia's *choice* to drink and Sunee's *choice* to drink? So would "they" be any different? Who are "they"? Who would Sunee be were she not an illiterate, self-hating, furiously resigned drunk? In any event, the darkness of her incompletion, such as it is, may approximate the darkness of my own blindness. Once the habit of poverty, like Natalia's alcoholism, becomes given to the generations, does it then become a sacred *choice* of the personality? I say that it does; I would never tell her not to cleave to it. But what if Natalia were rich? And my mind turns again to the rich people I know. How much knowledge have they gained? Sometimes I perceive the desperate burden of a leisured consciousness to those for whom survival comes easy; I enter their expensively barren houses, and I pity them. The ones who wrinkle their noses at the poor sometimes excite my anger. And Natalia's children, lost or abandoned by her no matter which version she told, likewise raised up my anger against her. So what would I want Natalia, or myself, to be? What is my model? I don't believe that most of us know what anything means. What should Natalia be called? What is her soul? Is poverty one of her fundamental qualities?

4

You and I are rich. Others are poor; and out of their hordes now hovers before my closed eyes the closed eyes, tilted head, half smile and clasped mittened hands of the woman who supplicated my help beside her box house in the tunnel in Shinjuku on a winter night **[photograph 124]**; rounded and rendered massive by her sweater, jacket and wool cap, she comprised an island of human need, waiting to survive or be washed away. I gave her something, how much I no longer remember, and then I left her to sleep in the cold. Why have I done over my life in light of this inequality, and what should I have done, and whom have I helped and harmed, and what should I do now? Is the answer *more aid, better directed*? On my own part, how can it not be? But how can I better direct it?

In Phnom Penh a male of the human species clasps his hands to me **[photograph 126]**; his long narrow face, unformed like a boy's and grim-gaunt like a man's, with wrinkles beneath the eyes, is fixed upon me and his steepled fingers meet beneath his chin. He wears a thin checked scarf loosely tied around his throat. He smiles at me, but not with his eyes, which gravely ask my help. It is night, the street is very dark beside him, and clutching the crook of his elbow is a boy-child with a rounder, less haggard face who stares at me in a calmly curious spirit; from the neck up he is cleanly, delicately luminous against the humid black street-night, but his pale shirt is occupied by an army of stains which would have been less noticeable on the brother-father's more neutral-toned garments. They wait for me to do something. The man has clasped his hands together forever.

They wait for me to do something, but because I know not what to do, or else am too human to do it, they wait with the hard grimace of the girl from Bogotá's infamous Cartucho district who tilted her head forward and down to watch me beneath the hatbrim wrapped in her hood, her throat pulsing with belligerence **[photograph 89]**. *Hope dies last.* Then what?

The mother whose broad, firm, protective face tilts down like a sunflower toward the naked child she holds against her breast, what will she not do, if necessary to you or me, to enrich him with life? *DONATE HERE and help keep me out of your neighborhood.*

TWENTY-THREE

MONEY JUST GOES TO WHERE IT GOES

(Japan, 2005)

The man with the white wrapping around his head said: We're getting moved out. What can you do for us?

Nothing, I said.

Then what do you want?

Why are some rich and others poor?

Well, money just goes to where it goes.

If only someone had explained this to me before! Then I never would have needed to annoy myself with the subject of poverty, and you could saved the time you've wasted reading my book. At any rate, I was a good reporter; I turned over rocks seeking deep meanings; so I persisted:

Is that due to luck or some other reason?

There may be some reason, but anyway money just goes to where it goes, and to us it doesn't come.

I could not think of much to say in response to that. He might as well have been the narrator in *Tales of Times Now Past* (ca 1120) who explains why it is that when a poor man and his wife, in a despairing attempt to improve their luck, finally separate, she becomes the Governor of Settsu's wife while he falls deeper into filthy, leech-afflicted wretchedness: *People utter foolish complaints about their lot through igno-rance of the fact that everything is determined by karma from a previous existence.* In other words, money just goes to where it goes. So I looked into the river, and then I looked away from the river, and then I asked the man with the white wrapping around his head:

Why are they trying to move you away from here?

They just want to have no homeless here for this year, he replied calmly. They budgeted five hundred million yen* to remove us . . .

---

* Slightly less than five million dollars.

SOURCES

INCOME TABLE

1.   Thoreau was interviewed by ouijah-board.

2.   United Nations Development Programme (UNDP), *Human Development Report 1997* (New York: Oxford University Press, 1997), 146–48.

3.   Ibid., 244–45.

4.   At time of interview.

5.   She got 300 yuan per month.

6.   He got 400 yuan a month and remarked that the garbage lady's 300 yuan was not enough to live on in Nan Ning, where they both dwelled.

7.   This Nan Ning resident also got 400 yuan a month and likewise remarked that the garbage lady's 300 yuan was not enough to live on then.

8.   Averaged over this time period's variable exchange rate of 105 to 130 yen.

9.   Half of the $25.53 to which 3,000 yen is equivalent.

10.   From street interviews in Almaty and Atyrau, calculated from a quoted figure of $100 per month. In Tajikistan, some people said, it was $10 per month. I have not been there and cannot verify that tenfold impoverishment of the Kazakh average. One flat in Atyrau contained six students whose rent was $200 per month, or $1.11 per day each. Paying this was extremely challenging for them. There was no water above the third floor; the first floor reeked of excrement.

11.   The exchange rate over this time period actually varied from 9 to 12 pesos, but most of this book's interviews took place in 2004–2005, when it was 10.5.

12. Thus was "to live normally." He earned this much from begging and accordion playing "only sometimes."

13. Based on a salary of 300 rupees per month, which the teachers said was "very small." I interviewed only the lady teachers, but they assured me that their male colleagues earned the same amount.

14. Supplement to other income, amount unknown.

15. All-night fee. This amount was duly receipted as "long time salary" on the letterhead of the Silver Dollar Bar, which took an unspecified commission. Juvy rarely got bought out for an entire night.

16. She estimated that her maximum daily take was 100 to 120 rubles, so I calculated the average. Her daughter Nina, one of Oksana's four dependents, told me that the family actually needed 200 rubles per day, plus an additional 300 if they were to make the rent. Oksana was not the sole breadwinner; a cousin paid some or all of the rent.

17. Calculated from 5,000 baht per month divided by 30, since she worked seven days a week.

18. Calculated from 5,000 baht per month, for the same reasons. She spent half her salary for rent in the Ratchutori district, a 20 minute walk from where she worked.

19. Thoreau's project at Walden Pond endured from March 1845 (he moved in on 4 July) through October 1847. So I took 1846 as a benchmark year. In 1846, the consumer price index (CPI) for all items was 27 @ 1967 = 100. In other words, 1846 prices were 27 percent of what they were in 1967. So one 1967 dollar = 27 1846 dollars. One 1867 dollar equaled 3.7 1967 cents. (Source: US Department of Commerce, Bureau of the Census, *Historical Statistics of the United States, Colonial Times to 1970, Bicentennial Edition, Part 1* [Washington, DC: US Government Printing Office, 1975, 211, Series E 135–166, Consumer Price Indexes (BLS)—All Items, 1800 to 1970 . . .]. According to a Google-linked web page for CPI, at 1967 = 100, 2001 = 531.9. In other words, to convert from 1967 dollars to 2001 dollars one needs to factor in an additional 5.32. Therefore, one 1846 dollar equals 143.64 2001 dollars, and one 2001 dollar equals 7/10 of an 1846 cent.

20. Figures on the average daily wage in 1846 were not available. In *A Statistical Abstract Supplement: Historical Statistics of the United States, Colonial Times to 1957, Prepared by the Bureau of the Census with the Cooperation of the Social Science Research Council* (Washington, DC: US Government Printing Office, 1960), I found on page 90 (Series D 573–577: Daily Hours and

Indexes of Average Daily Wages in All Industries . . .) that in 1860, the earliest year on record, the average working day lasted eleven hours. The year 1860 was set at a 100 index value, with a weighted index for 1890 (average working day ten hours) of 168.2. Furthermore, on page 91 (Series D 603–617: Average Annual Earnings in All Industries . . . 1890 to 1926), I learned that the average 1890 workweek lasted sixty hours, and the average wage was $0.199 per hour. Dividing this final number by 1.682 gave me $0.118, which I multiplied by eleven hours to get an average daily wage for 1860 of $1.30. Even if the average 1846 daily wage were as little as half of this—an unlikely proposition—it still seems that Thoreau's income was relatively very low. However, it also seems that in real dollars the 1860 wage was exaggeratedly high.

21. Call Thoreau's thirty Walden-associated months 900 days. His house cost him $28.12½ (*The Illustrated Walden*, ed. J. Lyndon Shanley, with photographs from the Gleason Collection [Princeton: Princeton University Press, 1973], p. 49). In the first year he spent $14.72½ for seed, tools, etcetera (p. 55). He laid out $8.74 for food for eight months, not "considering the value of what was on hand at the last date" (p. 59). After this he lived "on rice, mainly" (p. 61). Clothing and oil for the first eight months cost him $10.40¾. He made $23.44 from his crops (p. 55) and $13.34 from carpentry, surveying, and day labor (p. 58). There is no completely satisfactory way to amortize these numbers, since their durations vary and since some of them are omitted. I will therefore tot them up individually as best I can. Over the 900 days, his house cost him 3.1 cents per day. Over the first year his farm expenses were 4 cents a day. Later on they would have been less, but we don't know how much less. Clothing and oil for eight months cost 4.3 cents per day. It is unclear how much time it took to bring in his miscellaneous income; by context it seems to have been garnered in over the first year, so let us ignore what we do not know and calculate a total income of $36.78 per 365 days, or 10 cents a day. I suspect that he continued to work sporadically but got bored with keeping accounts. Thus his total expenses were 11.4 cents per day—a slight excess on his income. Since he resisted going into debt and since his figures bear the stamp of imperfect exactness, let us simply make his income equal his outgo at 10 cents a day. (And let us set aside the fact that he was exempt from mortgage payments, being a squatter on his friend Emerson's land.) There being no net gain, I have considered this figure to be the minimum Thoreau needed to get by, and placed the telltale asterisk before his name.

22. US Department of Commerce, *Statistical Abstract of the United States 2004–2005*, 124th ed. (Washington, DC: US Census Bureau and other

agencies, 2004), p. 619 (No. 619: Average Hourly Earnings by Private
Industry Groups: 1990 to 2003). Farmworkers, supervisory employees
and some other workers excluded. The 2003 weekly value was 517.36,
which divided by 5 equals 103.47. Hourly values were also given in this
table, but it seemed better not to use them since a simple multiplica-
tion by 8 would have clashed with page 378 (No. 584: Persons at Work
by Hours Worked: 2003), which informs us that the average weekly
hours for "persons at work" was 39.0; for "persons usually working full
time," 42.9.

23.   Ibid., 411 (No. 623: Full-Time Wage and Salary Workers—Number and
Earnings: 2000 to 2003). All workers: Median weekly earnings, 2003:
$620, which divided by 5 equal to $124.00.

24.   Midrange, $11.08 per hour. I assumed an eight-hour working day. Joyce
P. Simkin, ed., *American Salaries and Wages Survey*, 8th ed. (San Francisco: Thomson Gale, 2005), p. 793.

25.   Midrange, $9.36 per hour. Again, I assumed an eight-hour working day.
Ibid., p. 869.

26.   Based on three to five dates per week at $200, divided by 7. In fact she
frequently got tipped; her dates sometimes lasted longer, and she received
income from other sources. I would therefore speculate that her daily income was closer to $150, out of which she paid a mortgage, supported two
children from a previous marriage, and added to her husband's income.

27.   She needed $2,000 per month to support her household of five. Her hus-
band brought in some of this. She thinks that if she were alone she could
manage on $1,000 a month, or $33.33 per day. Her greatest expense is rent.

28.   He slept in a garage not far from a light rail stop known for drug dealing.
From a market he freqently got a slice or two of pizza which had gone too
soggy to sell. He also ate many meals at the homeless shelter. Doubtless
many of the other individuals in this income table counted on in-kind
donations to supplement the cash minimum which they told me they required.

29.   Why didn't I simply write "beggar"? Because he begged only opportunis-
tically, not steadily and overtly.

30.   After taxes. The bulk of this was mortgage payments.

31.   He required (my per capita calculation) 16,000 to 23,000 dong per day, so
I took the average.

32.   Street rate.

33. She estimated between 400 and 500 ryals, so I took the average. Sometimes she earned only 300.

34. He estimated between 2,000 and 3,000 ryals, so I took the average. He needed 1,000 to 1,500 to live, and spent the surplus on "the motor of my boat."

INTRODUCTION

XIV Great writer: "Poor people never, or hardly ever . . ."—Louis-Ferdinand Céline, *Journey to the End of Night*, trans. Ralph Mannheim (New York: New Directions, 1983; orig. French ed. 1934, repr. w/ new intro. 1952), p. 130.

SELF-DEFINITIONS

ONE: I THINK I AM RICH

3–27 Thailand interviews—These took place in September 2001. My interpreter was D. The "bombing" of the World Trade Center was, of course, the September eleventh atrocity.

All economic data not supplied by the interviewees themselves derive from Alpha Research Co.'s *Pocket Thailand in Figures*, 4th edition (Bangkok, 2001), pp. 18–19 (Tables 1–3: Area, Population, December 31, 1999, Gross Regional Product, 1997), p. 54 (Table VII.1: Minimum Wage per Day: By Province), p. 55 (Table v.3: Average Wage of Daily employees, by Size of Establishment and Region, 1999), p. 189 (Table 5.2: Average Household Monthly Expenditures—Greater Bangkok), p. 218 (Table 8: Household Income for Bangkok Metropolitan Province).

16 Footnote: Both Lu Xun extracts—Philip Lopate, ed., *The Art of the Personal Essay: An Anthology from the Classical Era to the Present* (New York: Anchor/Doubleday, 1995 repr. of 1994 hdbk ed.), p. 330 (Lu Xun, "Death").

23 Marx: "Because the labor required to produce horses and machines . . ."—Karl Marx, *Capital: A Critique of Political Economy*, vol. 1, trans. Ben Fowkes (New York: Vintage, 1977), p. 517 ("The Value Transferred by the Machinery to the Product").

TWO: I THINK THEY ARE POOR

29–30 Yemen interviews—These took place in September 2002. The interpreter was Ahmed Al-Rabahi.

30   "Narrated Imran bin Husain Al-Bukhari . . ."—*The Translation of the Meanings of Sahih Al-Bukhari, Arabic-English*, tr. *Dr. Muhammad Muhsin Khan* (Al-Medina Al-munauwara: Islamic University, n.d.), vol. 9 [of 9], p. 306 (LXXVI.16).

32   Gandhi's apology for the violence of others—Quoted in Judith M. Brown, *Gandhi: Prisoner of Hope* (New Haven: Yale, 1989), p. 376. See also pp. 132 (self-castigation for the Amritsar atrocities, 1919), 285 (self-castigation for the relative failure of Indian non-violence generally, 1938).

33   United Nations report: "A quarter of the world's people remain in severe poverty . . ."—United Nations Development Programme (UNDP), *Human Development Report 1997* (New York: Oxford University Press, 1997), p. 2.

33   Pulitzer Prizer winner: "Billions of Third World citizens . . ."—Jared Diamond, *Collapse: How Societies Choose to Fail or Succeed* (New York: Viking, 2005).

33   1911 *Britannica* remarks on shiftless poor, rogues and vagabonds, etc.—*The Encyclopaedia Britannica*, Eleventh Edition (New York: The Encyclopaedia Britannica Co., 1911), vol. XXVII (Tonalite to Vesuvius), pp. 578 (entry on unemployment), 837 (entry on vagrancy).

34   Replacement of resource poverty by money poverty—Jeremy Seabrook, *The No-Nonsense Guide to World Poverty* (Oxford, U.K.: New Internationalist Publications Ltd., in association with Verso, 2003), p. 54.

34   Footnote: "The benefits of the Western way of wealth . . ."—Ibid., p. 63.

35   "Standard of living is defined as the amount and quality of commodities . . ."—Andres V. Castillo, Ph.D., *Philippine Economics* (Manila: Privately printed?, 1949), p. 626.

35   Problematic comparison: Income of a peasant vs. a town worker—Samir Amin, *Unequal Development: An Essay on the Social Formations of Peripheral Capitalism* (New York: Monthly Review Press, 1976; orig. French ed. 1973), p. 219.

36   Nina Leonigovna Sokolova interview—Petersburg, Russia, 2005. See next chapter.

37   Descriptions of conditions in Pakistan—Kachagari Camp, near Peshawar, 2000.

38   Footnote: agrarianism as nutritionally inferior to nomadism—Kenneth F. Kiple and Kriemhild Conèe Ornelas, general editors, *The Cambridge*

World History of Food, vol. 1 (Cambridge, U.K.: Cambridge University Press, 2000), p. 15 (1.1: "Dietary Reconstruction and Nutritional Assessment of Past Peoples: The Bioanthropological Record," by Clark Spencer Larsen).

38   A novelist of post-Soviet Poland—Andrzej Stasiuk, *Tales of Galicia: A Novel*, trans. Margarita Nafpaktitis (Prague: Twisted Spoon Press, 2003), p. 18.

39   "The subsistence which they find there . . ."—Adam Smith, *An Inquiry into the Nature and Causes of the Wealth of Nations, Selections, Book I* (Chicago: Henry Regnery Co., 1953, 3rd printing; orig. ed. 1776), p. 128.

39–42   Description of Vietnam—Visited in 2003.

40   "The use . . . of slaves hardly differs at all from that of domestic animals . . ."—Aristotle, *The Politics*, trans. T. A. Sinclair (New York: Penguin Classics, 1973 repr. of 1962 ed.; orig. Greek ed. bef. 322 B.C.), p. 34.

41   Montaigne on the anticipation of poverty—*The Complete Essays of Montaigne*, trans. Donald M. Frame (Palo Alto, California: Stanford University Press, 2002 repr. of 1965 pbk ed.; trans. first pub. 1957; based on final (5th) ed. of 1588), p. 54 ("Of fear").

42   "Through virtue in past lives . . ."—*The Confessions of Lady Nijo*, trans. Karen Brazell (Stanford, California: Stanford University Press, 1976 repr. of 1973 Doubleday ed.; orig. Japanese ms. *[Towazugatari]* wr. 1307), p. 17.

42–43   Colombia interviews—Bogotá and Medellín, 1999. The interpreters whose work figures in this book were Carlos Andrés Ruiz Arango, Diana Andrea Pereira Velasquez and Marcos Lopez.

43–44   Mexico interviews—Mexicali, 2005.

44   Leonard Knight—Interviewed September 2005 at Salvation Mountain (Niland, California). Terrie Petree was present.

45   "I see no reason whatever to think . . ."—I. A. Richards, *Practical Criticism: A Study of Literary Judgment* (New York: Harcourt, Brace & World, Inc. / A Harvest Book, ; n.d. but prob. pub. ca. 1980; orig. pub. 1929), pp. 4–5.

45   "The chief cause of ill-appropriate, stereotyped reactions . . ."—Ibid., p. 232 ("withdrawal from experience" emphasized in original).

46   "Depending on how resources, poverty lines and equivalence scales are defined . . ."—Anthony B. Atkinson and François Bourguignon, *Handbook of Income Distribution*, vol. 1 (Amsterdam: Elsevier, Handbooks in

Economics ser., no. 16, 2000), p. 362 (ch. 6, M. Jäntti and S. Danziger, "Income Poverty in Advanced Countries").

46   Rousseau's savage: "The only goods he recognizes in the universe are food . . ."—Jean-Jacques Rousseau, *A Discourse on the Origin of Inequality, A Discourse on Political Economy, The Social Contract*, trans. G. D. H. Cole (Chicago: Encyclopaedia Britannica, Inc., Great Books ser. [bound with Montesquieu], no. 38, 1952), p. 338 (*Origin of Inequality*, orig. date [of dedication] 1754).

48   Japan interviews—These took place in April 2004 and May 2005. Ms. Kawai Takako interpreted.

48   Interview with the withered man on the bicycle—Homeless camp by the river, Taito City, Sumidagawa Ward, Tokyo, 2004. Ms. Kawai Takako interpreted.

THREE: NATALIA'S CHILDREN

49–79   Russia interviews—These took place in July 2005. My interpreter for most of the interviews was Mariya Grusev, although with two brief Oksana interviews I was helped by the prostitute N.K.

56   Footnote: United Nations: "Eastern Europe and the countries of the Commonwealth of Independent States . . ."—UNDP report, p. 3.

62   "The other woman only wanted to get our housing and to worm her two children into it."—Mariya's translation was actually "the other woman only wanted our housing and to get her two children into it." I thought that my "re-translation" accurately preserved the sense while reducing awkwardness and monotony.

62   Footnote: "Don't you know us gypsy girls?"—Ivan Turgenev, *A Sportsman's Notebook*, trans. Charles and Natasha Hepburn (New York: The Ecco Press, 1986 repr. of 1950 Viking ed.; orig. stories written 1848–1850, pub. in Russia 1852), p. 326 ("The End of Chertopkhanov").

69   Views of an oncologist regarding irradiation of head—Personal communication from Dr. Janice K. Ryu, September 2005.

69   Tale of the Japanese radiation accident in 1971—International Atomic Energy Agency, *Handling of Radiation Accidents: Proceedings of a Symposium, Vienna, 28 February–4 March 1977* (Vienna: IAEA Proceedings Series, 1977), p. 35 (T. Kumatori et al, "Radiation Accident Caused by an Iridium-192 Radiographic Source"). Some of the characteristic symptoms which resulted were (p. 37) nausea, skin lesions, blisters, anemia,

temporary sperm count decreases. The long-term effects included skin depigmentation, atrophy of the hands which had handled the iridium and contraction of the fingers.

74   "To date there is no broad scientific consensus . . ."—www.chernobyl. info/index, sponsored by the Swiss Agency for Development and Cooperation (partners: the United Nations Development Programme, the Ukraine Ministry of Emergencies and Affairs of Population Protection, etc.; the Chernobyl Committee and the United Nations Office for the Coordination of Humanitarian Affairs), accessed 6 September 2005. Section titled "The impact of radiation."

74   "Not based on statistical evidence . . ."—Ibid., section titled "Other diseases in children and adults." Arteriosclerosis was not associated with radium intoxication among Hiroshima-Nagasaki survivors. Nor did it seem to be among American radium dial painters, although these women, typically for their time, showed high atherosclerotic incidence. See *Environmental Research*, vol. 8, no. 3 (December 1974), p. 221 (William D. Sharpe, "Chronic Radium Intoxication: Clinical and Autopsy Findings in Long-Term New Jersey Survivors"), p. 291. There was, of course, a high incidence of malignancies, and possibly accelerated aging.

74   No mention of infection through interpersonal contact—chernobyl.info website, section titled "Low level radiation."

74   Follow-up study of American radium dial-painters—*Environmental Research*, vol. 15, no. 2 (April 1978), p. 252 (Anthony P. Polednak, "Long-Term Effects of Radium Exposure in Female Dial Workers: Differential White Blood Cell Count"). The subjects were American women who painted radium dials before 1930, those with malignant neoplasms and certain other complications excluded. Radon was measured in their exhalations. The study found (p. 258) that the comparatively low doses did not decrease these women's leukocyte levels; beagles receiving a higher dose in other experiments were, however, impaired in this respect. Polednak found a "possible dose-related depression in eosinophil level" (p. 259). He believed that plutonium exposure might have worse effects.

74   Footnote on luminous kisses—*Environmental Research*, Sharpe article, p. 243. The result from this bit of amusement (and also from licking the tips of brushes): radium related anemias, jaw necrosis, osteitis, mouth lesions, osteogenic sarcoma, aplastic anemia.

74   "Dependence, victimization"—chernobyl.info website, section titled "Psychological Effects."

74–75   Other extracts from same website—Section titled "Overview of Health
        Consequences."

75   *The New York Times*, vol. CLIV, no. 53,329 (Tuesday, September 6, 2003),
        p. A12 (Elizabeth Rosenthal, "Experts Find Reduced Effects of Cher-
        nobyl"). The report seems to be the so-called Chernobyl legacy docu-
        ment released by the Chernobyl Forum and criticized as "inappropriate"
        by Chernobyl relief organizations. The sentence on pediatric thyroid
        cancers was taken from the news section of the www.chernobyl.info/
        index website.

FOUR: EVERYTHING YOU SHOULD DO BY YOURSELF

81–92   Chinese interviews—Nan Ning, summer 2003. My interpreters were Mai
        (interviews with retired road mender, retired railroad worker, garbage
        lady), and Michelle [Wei Xiao Min] (all other interviews). Ben Pax was
        present.

FIVE: THE TWO MOUNTAINS

93–98   The interview with Big Mountain and Little Mountain—These took
        place in Kyoto in 2004 and 2005. Ms. Kawai Takako interpreted.

PHENOMENA

PHENOMENA [INTRODUCTORY NOTE]

101   "Dimensions of poverty"—UNDP, p. 5.

SIX: INVISIBILITY

103–22   Afghan and Pakistani interviews—These took place in 2000. M. Ekram
         interpreted, except for the interview with the man in smoked glasses, which
         occurred in English.

108–10   Interview with the Algerian woman Amel—This occurred in Sacramento
         in July 2005.

111   Description of poverty in Rangoon—From a visit in 1993.

113–14   Description of the train tracks in Salinas—From a visit in 2005.

117–19   Interview with Hong—Hanoi, 2003.

119   Description of the policewomen in Budapest—From a visit in 1998.

119–20   Description of the Inuit drunks in Nome—From a visit in 2000.

SEVEN: DEFORMITY

123   "The day before yesterday I saw a child . . ."—Montaigne, p. 538 ("Of a
       monstrous child").

124   The old man who stank of urine—Sidewalk near the steps that led down
       to the homeless camp by the river, Taito City, Sumidagawa Ward, Tokyo,
       2004. Ms. Kawai Takako interpreted.

EIGHT: UNWANTEDNESS

127   A well-wisher of West Bengal: "Industrialisation, being the basis of
       urbanisation . . ."—D. S. Ganguly, Project Director, Professor and Head,
       Department of Commerce, University of Burdwan, West Bengal, *Re-
       gional Economy of West Bengal: A Study of Urbanisation, Growth Potential
       and Optimisation of Industrial Location* (Calcutta: Orient Longman, 1979),
       p. 181.

127   Motivations of "in-migrants"—Ibid., p. 41 (Table 3.6: Migration on Eco-
       nomic and non-Economic Consideration . . .").

128   "A depression is a time . . . when millions of individuals . . ."—Geoffrey
       Crowther, Managing Director and former Editor of *The Economist*, Lon-
       don, *The Wealth and Poverty of Nations* (Claremont, California [lectures],
       1957), p. 37.

128   "During the 1920s, many Americans had begun to equate self-
       worth . . ."—Robert S. McElvaine, editor in chief, *Encyclopedia of the Great
       Depression*, vol. 2 (New York: Macmillan Reference USA / Thomson
       Gale, 2004), p. 112 ("Psychological Impact of the Great Depression").

129   "Because native-born Americans mainly saw poor and ill-kempt common
       laborers . . ."—Andrew Rolle, *The Italian Americans: Troubled Roots* (New
       York: Macmillian / Free Press, 1980), p. 60.

129   "We were never taught that *Caucasians were better* . . ."—Yasuko I.
       Takezawa, *"Breaking the Silence": Ethnicity and the Quest for Redress among
       Japanese Americans*, dissertation for Doctor of Philosophy degree, Uni-
       versity of Washington, 1989, p. 97 (italics in original).

NINE: DEPENDENCE

131   Aristotle on slavery—Op. cit., pp. 26, 27, 37.

132   "The common run of men today . . ."—Montaigne, p. 191 ("On the ine-
       quality that is between us").

133   Interview with Colombian street vendor—Bogotá, 1999.

133   The Afghan refugee—Interviewed in Peshawar, 2000. Interview in English.

134   "All are often supplied . . ."—Smith, pp. 2–3.

134   "A carpenter in London . . ."—Ibid., p. 146.

TEN: ACCIDENT-PRONE-NESS

135   Scene from sanctioned Iraq—Witnessed in 1998. Saddam City was a slum within greater Baghdad.

135   Scene from sanctioned Serbia—Witnessed in 1994, in Beograd.

136   Encounter with Australian runaway-prostitute—This took place in 1994.

137   Interview with the poor man in Imperial County, California—1997.

138–39 Colombia interviews—1999. The black schoolgirl in Nueva Esperanza and her mother are depicted in a photo in the unabridged version of my *Rising Up and Rising Down* (San Francisco: McSweeney's, 2003), portfolio 4, plate 2.

138   The Albanian street vendor—Described in my notebook from that visit, 1998.

139   "No free person of color within their reach . . ."—*Free Man of Color: The Autobiography of Willis Augustus Hodges*, ed. Willard B. Gatewood Jr. (Knoxville: The University of Tennessee Press, 1982), p. 20.

139   "The sound of the whip . . ."—Ibid., p. 18.

140   "The multiplicity of unhealthy trades . . ."—Rousseau, p. 365. But he thinks the indulgences of the rich are also harmful to them.

140   The consumptive woman's room in 1889—*Irish University Press Series of British Parliamentary Papers: Third Report from the Select Committee of the House of Lords on the Sweating System with Minutes of Evidence and Appendices, 1889: Industrial Relations 15* (Shannon, Ireland: Irish University Press, 1970); p. 5 (*Reports from Committees: Eight Volumes*, vol. 5: Sweating System, Session 21, February 1889–30 August 1889, vol. XIII, Minutes of Evidence; testimony of Mr. Edward Squire, M.D.).

ELEVEN: PAIN

142–43 Descriptions of Malagasy beggars—From my second visit to the island, 1994.

TWELVE: NUMBNESS

146   Infant mortality among Highland Scots—Smith, p. 141.

147   "The morgue pathologist in Bogotá"—Dr. Gloria Suarez, interviewed in
        1999. For further details of this interview, see the first Colombia chapter
        of my essay *Rising Up and Rising Down*, unabridged ed.

147   Interview with Jose Gonzalez—Mexicali, September 2005. Terrie Petree
        interpreted.

148   The drunk in the grass in San Francisco—1998.

148   "I have seen several boys under twenty years of age . . ."—Smith, p. 14.

148   Interview with lady teacher in Kachagari Camp, Pakistan—2000.

THIRTEEN: ESTRANGEMENT

153   Homeless Mary—Interviewed on two occasions in San Francisco, 1998.

154   The tale of Mary O'Brien—*Irish University Press Series of British Parliamen-
        tary Papers: Papers Relating to Proceedings for the Relief of Distress and the State
        of the Unions and Workhouses in Ireland [Sixth Series] 1847–1848; Famine Ire-
        land 3* (Shannon, Ireland: Irish University Press, 1970) p. 809 (*Accounts and
        Papers: Twenty-Eight Volumes,—(18)—, Relief of Distress and Union Work-
        houses (Ireland), Session 18 November 1847–5 September 1848*, vol. LIV; Cap-
        tain Kennedy to the Commissioners, in reply: —*March 26*, 1848).

155   "One poor beggar is quick to espy another . . ."—Ivan Turgenev, *Fathers
        and Sons* and *A Nest of the Gentry*, trans. Bernard Isaacs (Moscow: Prog-
        ress Publishers, 1974 repr. of 1951 Russian ed.; *A Nest of the Gentry* orig.
        pub. 1859), p. 301 ("A Nest of the Gentry").

155   "The lot of the poor can easily be imagined . . ."—Castillo, pp. 629, 630.

156   Sarajevo interviews—1992.

156   Criminal convictions in Syria—Syrian Arab Republic, Office of the
        Prime Minister, Central Bureau of Statistics, *Statistical Abstract 1969–
        1970: Twenty-second and Twenty-third Year* (Damascus: Government
        Printing Office, 1971), p. 388 (Table 208: Convicted Persons in Syrian
        Courts During 1963–1968, By Offences). These convictions (269,829 in
        total) were suffered by about 4.3 percent of that year's population (which
        was 6,244,418 according to p. 41 [Table 10: Number of People Regis-
        tered in Civil Registration by Sex, at the End of the Years 1943–1968].

157   Kenyan employment data for 1972—Simplified from [Republic of Kenya], Central Bureau of Statistics, Ministry of Finance and Planning, *Statistical Abstract 1975*, p. 241; Table 225, "Wage Employment by Occupation and Citizenship, 1972–1974."

157   The 1974 consolidated minimum wage in Nairobi—Ibid., 266, Table 240.

157   Footnote on U.S. dollar equivalents for minimum wages—As computed from the same source, p. 164, table 137, "Foreign Exchange Rates, 1972–1974." The dollar was about 7 shillings throughout this period.

158   Interview with Javier Armando Gomez Reyes—Mexicali, September 2005. Terrie Petree interpreted. Señor Reyes makes another appearance in my book *Imperial*.

161   "It is indeed cause for envy . . ."—Helen Craig McCullough, comp. and ed., *Classical Japanese Prose: An Anthology* (Palo Alto, California: Stanford University Press, 1990), pp. 212–13 (Akazome Emon and anon., *A Tale of Flowering Fortunes*, written mainly 1030–1045).

CHOICES

FOURTEEN: AMORTIZATION

165   Definition of the fair price for a commodity—Amin, pp. 153–54.

166   Lotus—Interviewed in California on many occasions, 2005.

166–69   Erica—Paid interview in a late-night coffee shop in the Kabukicho red light district of Tokyo, 2000. Ms. Kawai Takako interpreted.

169–70   Tiffany—Interviewed in San Francisco, 1993.

FIFTEEN: CRIME WITHOUT CRIMINALS

173–95   Kazakhstan interviews—These took place in winter 2000. My interpreters were, in order, xx, xx, xx and (best and bravest) Asel.

174   The consortium's press release: "The world's deepest supergiant oil field."—Tengizchevroil fact sheet (October 2000), some of whose data supersede the figures in the TCO booklet cited below.

174   A glossy booklet published by TCO: "Tengizchevroil's goal is to be a model of industry, ingenuity and accomplishment . . ." and "Tengizchevroil and all those working for TCO are very proud . . ."—TCO booklet, "Working for the Future of Kazakhstan, 2000," pp. 2, 4 (unnumbered).

175   My guidebook: "If you're not in the oil or gas business . . ."—Bradley
        Mayhew, Richard Plunkett and Simon Richmond, Lonely Planet guide:
        Central Asia (Oakland: Lonely Planet Publications, 2000), 2nd ed., p. 226.

183   "It also burned off much of the fuel that was ostensibly being refined."—
        In 1974 about five-twelfths of the 2,400 million tons of fuels produced by
        refineries was lost or burned off (*Toxicological and Environmental Chemis-
        try*, vol. 5, no. 2 [1982], p. 168 [Ernest Merian, "The Environmental
        Chemistry of Volatile Hydrocarbons," 1981]. I had hoped that by 2000
        refinery procedures had reduced that 42 percent wastage rate to some-
        thing more reasonable, but those flames in the Tengiz were awfully
        bright.

194   Comparison of reported symptoms of sulfur poisoning in Atyrau with
        available medical information—You will recall that the symptoms men-
        tioned by my informants in Atyrau were (I) headaches, allergies, nose and
        eye "problems," heart trouble (which might actually be chest pain),
        breathing difficulties, (II) leg aches, hair loss, anemia, unexplained deaths
        of people in their prime, and for children developmental delays and white
        hair. The symptoms in Group (I) are all documented in the toxicological
        sources I consulted, as you will see below. The symptoms in Group (II)
        are not.

        I am not a chemist, and cannot tell you (especially since I was not al-
        lowed to visit the refinery) precisely which forms of sulfur and other
        chemicals were being given off in the Tengiz. Let's commonsensically
        assume that they were sulfur oxides.

        Sulfur dioxide can cause contraction in the airway above the larynx,
        thereby reducing oxygen intake (J. O'M. Bockris, ed., *Environmental
        Chemistry* [New York: Plenum Press, 1977], p. 248 [B. G. Baker, "Control
        of Noxious Emissions from Internal Combustion Engines", sec. 2.2, "Ef-
        fects of Exhaust Pollutants"]. This would account for many of the symp-
        toms reported in Group (I). Furthermore, sulfates from burning coal and
        oil are "associated with acute adverse health effects including: increased
        acute lower respiratory illness rates . . . and increased asthma attack rates"
        (*Environmental Research*, vol. 19, no. 2 [August 1979], p. 307 [Rebecca T.
        Zagraniski, Brian P. Leaderer and Jan A. J. Stolwijk, "Ambient Sulfates,
        Photochemical Oxidants, and Acute Adverse Health Effects: An Epide-
        miological Study"]. These latter researchers noted the prevalence of the
        following symptoms in their study population (p. 315): headache, eye and
        nose irritation, sneezing, runny nose, allergy, head cold. Only 2.7 percent
        of their sample felt chest discomfort. They concluded (p. 317) that sus-
        pended sulfates are not as poisonous as photochemical oxidants such as

ozone. They admitted (p. 319) that their study did not address chronic exposure effects. On the other hand, their study region, which included Connecticut, boasted "one of the highest levels of oxidants in the nation." They accordingly decided that only very sensitive people are harmed by sulfur oxides (by which they meant sulfur dioxide and suspended sulfates). The difference in exposure levels between Connecticut and Atyrau is unknown. Also, heavy smoking exacerbated these manifestations, and the people I met in Kazakhstan were often heavy smokers.

According to *Environmental Research,* vol. 16, nos. 1–3 in one vol. (July 1978), p. 302 (John McK. Ellison and Robert E. Waller, "A Review of Sulphur Oxides and Particulate Matter as Air Pollutants with Particular Reference to Effects on Health in the United Kingdom"), sulfur oxides reached lethal concentrations in Belgium in 1930. In 1952, four thousand people died in the infamous London fog (ibid., p. 310). Much of the mortality was due to bronchitis, which increased by a factor of ten. These researchers concluded (p. 312) that mortality increases when daily mean concentrations of both smoke and sulfur dioxide exceed 750 micrograms per cubic meter; while 500 micrograms of sulfur dioxide plus two hundred and fifty of smoke would induce chronic effects: respiratory infections, asthma, et cetera. Findings in children remained "ambiguous" (p. 316). Stunted growth and other developmental disabilities were still under study.

Other chemicals given off by burning petroleum include benzene, which Bockris (loc. cit.) calls "the most volatile, most water soluble and most toxic of the aromatic one- or two-ring hydrocarbons." It is also possible that carbon monoxide may be implicated in the reported deaths at Sarykamys. In any event, I did not see any dead people, and so the accusations against TCO remain unproven, although I personally am inclined to believe them.

194–95   Footnote: Interview with one of the female snow-shovelers—This woman had given her address not just willingly but enthusiastically (the other two women refused), so I visited her on a Sunday when I knew that she would not be at work, and we chatted briefly in front of the house she rented, her words apprehensive and resentful. She went inside after awhile and hid. A man came and explained for her that she was too busy.

SIXTEEN: SNAKEHEAD FEAR

197–217 Japan interviews—These took place in January 2001. My interpreters were Ms. Mari R. and Ms. Kawai Takako.

203   We "cannot even face the fact of nature . . ."—James Agee and Walker Evans, *Let Us Now Praise Famous Men* (Boston: Houghton Mifflin Co., 1960; orig. text and photos 1939–1940), p. 247.

215   Footnote: "Five millionaire gangsters have been identified . . ."—From *The Japan Times*, Saturday, February 14, 2004, p. 3 ("Best of . . . The Award-Winning Newspaper *The Observer*; Anushka Asthana and Tony Thompson, 'Police hunt bosses of "cockle slaves": 19 illegal Chinese immigrant drown' ").

HOPES

221   United Nations policy recommendations—UNDP report, pp. 6–11.

222   Footnote on unemployment figures from the Indian census—A. Mitra of the Indian Civil Service, Registrar General and ex-officio Census Commissioner for India, *Census of India 1961*, vol. 1: India, part V-A(i): Special Tables for Scheduled Castes, pp. 428–29 (SC-1—Persons Not At Work Classified by Sex, Type of Activity and Educational Levels for Schedules Castes—*contd.*)

222–23 The Chinese bookstore where people were reading books they could not afford—Nan Ning Shu Cheng (Nan Ning Book City), in Nan Ning, obviously, in 2002.

223   Interview with the two homeless men on Sumidagawa Terrace—Homeless camp by the river, Taito City, Sumidagawa Ward, Tokyo, 2004. Ms. Kawai Takako interpreted.

NINETEEN: UNDER THE ROAD

237   Cambodia as 1 of 7 countries with UN HPI higher than 50 percent—UNDP report, p. 6.

238   "Every item and every strand of meaning . . . —Richards, p. 231.

239   Julio the drunk—Interviewed in Calexico, July 2005, in English. Micheline Marcom was present.

240   Okura's "Dialogue on Poverty"—Robert H. Brower and Earl Miner, *Japanese Court Poetry* (Palo Alto, California: Stanford University Press, 1997 pbk repr. of 1961 ed.), pp. 121–23 (parallel text).

241 Happy afternoons in a Cambodian beauty shop far in the ricefields—Battambang, 1996.

241 Rainy afternoon in Burma—Notes from Rangoon, 1993.

241–42 Scene at the Cinnabar—San Francisco, 1998.

242–43 Description of the tea-seller and his customers—Pakistan, 2000.

243 "Poverty has nothing to be feared but this . . ."—Montaigne, p. 38 ("That the taste of good and evil depends in large part on the opinion we have of them").

244 "He who has learned how to die . . ."—Ibid., p. 60 ("That to philosophize is to learn to die").

244 "Greatness of soul . . ." Seneca, *Moral Essays*, vol. 1, trans. John W. Basore (Cambridge, Massachusetts: Harvard University Press, Loeb Library, 1994 rev. repr. of 1928 ed.; "On Mercy" orig. written A.D. 55 or 56), p. 371 ("On Mercy," I.V.3).

246 Descriptions of Madagascar—Notes from my first visit (1994).

247 "Every man is rich or poor . . ."—Smith, p. 51.

251–54 Colombia stories and interviews—From my first visit in 1999.

251 The four-year-old shantytown in Ciudad Bolívar—Nueva Esperanza, 1999.

251 The president of another such community in Ciudad Bolívar—Pedro Jose Arías, interviewed 1999.

253–54 Dr. Carlos—Interviewed in his clinic in Ciudad Bolívar, 1999.

PLACEHOLDERS

TWENTY-ONE: I KNOW I AM RICH

261 Footnote: Fanon on natives and settlers—Frantz Fanon, *The Wretched of the Earth,* trans. Constance Farrington (New York: Grove Press, 1968; orig. French ed. 1961), p. 39.

266 Footnote: Engel's First Law of Consumption and the Filipino case—Castillo, pp. 632, 630.

269 "The rich having feelings . . ."—Rousseau, p. 356.

270 Encounter with the legless beggar—Serbia, 1998.

270   Encounter with the beggar in Battambang—Cambodia 1996.

271   "For no friendship can be knit . . ."—Montaigne, p. 195 ("Of the inequality that is between us").

272   Incident in Minneapolis—1994.

274   "Women of town origin who become concubines and attendants . . ."—*Monumenta Nipponica: Studies in Japanese Culture* [Sophia University, Tokyo], vol. 26, no. 2 (summer 2001; remainder of trans. in preceding issue), p. 186 (Janet R. Goodwin et al., "Solitary Thoughts: A Translation of Tadano Makuzu's *Hitori Kangae*"). The translation used the absurdly politically correct "of townsperson origin" and placed "who become concubines and attendants" in brackets. Hopefully my "retranslation" is more readable.

276   Interview with Hugo Ramirez—Mexicali, September 2005. Terrie Petree interpreted.

276   Description of first-class train compartments shutting their doors—Romania, 1996.

277   The developer Scarpia—Interviewed on one of his vacant lots in downtown Sacramento, 1997.

279   My commercial photographer friend Kent—Interviewed in his studio, 1997.

283   Encounter with the Palestinian postcard vendor—Jerusalem, 1993.

284   "It then became apparent how great would be the impending danger . . ."—Seneca, p. 421 ("On Mercy," I.xxiv.1).

285   "That seemingly wealthy, but most terribly impoverished class . . . " + "the degraded poor . . ."—Henry D. Thoreau, *The Illustrated Walden, with Photographs from the [Herbert Wendell] Gleason Collection*, ed. J. Lyndon Shanley (Princeton: Princeton University Press, 1973), pp. 16, 34–35.

TWENTY-THREE: MONEY JUST GOES TO WHERE IT GOES

293   Interview with the man with the white wrapping around his head—Homeless camp by the river, Taito City, Sumidagawa Ward, Tokyo, 2004. Ms. Kawai Takako interpreted.

294   "People utter foolish complaints about their lot . . ."—McCullough, p. 282 (*Tales of Times Now Past*, "How An Impoverished Man's Deserted Wife Became the Spouse of the Governor of Settsu").

294   "They budgeted five hundred million yen . . ."—The translation originally read: "They had five hundred million yen." But the interpreter later
confirmed with me that the "they" this man was talking about meant "the
authorities." She agreed that my word substitution improved the clarity
of the sentence.

ACKNOWLEDGMENTS

I would like to thank Mr. Karl Greenfeldt and Mr. Zoher Abdool-carim of *Time Asia* for sending me to China. I am also obliged to Mr. John DeCaire for several library excursions.

Mikhail Iossel invited me to give a speech or two in Petersburg, which is how I met the people portrayed in "Natalia's Children." He has my grateful friendship, as does Deborah Triesman for recommending me.

Dan Halpern and Millicent Bennett were very patient with me. Susan Golomb and Casey Powell were helpful in many matters.

Mr. Ben Pax has been a trustworthy companion and friend for many years. He was with me in several of the places mentioned in this book.

PHOTOGRAPHS

PHOTOGRAPHS

1. Woman of the Burned Land, Madagascar, 1994.
2. Hugo Ramirez, Mexicali, Mexico, 2005.

Homeless camp under the freeway, Miami, 1994.

3. Ellen in her shack.
4. Ellen at the group toilet.
5. Ellen's waterfall picture.
6. Ellen crossing herself.
7. Ellen getting water.
8. View of the camp.
9. Couple who lived near the toilet.

People and streetscapes, Riverton, Jamaica, 1995.

10. Fab ice.
11. Two children.
12. Under the awning.
13. Garbage and canal.
14. Two shanties.
15. Woman.

Beasts of burden.

16. Poussepousse driver, Madagascar, 1994.
17. Porter boy, Aranyaprathet, Thailand, 1996.
18. Group pull, Aranyaprathet, 1996.

"I Think I Am Rich," Bangkok, 2001.

19. Sunee and her mother at the mother's home, Klong Toey slum.
20. Sunee and Vimonrat, Sunee's home, Klong Toey.
21. Sunee and Vimonrat. *See also 110.*
22. Office cleaning lady, downtown.
23. Office cleaning lady just off work, beside Colonel Sanders, downtown.
24. Wan, at Central Railroad Station.

"I Think They Are Poor."

25. Annah, beggar woman in Yemen, 2002.
26. Beggar near Shinjuku Station, Tokyo.
27. Beggar in Beijing, 2002.
28. Congolese beggar boy, 2001.
29. Congolese beggar girl, 2002.
30. Unknown sleepers.
31. Old poor woman, Cebu, Philippines, 1995.

"Natalia's Children," Petersburg, Russia, 2005.

32. Natalia.
33. Oksana.
34. Nina.
35. Nikolai.
36. Elena. *See also 111.*
37. Oksana's family (except for Marina).

"Everything You Should Do By Yourself," Nan Ning, China, 2002.

38. Garbage lady.
39. Man in rubble of houses destroyed for a highway.
40. Man with photo and title deed of his destroyed house.
41. Man in rubble.

"The Two Mountains" and their colleagues, Japan, 2001–05.

42. Panorama of box houses, Sumidagawa Terrace, Tokyo.
43. Box house in tunnel, Shinjuku, Tokyo.
44. Interior of box house, Sumidagawa Terrace.
45. Man and comic on sidewalk, Sumidagawa Terrace.
46. By the river, Kyoto.
47. At home, Kyoto.
48. Big Mountain and Little Mountain.
49. Big Mountain.

"Invisibility."

50. Woman in burqa, Sana'a, Yemen, 2002.
51. Beggar in burqa, Peshawar, Pakistan, 2000.
52. Mother in headscarf, Islamabad, Pakistan, 2000.
53. Headscarfed woman in Afghan refugee family group, Kachagari Camp, Pakistan, 2000.
54. Street prostitute in burqa approaching rickshaw, Peshawar, 2000.
55. Burqa, baby, hand, Peshawar, 2000.
56. Beggar-women sharing food under burqa, Peshawar, 2000.
57. Beggar in burqa on main road, Kabul, Afghanistan, 2000.
58. Two views of a woman (1), Kabul, 2000. She is standing before the ruins of her house, which was destroyed in the civil war.
59. Two views of a woman (2). She shows her face.
60. Beggar in burqa, with baby, Peshawar, 2000.
61. Afghan refugee washing her pots in canal, Peshawar, Pakistan, 1982.
62. Huddled beggar, Bogotá, Colombia, 1999.
63. Homeless man reading newspaper in park, Tokyo, 2005.
64. Hong, Hanoi, 2003.
65. Three drunks, Nome, Alaska, 2000.

"Deformity."

66. Beggar-girl with deformed nose, Aranyaprathet, 1996.
67. Old Russian beggar-lady, Atyrau, Kazakhstan, 2000.
68. Man out of line in subway station, Osaka, 1995.
69. Beggar who pretended to be armless, Bangkok, 2001.

"Accident-Prone-ness."

70. Family in front of their bullet-pocked house, a relic from the civil war, Brazzaville, Republic of Congo, 2001.
71. Man in front of his destroyed house, a relic from the civil war, Kabul, Afghanistan, 2000.
72. Victim of robbers, near Tuléar, Madagascar, 1994.
73. Father and daughter. Refugees from rural violence, city Colosseum, Cúcuta, Colombia, 1999.
74. Young children eating rice. Refugees, Cúcuta, 1999.
75. Section of wall assigned to individual refugee families: Dollscape. Cúcuta, 1999.
76. Refugees from rural violence, Red Cross headquarters, Bogotá, Colombia, 2000. Street view from above. Note police guard.
77. Refugee from Kobe earthquake, Japan, 1995.
78. Karenni refugees in church they built themselves, guerrilla village in Shan State, Burma, 1994.
79. Beggar-woman, Tuléar.
80. Beggar-woman, Antananarivo.
81. Woman with fever, Tamatave.

"Numbness."

82. José González playing his accordion, Mexicali, Mexico, 2005.

"Estrangement."

83. Javier Reyes, Mexicali, 2005.
84. Beggar and hand, Bogotá, 1999.
85. Beggar and rich girl, Bogotá, 1999.
86. Beggar and wall, Bogotá, 1999.
87. Snarling beggar, Bogotá, 1999.
88. Beggar with twisted face, Bogotá, 1999.
89. Feral girl, Cartucho, Bogotá, 1999.
90. "DONATE HERE TO GET ME OUT OF YOUR NEIGHBORHOOD," Portland, Oregon, 2003.

"Crime Without Criminals", Kazakhstan, 2000. See also 112-16.

91. Group portrait of the "Moskva" snow shovelers' brigade, Old Town, Atyrau.
92. Two brigade members at work.
93. Brigade member.
94. The TCO refinery by night, near Sarykamys.
95. Sarykamys family.
96. Man and child, Sarykamys.

"*Under the Road.*"

97. Slum children and puppies, near Phnom Penh, 1996.
98. Children in Ihosy, Madagascar, 1994.
99. Mother and child, Phnom Penh, 1994.
100. Fishmonger, Abyan, Yemen, 2002.
101. Boy on blanket, near Islamabad, Pakistan, 2000.
102. Julio, Calexico, California, 2005.
103. Homeless men at leisure, Sumidagawa Terrace, 2004.
104. Yemeni men in rocks by Sana'a road, 2002.
105. Afternoon on Avenue de la Mort, Brazzaville, 2001.
106. Afghan boys playing in wrecked Soviet plane, 2000.
107. Close-up of same.
108. Poor Ainu woman at home, Obihiro, Japan, 2001.
109. The same, in traditional costume.
110. Drawing by Vimonrat, Klong Toey, 2001.
111. Drawings by Elena Sokolov, Petersburg, 2005.

"*Under the Road.*" Series of views of Atyrau's Old Town and its house decorations, 2000. Many or most of these houses have now been demolished.

112. Man walking past house.
113. Two boys in yard of house which was to be demolished in spring 2001.
114. Wheel-like floral decorations.
115. Window.
116. Tulip-like floral decorations.

"*Under the Road,*" continued.

117. Improvised house, Nueva Esperanza, 1999.
118. Another improvised house in Nueva Esperanza.
119. Map of proposed legalization of Nueva Esperanza, 1999.
120. Gladys, Ciudad Bolívar, 1999.
121. Two girls in interior of home in more built-up portion of Ciudad Bolívar, 1999.
122. Street tailor, Yemen, 2002.

Wais.

123. Panhandler making peace sign, Haight Street, San Francisco, California, 1992
124. Homeless woman making *wai*, winter night in tunnel, Shinjuku, Tokoyo, 2001.
125. Beggar-girl's *wai*, Phnom Penh, 1994.
126. Beggar's *wai*, son beside him, Phnom Penh, 1996.

Night and day.

127. Street children at night, Cebu, Philippines, 1995.
128. Shopping cart man near the railroad tracks, Marysville, California, 1997.

I.

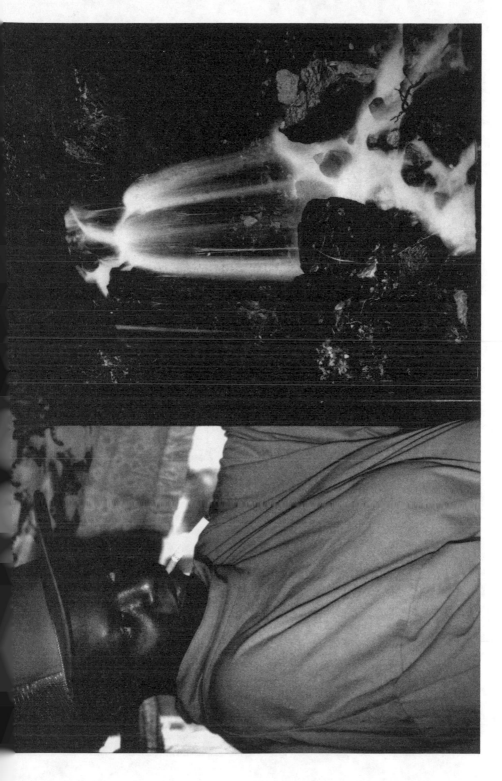

12.

13.

19.

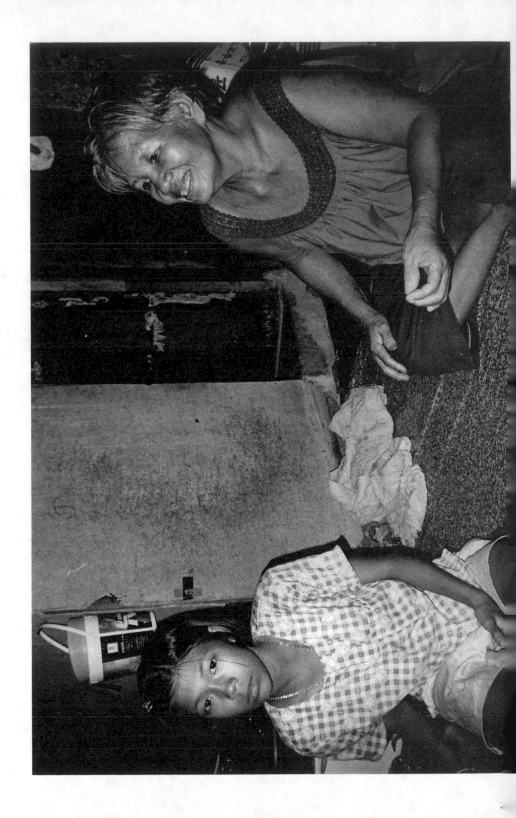

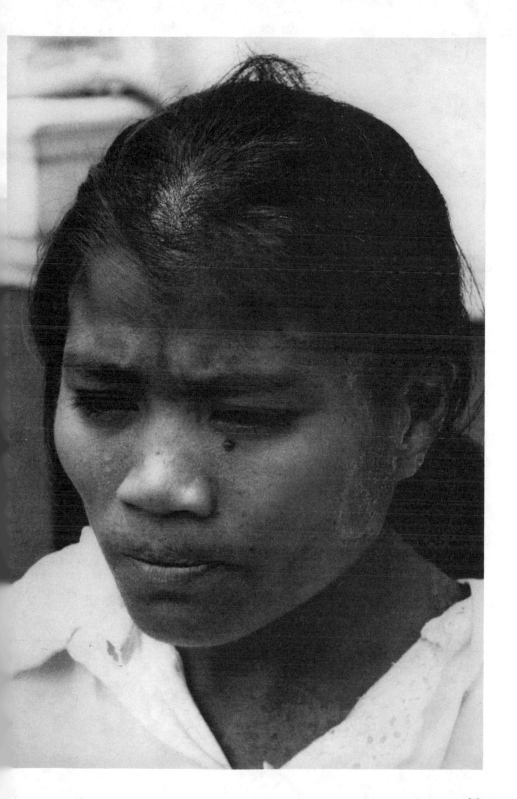

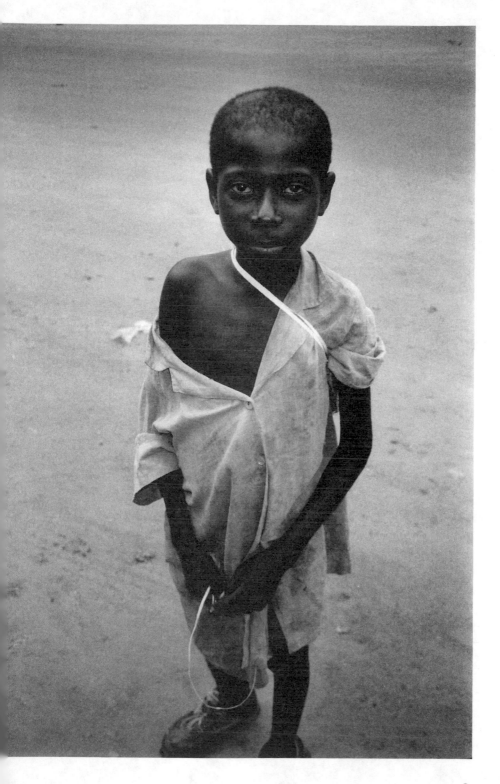

28.

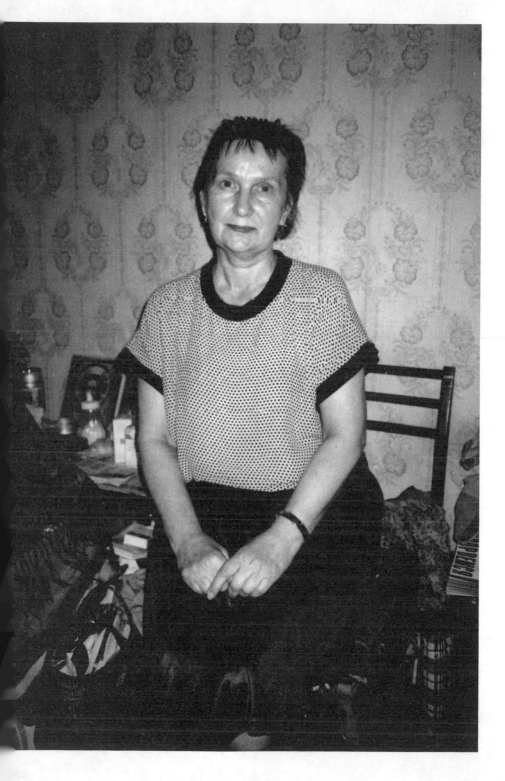

4

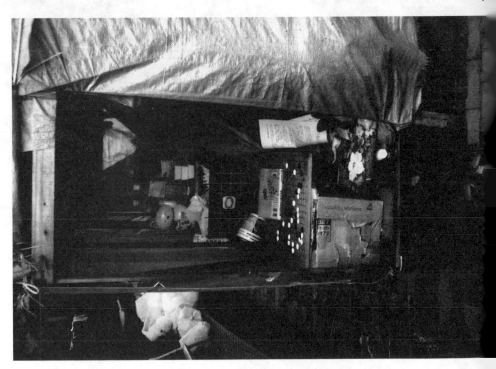

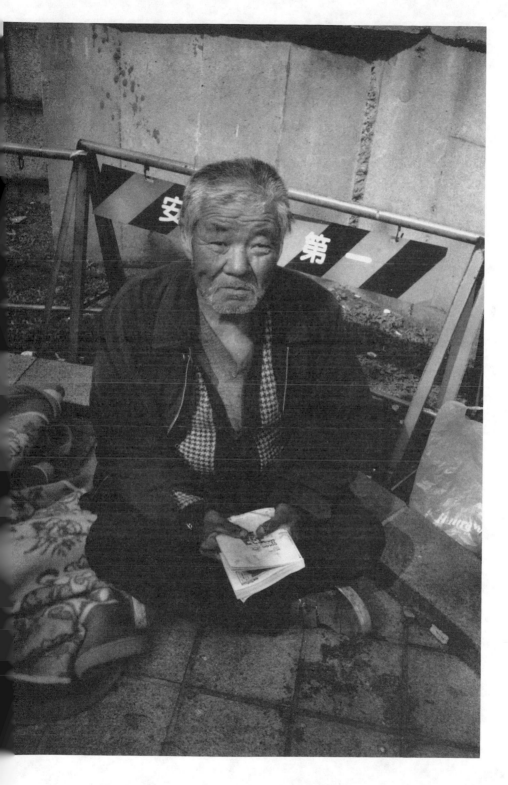

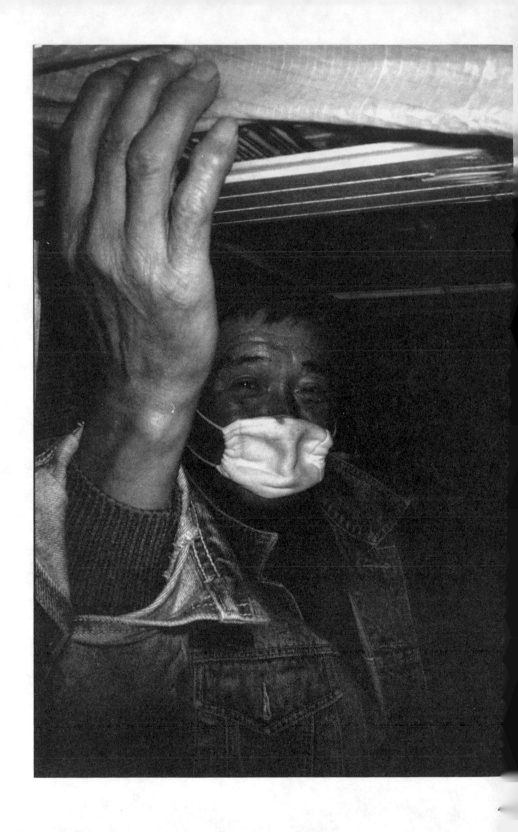

56.

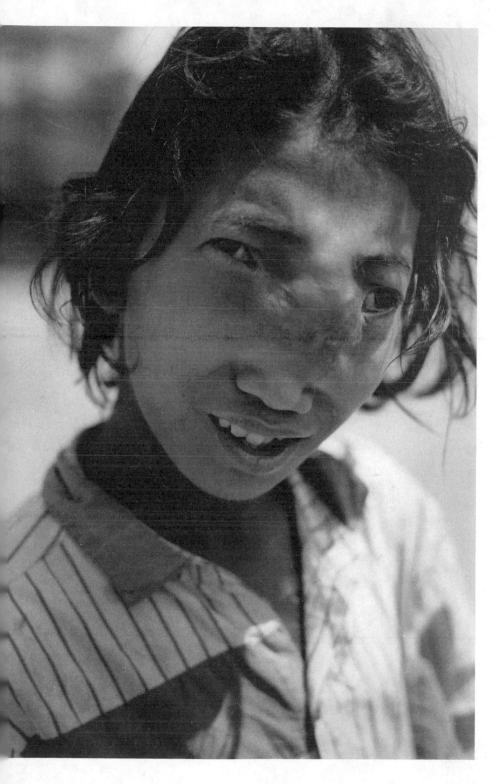

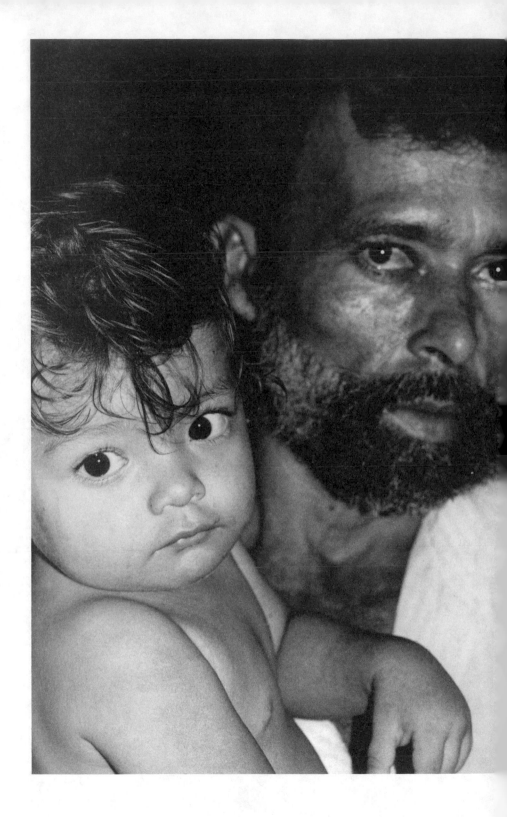

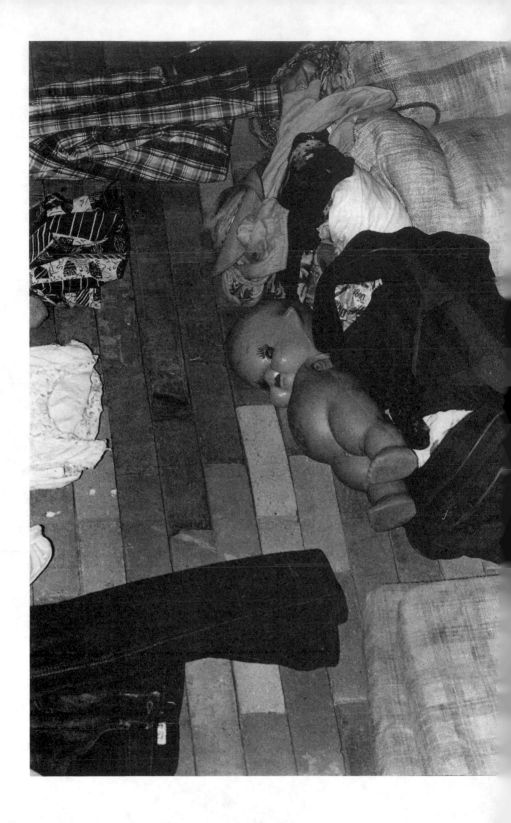

76.

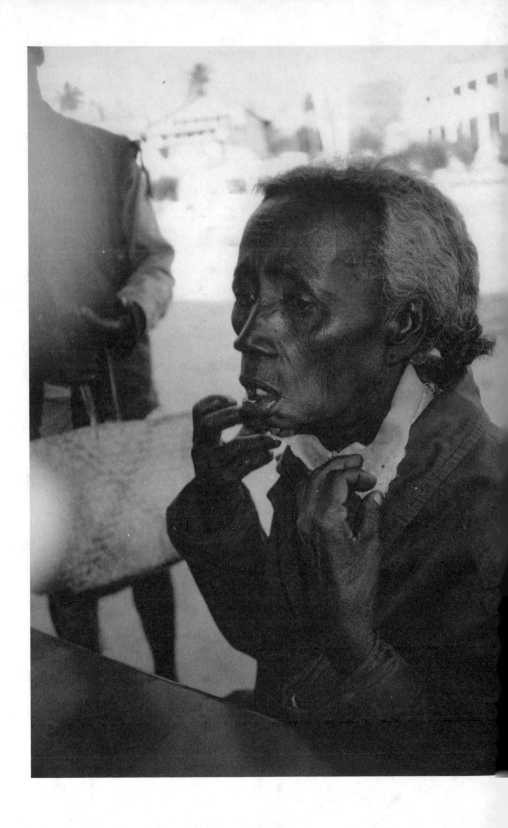

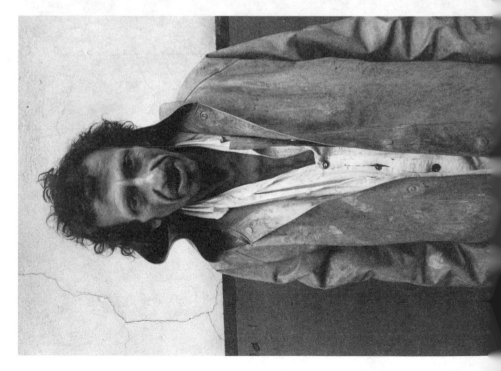

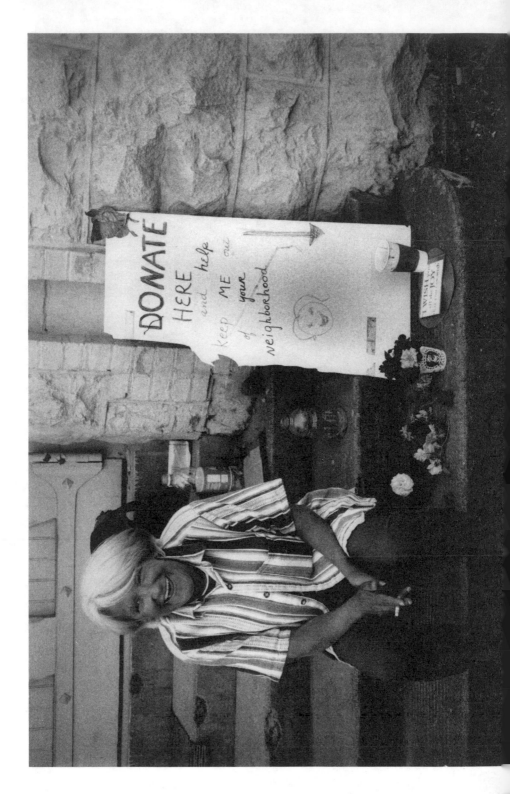

102.

103.

106. 107

112.

113.

114

11

116.

117

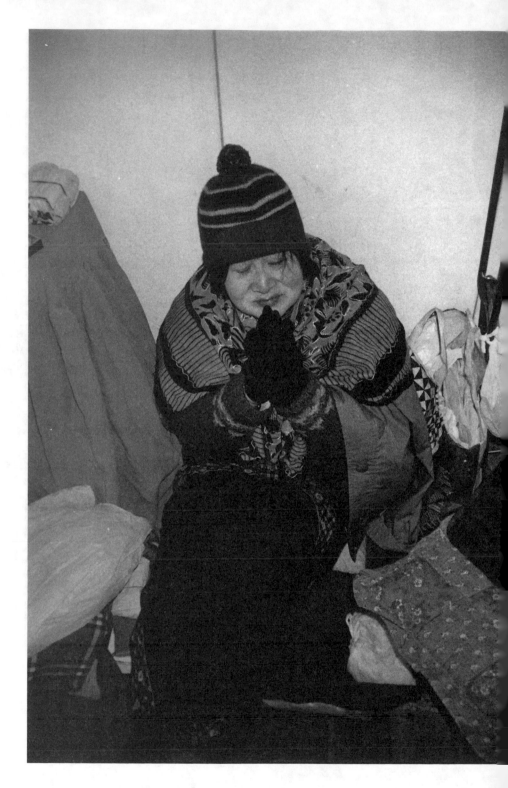